BLACK MONEY
&
FINANCIAL FRAUD

BLACK MONEY
&
FINANCIAL FRAUD

Thakur Shailendra Nath

Manas Publications
(We Convert Fighters into Writers)
New Delhi - 110 002 (INDIA)

MANAS PUBLICATIONS
(We Convert Fighters into Writers)
(Publishers, Library Suppliers, Importers & Exporters)
4402/5-A, Ansari Road (Opp. HDFC Bank)
Darya Ganj, New Delhi - 110 002 (India)
Phones: Off.: 011-23260783, 23265523, Res.: 011-23842660
E-mail: manaspublications@gmail.com
manaspublications@yahoo.com
Website: www.manaspublications.in

ISBN 978-81-7049-520-8
₹ 995.00

Designed at
Manas Publications

Printed in India at
R.K. Printers, Delhi
and published by Mrs Suman Lata for
Manas Publications, 4402/5-A,
Ansari Road (Opp HDFC Bank),
Darya Ganj, New Delhi - 110002 (INDIA)

To

the Fighters of India

who are

Fighting for Country

without

Fear or Favour

Preface

I am pleased to present my book *Black Money and Financial Fraud* before the readers.

There is a misconception about embezzlers and financial fraudsters. Generally they are regarded as one-shot offenders. They have the reputation of being good people who committed a bad act, who fantasized about and then carried out an embezzlement scheme. In fact embezzlers are white-collar criminals who are often repeat-offenders and share the same attitude towards crime as non-white-collar criminals. But they are innately non-violent or otherwise averse to criminal behaviour, blame others for his/her problems, display a sense of entitlement exploitative, egocentric, grandiose, difficult in taking criticism, and feel victimized. Offenders believe that they are entitled to commit fraud and feel victimized when that entitlement is challenged. Narcissistic psychopaths are then more likely to retaliate with violence or homicide.

Strain theory is one popular explanation of criminal activity. The theory argues that crime is the result of inequalities of wealth and opportunity. An individual commits a crime in order to satisfy his universal needs and wants. Because of his own poverty or due to prejudices in society, he lacks access to education and high-paying work. He sees others living richly, driving expensive cars, wearing expensive clothes, using the latest gadgets—and is frustrated that his own position keeps him away from having these things. Since he cannot pursue these comforts by legitimate means, he resorts to crime. Yet, millions of rupees are extorted and embezzled by highly educated men who are themselves symbols of white privilege who had opportunity to earn wealth legitimately but took to crime instead. In fact, in their capacity of manipulation and violence they have more in common with their street-crime cousins than their co-workers. The psychologists believe that they are the only real victims of their crime. The criminal act itself can betray a narcissistic perspective. It may seem remarkable that someone in a position with so much to lose sometimes flaunts his crime so carelessly, not even bothering to take simple steps to avoid detection.

The mind-set of white-collar criminals seriously discredits the notion that crime is a phenomenon of the poor inviting economic explanations. Whatever a person's income, they may choose to earn their way honestly or take the short-cut to wealth by stealing from others. Just as crime models based on family background cannot explain why one child of abusive parents turns to crime while another does not. Strain theory is unable to explain why most residents in poor neighbourhood do not become robbers and thieves despite suffering the same conditions. The common denominator of criminal behaviour here is not income or social barriers or prejudices but lack of personal responsibility for one's own actions and feelings of entitlement to the work and property of others.

The story of the rise and fall of Rajat Gupta, worldwide head of McKinsey is incomplete as a fairy tale without a happily ever after conclusion. As a real-life drama, it can't be bettered. If his rise to the top of the consultancy major was the culmination of a dream run that began as an orphaned immigrant who made it good through sheer dint of hard work and determination, his subsequent fall from grace and conviction for being party to insider trading must evoke a sense of bewilderment. This explanation of grading hollows in the case of Rajat Gupta. He'd already made more money than most could dream of in a lifetime. Moreover, there is no evidence that he actually made money in the process. He fed inside information to Galleon Group's Raj Rajaratnam, now serving an 11-year sentence on charges of insider trading. There are no definite answers. It is this inability to find a reason, this gnawing sense of a lack of plausible explanation that is, perhaps, the most disturbing aspect of Gupta's conviction. His actions defy understanding. It is, perhaps, why two of the jurors were reportedly in tears even as they reached a unanimous verdict to convict Rajat Gupta.

Frauds and fraudsters never make happy reading. Ramalinga Raju's fraud at Satyam was deeply disturbing, as was Bernie Madoff's. The questions are invariably the same in the Satyam case, for instance, the nagging question was—why would a man who had the vision to create a software giant virtually from scratch have behaved like a common criminal? There was an answer, however damning. It was greed. Raju and his family benefited. In the case of Rajat Gupta, however, even that benefit seems to be missing. Hence this void; this sense of incompleteness.

I am obliged and indebted to my department and senior officers and colleagues who have provided necessary help and guidance in writing of this book. I am also thankful to Manas Publications, who agreed to publish this book.

I owe a deep debt to my family members for their reverential and encouraging attitude. I would not have found a congenial environment at home for undertaking the onerous task of writing this book in difficult times, covering a wide range of complex issues.

I shall welcome all criticism and suggestions for improving the quality of this book from readers.

Thakur Shailendra Nath

Gwalior
Phone : 07697014309
Mobile : 09826085246
E-mail : thakurshailendranath@gmail.com

Contents

1. Introduction

To fully understand the predicament over black money, one should not have mind. This story explains the present scenario—an anatomy professor in a medical college once asked a tricky question to one of his female students: which part of the human body can expand several times its size under excitement. She went red and refused to answer saying it is unfair to ask her such question. The professor smiled and said three things to her: (1) she had not been reading her notes; (2) she has a dirty mind; and (3) she was probably in for disappointment when she got married. The right answer to question of course is the pupil of the human eye. Everybody has his own presumptions. Of all the astronomical figure-work touted in the name of corruption, black money was the most inflated one. But no one checks the basic facts. Any black money could only be a fraction of the overall economy. For Indians, with black money, a Swiss or foreign bank account is no longer the preferred option. It is real estate, unrealized capital gains, Satta Bazar, in every conceivable things from cricket to elections to commodities to weather and the most favoured place, under the bed or mattress. Some bit of exaggeration at the time of election is acceptable but a clear cut line should be drawn between activism and sensationalisation. It appears, we are yet to learn lessons from the past like Bofors scandal, Coalgate and 2G spectrum. Indian telecom growth has been held to ransom by the ₹1.76 lakh crore mythology. India suffered due to damming of a fine weapon like Bofors. While nobody has yet been punished nor the money recovered. We need to combine the efforts of bringing black money in conformity to national law and international commitment. The country has been restless for long and wants to see some tangible action on the issue of black money. We must try to plug further generation of black money. FEMA (Foreign Exchange Management Act), 1999 should be amended suitably to allow the agency to confiscate the property of similar value in India if a person has stashed money abroad and is under investigation.

Under pressure from India and other countries, Switzerland has made key changes in its local laws governing assistance to foreign nations in their pursuit of extracting black money allegedly stashed in Swiss banks. These amendments, which have come into force at present, would allow India and other countries to make group requests for information about suspected black money hoarders.

While Swiss authorities would not give prior intimation to suspected individuals or entities before sparing their details, however, the onus would be on India (or any other requesting nation) to establish that any prior intimation to the account holders before information exchange would defeat the 'purpose of the administrative assistance' and the success of investigation would be thwarted.

In one of the major roadblocks to effective and timely exchange of information with foreign authorities about suspected illicit account holders, the Swiss laws provide that the person concerned would get a prior intimation of any such international assistance and he or she is also given an opportunity to appeal against this decision and inspect the files before being transmitted to the requesting nation.

While Switzerland has decided to retain these clauses in its amended Federal Act on International Administrative Assistance in Tax Matters, it has now incorporated at least 10 changes in this Act to lower guard on its famed banking secrecy walls to improve its information-exchange framework.

According to one of these amendments forming part of a new Gazette Notification:

> "If the foreign authority demonstrates grounds for secrecy regarding certain case documents, the FTA (Federal Tax Administration) may refuse to allow a person entitled to appeal to inspect the corresponding files."

Swiss Federal Council decided to relax this key legislation, following an intense pressure from India and other countries probing cases of suspected tax crimes.

The Swiss Parliament approved revision of this Act in March, 2014, while a referendum deadline for the proposed amendments expired on July 10, 2014.

In reply to queries on the status of the new Act, a spokesperson for Switzerland's State Secretariat for International Financial Matters told PTI,

> "I can confirm that the revised Federal Act on International Administrative Assistance in Tax Matters entered into force on August 1."

However, the new Act explicitly mentions that the Swiss authorities would not consider a request if "it constitutes a fishing expedition" or "if it violates the principle of good faith, particularly if it is based on information obtained through a criminal offence under Swiss law."

In its effort to unearth black money stashed away abroad, India has received data on over 24,000 instances of alleged tax evasions and dubious funds which has been detected in foreign shores in the last financial year. These cases are now under investigation by the taxmen even as the Special Investigation Team (SIT) on black money has set its eye on tracking the outcome of this classified information which has been received from over a dozen countries during the 2013-14 fiscal year. The bulk of the information on these foreign accounts and statements, with a basic fledgling domestic connect in each of them, has been received from New Zealand, followed by Spain, the United Kingdom, Sweden and Denmark—PTI.

It is no longer a crime to maintain bank accounts abroad by resident Indians. On June 1, 2000, the Foreign Exchange Regulation Act (FERA) was replaced by the Foreign Exchange Management Act (FEMA). By that change, a criminal offence became a civil contravention. So, nobody can be prosecuted for violating FEMA, much to the relief for black-money owners.

The clamour doing the rounds now to prosecute every foreign account holder appears silly. No prosecution under FEMA, or the Prevention of Money Laundering Act (PMLA), is possible since FEMA is not a scheduled offence under the PMLA. Prosecution can be launched only under the Income Tax Act for 'concealment' of income, not for parking funds abroad.

Parking funds abroad without concealing income does not contravene the Income Tax Act. The destination of concealed income—in India or abroad—is irrelevant under the Income Tax Act. The consequences of concealment under the Income Tax Act are slapping additional tax, interest, penalty and prosecution. But every concealment does not give rise to prosecution. Income tax authorities can exercise discretion whether or not to prosecute, depending on the gravity of each offence detected. However, the tendency to 'pick and choose' names to prosecute and to selectively reveal names under the garb of firming up an 'agreement' with Swiss authorities is unlikely to withstand any judicial scrutiny.

Before disclosing any name, several questions need to be answered—

1. When was the foreign account opened? If opened while the person was a non-resident Indian under FEMA, he would be entitled to maintain and operate that account for the rest of his life, even after becoming a resident of India.

2. One has to know if the account has been opened within the limit prescribed by the RBI, applicable to residents. If it has, then it would be in order.
3. If the funds have been generated abroad when the person was an NRI under the Income Tax Act. If they have been generated abroad, these funds would not be taxable in India.
4. One must ascertain if the funds have been generated abroad while the person was a resident under the FEMA and whether these have been repatriated through the banking channel. If so, it would be in order.
5. If funds have been stashed away abroad through the hawala route, whether the Enforcement Directorate (ED) has commenced any adjudication proceedings under FEMA.
6. Whether the income tax authorities have issued a notice to ascertain if the tax has been paid on funds generated in India and parked abroad.

These issues would require investigation by ED and Income Tax authorities. The passport of each account holder would require scrutiny to ascertain residential status at various points in time.

For ascertaining residential status of a person under the FEMA, full opportunity must be given to explain his employment, business and vocation from the date of opening his account. The total number of days that he has remained in India and outside in each financial year must also be ascertained. The residential status would have to be separately determined under the Income Tax Act.

The yardsticks for determining residential status under the Income Tax Act and the FEMA are different, with vastly varying implications. Simply declaring names to brand them 'criminals' without proper investigation would be catastrophic. The court is sure to come down heavily against the government if it carries out any slipshod exercise in a hurry.

So, the stand of the government not to disclose names at this stage is correct, even though the reasoning is wrong. The government is taking shelter behind treaty obligations with foreign countries. It is a settled law that in a conflict between any treaty obligation and domestic law, it is the domestic law that prevails. Even if the treaty obligations had allowed disclosure of names, the government cannot brand anyone a criminal without a proper and cogent inquiry.

Consequently, the government must expeditiously conclude an inquiry under domestic laws and then proceed. The question is, if prosecution is launched under the Income Tax Act for concealment of income abroad, what about prosecuting those concealing income in India? The Income Tax Act does not recognise the colour or origin of currency notes.

Repatriation of Funds

Under the Income Tax Act, an assessing officer has no power either to confiscate on behalf of the central government any asset or to direct any foreign bank account holder to repatriate funds. These powers lie with the ED under the FEMA. The ED hasn't even commenced any adjudication so far. In any event, residents today can hold, own, transfer and invest foreign assets in many situations.

Repatriation of funds is almost unachievable and collecting tax will be minuscule in a $2-trillion economy. So, the fact of the matter is, all this noise about bringing back stashed away funds into the country isn't about economics, but manipulating politics.

Swiss Accounts

The deal struck by the nation, which once seemed a pioneer in combating tax evasion, is emerging as a cautionary tale for a growing number of nations that are desperate to reap revenues from secret accounts held by the wealthy magnets.

When the British tax authorities struck a landmark deal with the Swiss to crack down on tax evasion, they sat back and waited for the cash to flow in. Almost three years after, they are still waiting. So far, only about $1.7 billion of the $8.4 billion windfall they once expected has materialized, and sheepish tax authorities now hope to eventually collect just one-third of their original estimate. The amounts at stake are enormous. In 2012, the British government estimated that Britons had amassed more than ¢68.5 billion in Swiss banks. Some conservative estimates of the amount of money tucked away in tax havens and out of reach of governments worldwide range as high as $21 trillion—more than the gross domestic product of the United States. British tax authorities are now facing increasing pressure to act more aggressively. But as the British deal has shown, the efforts to reduce tax avoidance by striking deals with individual havens are akin to plugging one hole in a colander. Britain's tax collection authorities said that it was "a concern we have had all along that as the Swiss agreement began to bite, people would then move their money elsewhere." In short, conceded the authorities, they took the money and ran.

The lesson that you cannot rely on a black hole to get income organization is developing standards for a broader international deal. So far 60 jurisdictions and nations, including Switzerland, have committed themselves. But that agreement is not expected to take effect until 2017, and critics are already pointing out loopholes.

Britain's deal with Switzerland had plenty of its own. For those who wanted to evade the British tax authorities, the agreement gave ample warning of 16 months-to shift money to other offshore havens or put it into gold, bearer funds, artwork, insurance or safe deposit boxes. The 16-month warning was "almost absurd," said Ian Swales, a Liberal Democrat and member of Britain's parliamentary Public Accounts Committee:

> "If you had £100 in your pocket and I told you that in a few weeks I would take a portion of it then you would'nt really keep £100 in your pocket."

Other money is hidden in even more elaborate mazes of offshore trusts and foundations often managed by trustees, usually foreign lawyers, allowing the real beneficiaries to remain hidden.

In July, *The Times* of London published the leaked data about a scheme called 'Liberty' deployed by 1,600 people, including celebrities like George Michael and the band Arctic Monkeys. The newspaper reported that they had sheltered money through a company in Leeds, England, that created offshore companies to generate paper losses.

Another example is the bribery trial in Germany of Bernie Ecclestone (age 85), a billionaire and Formula One tycoon considered one of the richest men in Britain. Ecclestone is accused of bribing a German banker, Gerhard Gribkowsky, with $44 million, for a favourable business deal. His defence is that he lavished the money to prevent the banker from alerting British tax authorities that it was he, and not his former wife, Slavica, who controlled a family trust set up in Liechtenstein, another famous tax haven.

Ecclestone denies that he controlled the trust and says the $44 million was extorted by the banker, to keep him from making false claims.

The finances of the trust are so complicated, according to a document filed in the trial, that under a 2009 divorce agreement, Ecclestone's former wife agreed to pay him about $100 million a year. In effect, the authorities say, it is a kind of alimony 'inversion'. Ecclestone keeps a home in Gstaad, Switzerland, which offers a shield because the Swiss authorities do not disclose any account information about legal residents. And his ex-wife is a Croatian who is not a British resident, which fact has also allowed Ecclestone to keep the money out of the reach of British tax authorities.

"This kind of multi-jurisdictional trust shows how difficult it is to break open these structures," said Markus Meinzer; a senior analyst based in Germany for Tax Justice Network which lobbies for transparency on tax issues.

> "They are basically impossible to penetrate without a whole array of lawyers and public prosecutors."

The British-Swiss deal was always contentious, with critics arguing that it amounted to an amnesty to tax evaders. The German government abandoned efforts to sign a similar agreement with Switzerland.

Under the deal with Switzerland about 18,000 Britons disclosed their names to the British authorities. Those who did not want to be identified paid a one-time levy of up to 34% to settle past taxes. Then the Swiss started deducting a regular 'withholding tax' on the interest on behalf of the British authorities. But recently, the Swiss sent the British a list of the international jurisdictions that had received money from accounts held by Britons in Switzerland before the deductions could be made. Jason Collins, a tax lawyer with Pinsent Masons in London, said that the likely locations include Singapore and Dubai. Other experts view the money shifting to Mauritius, Seychelles and Hong Kong.

The British tax authorities still insist they did the right thing by striking the agreement, even as they quietly lower expectations of its likely value. Supporters of the government argue that essentially it came down to this deal or nothing.

But Swales, the lawmaker, said that he wanted to see more naming and shaming of individuals. The Swiss, he said, were aware of many cases involving "people that they know are engaged in some form of criminal activity like tax evasion." The government was on severe grief that fell on it in the form of a

Supreme Court hearing on ill-gotten, untaxed 'black money' held in foreign banks. The change in fortunes was precipitated by its admission in court that the names of Indians (secretly) holding bank accounts abroad cannot be revealed owing to double taxation avoidance treaties with other countries. A public roasting ensued—expectedly.

Fortuitously for the government, a team of Indian officials had almost simultaneously rounded off talks with Switzerland, which they believe is the epicentre of black money. The Swiss banking system is steeped in secrecy and Indian attempts to even extract information have always proved futile. The government gave the impression that it had at long last achieved a major break-through in Switzerland.

Let's look at the joint statement signed by Indian Revenue Secretary and Swiss State Secretary that describes the talks. The two officials met in Berne as "part of the regular dialogue conducted by Swiss and Indian authorities." Though this deflates the impression of Indian spooks chasing bad guys, it would be wrong to surmise that nothing good came out of the meeting. There were two gains. The first was the willingness expressed by Switzerland to examine Indian requests for which investigations have been carried out independently. Indian authorities possess a so-called 'HSBC list' that contains names of Indians who have stashed wealth in the Swiss unit of the banking major. But Switzerland had since long maintained that there is no international standard to provide assistance based on information illegally obtained and Swiss legislation does not allow cooperation in such cases. The Swiss had finally relented, if only a little.

The second gain was the statement by Adrian Hug, Director of the Swiss Federal Tax Administration, that a competent Swiss authority would assist in confirming the genuineness of bank documents. The Indian Press reported on October 2014 that the government is about to send a batch of 50 names to Switzerland to confirm the authenticity of the HSBC list.

The gains end here. India's attempt to conclude an Automatic Exchange of Information Agreement (AEIA) with Switzerland "after completion of domestic procedures at the earliest" too was bandied about as another triumph. But only a diehard optimist would take solace from 'domestic procedures' and 'at the earliest'. Switzerland is yet to introduce the new global standard on AEIA in tax matters with partner States and the Swiss parliament will vote on the standard only next year. A statement on October 8 by the Swiss Federal Council says the first exchange of information could take place in 2018 but is subject to parliament and voters approving the necessary laws and agreements. The referendum has become necessary because, as a recent *The New York Times* report said, though Swiss authorities have nodded at cooperation with frustrated governments abroad, "at home, laws on the books since 1934 make violating client confidentiality a crime". There is no telling how the referendum will swing. But the *NYT* report said, "a backlash is building to protect the vaunted traditions of secrecy."

Andres Knobel, an analyst for the Tax Justice Network, an advocacy group that promotes transparency in international finance, said Switzerland has shown unwillingness to part with information, specially to developing countries. Switzerland has already expressed that it will require, among other things, reciprocity and confidentiality to exchange information, according to Knobel. The first caveat does not bode well for India because New Delhi is not a tax haven and the chances of Swiss nationals parking money here are remote. As for confidentiality, the Double Taxation Avoidance Agreement (DTAA) with Switzerland—the basis of cooperation in tax matters between the two countries—allows disclosure of information to authorities and courts concerned with tax appeals. However, the DTAA insists on confidentiality until authorities file charges for prosecution. The problem is that there is likelihood, according to media reports, of the names being revealed prematurely.

These obstacles apart, there are problems with the government's singular reliance on DTAA to extract information on black money. As Prof Arun Kumar (Jawaharlal Nehru University) noted in an article in *ET Magazine*,

> "The government has projected DTAA as a step to tackle the menace (of black money) but it is for getting information about legally held capital abroad. Capital is taken out of the country through layering via different tax havens (of which there are more than 70) so that when it reaches its final destination, it does not appear to be Indian money but say, from Cayman Islands."

That means Indian tax authorities have plenty of sniffing and chasing to do. But historically, whistleblower revelations have proved to be the primary sources of information on secret bank accounts.

Fake Currencies

Elections and money have an uneasy relationship. We fear money's influence in elections, and how it might undermine trust in the democratic process. Yet, it is seen as essential, especially when campaigns are as protracted as this current one. Money pays for the logistics, the ads and even the food and drinks that, in large parts of the country, is seen as a necessary inducement to voting.

But money might be a source for further unease with this election. Several media reports have quoted sources in organisations like the Directorate of Revenue Intelligence (DRI) on the large amounts of fake currency notes flooding the country. They are usually alleged to have been printed in Pakistan, both to finance terrorism and destabilize the Indian economy by destroying trust in our currency, and smuggled into India from other neighbouring countries. ET recently reported a DRI alert for all international airports, ports and land transit roots to watch out for smuggled counterfeit notes. Law enforcement agencies know that in all counterfeiting operations the challenge is not just producing convincing notes, but also finding easy ways to distribute them and that is what elections provide. With so much money thrown around and no accounts asked for, its easy to pass out large amounts of fake notes. One report suggests that 4 out of every 1,000 currency notes might be fake and that the total value in circulation is well over ₹3,200 crore.

This is wildly in variance with what the Reserve Bank of India (RBI) claims. The RBI's annual report says that 4,98,252 fake notes were detected in 2012-13. This would be around 0.00067% of total Indian rupees in circulation, adding up to a value of around ₹25 crore. Central banks typically don't like talking about counterfeits, but in a detailed report in the Toronto Globe & Mail on how Canada tackled its burgeoning counterfeiting problem its indicated that alarm bells went off when the number reached 0.47% of notes, which was 10 times of what was acceptable in G20 countries.

By that norm India is still far from facing problems. The RBI's currency department, through the bank's spokesperson, says firmly: "The security features in genuine Indian banknotes have not been breached." A directive to withdraw by March 2014 (later extended to January 2015) all pre-2005 notes stirred rumours that it was meant to tackle counterfeiting, but RBI says it was simply a regular process: "Earlier we withdrew older series banknotes in a passive manner where the banks were instructed not to re-issue such notes and send back those notes to RBI for disposal," says the spokesperson. In the past few years, banks were told to do this for all notes of ₹100 and above printed prior to 2005. "In the current withdrawal plan we have involved the public also," says the spokesperson.

One response to this divergence in news might be that the RBI is understating the problem either because it is not convinced about the extent of counterfeiting or because it wants to dampen fears of its extent. After all, stories about Pakistan-printed notes are widespread. In January, 2014 a National Investigative Agency (NIA) judge awarded life sentences to six people caught in 2009 distributing fake notes and explicitly stated,

> "It is certainly a terrorist act in which neighbouring sovereign country, i e Pakistan is involved with the sole purpose and intention to damage and threaten the unity, integrity, economic security and sovereignty of this country...."

That would seem to state the matter plainly, yet there is room for some ambiguity in the issue and it is linked to the nature of money. Money, particularly paper currency, is in its essence just a matter of trust and this is why counterfeiting has always been seen as such a threat. Fake currency undermines trust and threatens the whole system of money, as can be seen from the NIA judge's strong words. A State's power is reflected in the trust its money commands, so counterfeiting is an attack on the State.

For this reason counterfeiting has always been punished very severely. The Romans varied the penalty depending on the value of currency—faking silver coins meant exile, but faking gold got you thrown to the lions. The British decreed hanging, drawing and quartering, which involved disembowelling the criminal before he was dead. The US also made it a capital crime, with a lesser penalty of being branded and having ones ears cropped. This no longer applies, but fighting counterfeiting is still the job of the US Secret Service, along with protecting the President.

Yet counterfeiting currency has always flourished. The gains seem too large and immediate—all you need to do is pass on the fake, and then it is literally out of your hands. Counterfeiting also appeals to an anarchic dislike for the State that many people harbour. Many counterfeiters in the US were acquitted by juries who felt it was a minor, 'clean' crime. When the State is the victim then all are, but few feel it that way. So, once currency was delinked from bullion reserves and governments printed money easily to cover their needs, people were cynical and wondered why they couldn't create value the same way.

Adding to cynicism is the fact that States have done their share of faking. Rulers have devalued their own currency to cover their reckless spending, but printing an enemy State's currency is also an established tactic. The most famous case is Operation Bernhard when the Nazis took Jewish artists into concentration camps and made them forge British pounds and US dollars which they planned to air drop to cause chaos in these countries. 'The Counterfeiters', an Austrian film based on this story, won an Oscar for Best Foreign Film in 2007.

But Jason Goodwin, in *Greenback*, a history of the US dollar, points out that the idea originated with the British during the American Revolution. The rebelling colonies printed their own currency, but the British felt this was illegal to start with, so it wasn't wrong to fake these notes. They were open about it: "The more public their operations, the more successfully they cast doubt on the currency," writes Goodwin, citing newspaper ads through which they offered the fakes to those travelling to the rebels.

Such brazenness was matched by Rajaram Waman Mudras who, *The Times of India* reported on April 12, 1960, was arrested when the police found a currency printing press in his office in Fort, Bombay. Mudras had an ingenious defence he was forging the Portuguese currency of Goa, still not part of India then. Mudras said he was fighting for Goa's freedom and "that one of the acts of hostility in this war was to print counterfeit notes and thereby inflate the value of the currency in the Portuguese set dement." The judge didn't buy this admirably anti-colonial argument and sentenced him to jail.

And then there is the Super Dollar. This is a very high-quality fake dollar that is said to be printed by an enemy State to the US—perhaps Iran or Syria. The first Super dollars may have surfaced in the 1980s, with more details emerging after the capture of two Lebanese born drug traffickers in 1992 who revealed the operation. The Super dollar story made much news at that time but then this is the interesting part it neither entirely went away nor developed much beyond that.

Super Dollar stories still emerge occasionally focusing on North Korea now, and always suggesting economic danger and imminent collapse of the dollar and then the story dies again. The US treasury department stonewalls, much as the RBI might be doing now. At the most there is tinkering with security features like new micro-printing panels or threads. The RBI is talking about polymer currency, the so-called plastic notes pioneered by Australia that are the most secure form of currency because the formula for the polymer substrate is closely guarded and does not as yet, seem to have been copied. Polymer notes are how Canadians solved their counterfeit problems with and they are now widely used by our neighbours including Bangladesh, Sri Lanka, Singapore and Nepal. The RBI has plans to try them in five cities—Shimla, Kochi, Jaipur, Bhubaneswar and Mysore—but this has been the case only for a while now. The RBI's plans for polymer highlights its durability and environmental benefits as much as its security. India may get polymer notes one day, but the RBI doesn't want to sound like counterfeiting is the compulsion.

Apart from the pre-2005 withdrawal proposal, quickly modified, the RBI has also not gone in for the wholesale withdrawal of bank note series. Countries like the UK which do this make it easier by doing a complete redesign of their notes each time. When new notes are introduced, with the latest security features, there are windows in which the old notes can be withdrawn, but after a point this closes. It is not a good idea to keep old UK pounds in your cupboard between trips.

As of now, India is like the US where every note printed in the independent country is legal tender (barring the high value rupee notes demonetized in 1978). Both countries also rarely change the basic designs of the notes, though the reasons probably differ—the US treasury feels it adds to the stability of the currency, whereas the RBI probably knows that any design change is likely to cause objections from politicians, so it's easiest just to keep things the same.

Yet such a static position is curious, given the frequency and urgency of allegations in both countries of fake currency printed by enemy States (claims of forged Indian notes in Pakistan go back to 1957). And perhaps there is a clue in Goodwin's statement of how the British felt that even claims of counterfeiting could undermine trust. When you are in a situation where even a claim of an attack might work as well as an actual attack, perhaps the best solution is not to even bother repulsing the attack, but pretending the attack never happened. It is a mind game, but then that is what money is about.

In any case, cash is becoming ever less important to central banks. This may not be the case with the RBI, given the extant of the cash economy in India, but the US treasury is clearly more concerned about digital dollars that trade invisibly and continuously across the world than their green and black real life counterparts. As for the Super Dollars, perhaps they are a threat, as just another sign, however backhanded the compliment, of the US's power. Certainly, the US treasury doesn't seem to want us to worry about them, and the RBI may feel the same way about fakes. Hence in the strange world of currencies, counterfeits and confidence, perhaps they may be right.

Expenditure in Election

Money whisked away abroad is tiny compared with the unaccounted money within India. Yet, the political system has long been barking up the wrong tree; the ongoing debate on black money has been no different. Indians hold assets abroad through multiple trails of offshore shell companies and hundreds of accounts in tax havens. Tax officials haven't shown the gumption or means to track these assets, leave alone confiscating them. All the authorities possess as evidence is a so-called 'HSBC list' that contains names of Indians who have hoarded wealth in the Swiss unit of the banking major. This is actually a stolen information by a bank employee, which the French government shared with India. *The Times of India*, quoting unnamed government officials, reported recently that the HSBC list is of no use because it contains no big names, the entries are too old and accounts have little money. Talk about an anti-climax. India's best bet is to join other countries in turning the heat on tax havens. But even this plan faces uncertainty owing to a Supreme Court order seeking full disclosure on illegal bank accounts held abroad. The court order has muddied the emphasis on secrecy in bilateral tax treaties that facilitate exchange of information. The government's peekaboo policy of revealing three names on the HSBC list too didn't help. No surprise then that India has delayed signing of crucial international agreement aimed at automatic financial information on tax evasion, which could help secure information about Indians hiding money in tax havens. Pretty bleak, right? Say, the government by a stroke of luck receives information. Good luck with that because prosecutions are painfully long.

Against this grim back drop, government's directive is welcome. But it too has not addressed the heart of the scourge of black money in India—the way political parties finance themselves. It is no secret that all parties depend on donations, but the manner in which they collect money is largely shrouded in secrecy. "Nearly 75% of their funds are from undisclosed sources," said SY Quraishi, former Chief Election Commissioner.

Even the records of money parties have submitted to the Election Commission (EC) show a kind of guile bordering on illegality. The Congress, for example, has declared that more than a third of its total income of ₹2,365 crore between 2004-05 and 2011-12 was generated by sale of coupons to, mostly its own workers and leaders, according to a study by Association of Democratic Reforms (ADR), an organization that pursues political reforms. EC officials say coupons are nothing but a tool to collect money from outsiders and source it to party members. One would expect Samajwadi Party to find donors aplenty in Uttar Pradesh, where it rules. But it has listed just three donors (in 2012-13), two of whom reside in West Bengal of all places. The duo made 11 contributions totalling ₹2.19 crore. Nine of those contributions came from Aditi Sen, a resident of Salt Lake City, Kolkata. Two contributions were made by Sundeep Sen, a resident of the same address as Aditi. There are plenty of similar examples for every major party, which look more air-borne as fictitious.

As it happens, the donations disclosed are peanuts as compared with the amounts parties raise in the run-up to elections. In June 2011, the government tasked a committee to study black money. Its observations make for startling reading. "The two major national parties claim to have incomes of merely ₹500 crore ($81 million) and ₹200 crore ($32 million). But this isn't even a fraction of their expenses. These parties spend between ₹10,000 crore ($1.6 billion) and ₹15,000 crore ($2.4 billion) annually on election expenses alone," said the report.

Indeed, it costs parties a bomb to run a decent campaign. Lakhs have to be spent on just a rally on publicity, choppers and vehicles, booze and money to lure volunteers and so on. "Election financing is the best example of the existence of black money in India," said a senior EC official.

The EC issued a set of guidelines aimed at bringing transparency and accountability in the funding of political parties during 'elections and other times'. The guidelines, call for parties to maintain records of all donations and make all payments beyond ₹20,000 by cheques or drafts. At least four major parties aren't pleased. The Congress has accused the EC of exercising unbridled powers and said the guidelines are legally untenable and liable to be set aside on judicial review. The CPI(M) was uneasy on petty sums and raised the prospect of misinterpretations. The party was also against maintaining records of all donations.

> "We have about 1 million members and 1 lakh Party units. About 31.2% of the income for 2012-13 has come from Party members and from membership fees. The rest are from millions of donors from 1 lakh units. There are practical difficulties in issuing individual acknowledgment or receipt on coupons in hundi collections."

Wrote General Secretary Prakash Karat in a letter to the EC. (In its stronghold Kerala, the CPI(M) is known for 'bucket pirivu' that has volunteers collecting money in a bucket.)

The BSP has said it is hard to record every transaction because its donors are not literate, adding that the denominations too are small (the BSP is the only national party that claims that all the voluntary contributions it receives are below ₹20,000 according to ADR). "Then the cost of recording transactions will exceed the value of contributions," wrote Satish Chandra Mishra, General Secretary, in a letter to the EC.

The RJD and JD(U) echoed the same sentiment as the Congress, cautioning the EC that it simply doesn't have the powers to impose such guidelines. These three parties said that a few provisions are vague and parliament must amend the Representation of the People Act, 1951 for such requirements to take effect. (The language used by the representatives of these parties in their objections is eerily similar.)

Only the CPI(M) was reserved in its response, asking the EC to make the changes in guidelines regarding hundi collections. A member of the CPI(M) politburo, its highest decision-making body, said his party had agreed to nearly every proposal in the draft guidelines on transparency.

> "We don't agree with the Congress's view that the EC has no powers. We are all for transparency."

RJD spokesman said his party opposed the EC norms because they will endanger the very existence of small political outfits like his. The big parties have the wherewithal and resources but we have to manage our affairs with the aid of small donations. Another EC official said,

> "The responses of these parties seem like threats to sue us."

The first EC official said,

> "They are objecting to audit reports because they will establish that expenses are at least ₹500 crore while the records they present to us will point to expenses of say, just ₹30 crore. No doubt, the guidelines will make life difficult for parties. The huge amounts of money used in elections can only be raised illegally. Neither the donor (an individual, corporate or contractor) nor the beneficiary (parties) would want transactions to be made public. Contributors to political parties can claim tax rebates but they don't because they have to reveal their own source of income."

That is not to suggest that parties are unduly worried about EC directives rather, they have pooh-poohed these rules. A similar fate awaits the transparency norms. That's because, as the parties themselves reminded the EC, it lacks powers other than to conduct free and fair elections despite the argument that the transparency guidelines aim at achieving that very objective. At best, the EC can de-recognize an erring party (cancel its symbol), but cannot de-register it. It has made campaign finance rules tougher—by capping the expenses of candidates and insisting they maintain a separate bank account to issue money—but that has only encouraged parties to raise money illegally. Most candidates violate rules (there are no limits on-expenses by political parties anyway) and they spend up to 10 times the cap on expenses on an election, said Quraishi.

The bigger danger is that illegal funding of parties breeds corruption. Quraishi said,

> "Donations may be tainted money from criminals corporate houses with promises of favours in return. There are no free lunches, remember."

It should not surprise one that India is often cited as a prime example of crony capitalism, where plenty of people get rich or grow richer thanks to their proximity to the government.

Jagdeep S Chhokar of ADR said that it is true the EC has no powers, but that doesn't mean its guidelines are not relevant. He said,

> "It is sad that political parties, which make rules through their representatives in parliament, have refused to make rules that will usher transparency. Instead, They are taking refuge in existing laws, which ironically they themselves made."
>
> "If the situation continues, people at large may lose faith in democracy. That will be a sad day for the country."

Political parties remain tone deaf to such arguments. A Central Information Commission order seeking to bring national parties under the Right to Information Act is hanging fire due to stiff opposition.

Changing the system won't be easy, but what is the way forward? Chhokar said change will come eventually by building public pressure and securing legal victories. As an example, he cites how the previous government had a change of mind on overturning a Supreme Court ruling last year that disqualified MPs and MLAs convicted of criminal charge due to public pressure.

ADR has filed a Public Interest Litigation calling for transparency on party finances. The organization will challenge the arguments made by parties against the EC's guidelines at the next hearing. But until a court intervention happens, it is safe to say parties will ignore the guidelines, said the second EC official. "No party takes us seriously."

Recovering Black Money

The government must exert its influence globally to curtail the shadow financial system, particularly within G20 where it plays a key role. There are things India can do by itself. In an analysis, trade mis-pricing is more responsible than any other mechanism for flow of illicit money from India and other countries. India should take a strong role in determining the identity of the real owners of entities that do business, particularly those established in Mauritius and other tax havens. We can accomplish this by instructing banks against receiving investments from abroad without knowing their origins. This is not difficult, but we need the will to do it.

Indians use the same techniques as everybody else, in particular the mis-pricing of trade. It is the biggest mover of illicit money and the toughest to curtail. Let us be realistic. It is very easy to mis-price a transaction by 5-15%. By looking at an invoice, we can never tell if it has been mis-priced.

Money has been moved from Switzerland to Singapore and Hong Kong. Dubai was a favourite destination until economic problems surfaced. But this is a favourable development. When we keep pressure on larger jurisdictions and force money to smaller ones, it will force money to even smaller ones until the problem is weeded out.

It is still possible to open secret bank accounts, hiding behind nominees and trustees. But the situation is getting marginally better.

Real Estate

A real estate developer joked that the engine of real estate in India has two wheels: one is white money that comes from genuine buyers and the other is black money. And, currently, both wheels have stopped turning.

He wasn't joking. Today, the market is stagnant because most genuine buyers can't afford to buy their dream home as the market is overpriced. The investors who were pumping in black money have also paused as prices have stagnated. Curiously, the escalation of prices itself has happened because of the large inflows of black money into realty. Even though no official figures are available, it is safe to assume that anywhere between 30% and 40% of real estate transactions be it the purchase of land or an apartment in a metro—involve black money.

Of course, higher the price tag of an apartment, bigger is the black money component. For instance, there is hardly any black money involved in an apartment priced between ₹15 lakh and ₹20 lakh but in a luxury apartment priced above ₹3 crore, the black money component could go up to 60%.

It starts right at the time the land is purchased, let's say for the construction of an apartment. In a city like Mumbai, virgin land isn't available. So invariably, developers have to buy land in outskirts or villages outside the city limits, where the ready reckoner rates (or circle rates) are low. Often, the people who own the land, ask for a significant part of the payment in black, sometimes as much as 25-30%, so that they can avoid getting taxed.

The next step is getting approvals, which invariably involves getting building approvals from local civic bodies which in turn are controlled by politicians and bureaucrats. That again involves significant amount of unaccounted money.

All these under-the-table payments mean that a developer has to have a significant kitty of black money. So, the developer starts putting price tags on things he isn't legally allowed to sell, parking in apartments, for instance. It is this chain of black money transactions that has raised the launch prices of apartments, resulting in the fact that most genuine buyers can't afford a home.

The only one who can afford a home are, unfortunately, not the salaried class but traders and other dubious buyers who have a steady flow of black money. Given that Indian tax norms favour people who are buying a second or third house more than a first-time buyer, most people who can indulge in inflated real estate transactions are investors who have black money. They have unyielding capital that they choose to invest in real estate.

Between 2001 and 2005, real estate in India boomed. Interest rates were low, housing was affordable and first-time buyers were entering the market. One could understand a bump-up in prices then. But, 2009 onwardss, something strange happened. Despite the fact that there wasn't a great wave of buying from first-time buyers, prices went upwards sharply. Most of this was fuelled by investors who invested in the premium and luxury segments and most of them involved black money transactions.

State governments have responded by reducing ready reckoner rates to almost the same level as market value but that alone hasn't been enough.

If the government is serious about achieving its stated goal of housing for all by 2022, then it will have to make a few systemic changes. One, incentivize first-time buyers. Two, make the process of getting approvals transparent. Make the process automated. Cut off all political discretions when it comes to granting approvals or buying land.

The Real Estate Regulation Bill is a first step towards that. But in its current form, there are some loosely defined terms in the draft and oversights which can be misused. For instance, approving authorities are not brought under the purview of the Bill. Most delays of housing projects happen because of delayed approvals.

India has a shortfall of 18.7 million homes—over 95% of this is in the economically weaker section. Only 1.4% of that demand is being met. If we want India's real estate sector to blossom again, this menace of black money needs to be weeded out.

Route of Black Money

In February 2008, R Prasad, the then Chairman of the Central Board of Direct Taxes (CBDT), led a team of tax sleuths to Port Louis, the capital city of Mauritius. Backed by a team from the ministry of external affairs, Prasad made an attempt to convince Mauritius officials to re-negotiate the Double Tax Avoidance Agreement (DTAA), which was resulting in massive tax losses to India.

The attempt was unsuccessful, but what discovered in the process was startling—a handful of persons acted as directors for about 30,000 companies located in that island nation. Also, companies there exist only on paper, as addresses of many of those begin with a mere post box number.

Mauritius and many other tax havens act as buffers to bring back India's black money as white. And the challenge before the investigators is to establish the criminality of those involved in such activities.

Now, the Supreme Court appointed Special Investigation Team (SIT) on black money wants such tax treaties to be re-drafted, a move that will put the government in a spot. Recently, a reluctant government had to hand over to the Apex Court a complete list of 627 Indians who have accounts in HSBC Bank, Geneva.

The debate so far has been that what comes first: investment or tax? Is India ready to sacrifice investments worth billions of dollars for the sake of some tax gain? So far as Mauritius is concerned, any retreat from India's side will allow China to woo the island nation. This explains why New Delhi hasn't been assertive with Mauritius, a nation where Indian defence forces harbour strategic interests.

While tax havens like Mauritius will help black money come back into the country as white, Indians continue to send illicit money abroad. This is done through various methods, hawala transactions—where money is transferred abroad without any real movement of funds—being one of them although, according to a finance ministry white paper on black money released two years ago, hawala transactions have actually dwindled over the past decade. The report says,

> "In recent years, after the 9/11 incident in the US, due to intense scrutiny of banking transactions, enhanced security checks at airports and ports and relaxation of exchange controls, transfer of money through hawala has reduced significantly."
>
> "...increasing pressure on financial operators and banks to report cash transactions has also helped in curbing hawala transactions."

However, there are other methods to siphon black money out of the country, two of which are manipulation of export invoices and setting up of trusts abroad. A large number of the accounts of the 627 names based on data stolen by an employee of HSBC, Geneva, would be of such trusts. The *modus operandi* adopted here is as follows: black money moves abroad through routes like hawala. Then a trust is formed in, let's assume, The Netherlands. The trustees in this case will be Dutch nationals, but the beneficiaries will be relatives of an Indian back home who put in the initial corpus. But they can initiate a probe only when money gets reflected in the accounts of the beneficiaries.

As the Income Tax department and the Enforcement Directorate (ED) will now work under SIT, one can expect more urgency in the mission to bring back unaccounted money. Yet, genuine hurdles may come in the way of that endeavour. The classic example of such a hurdle is seen in the case of Pune-based stud farm-owner Hasan Ali Khan, who was raided by the Income Tax department seven years ago. Documents and data in his laptop established that he had a Swiss bank account with a whopping $8 billion (roughly 48,000 crore) in deposits. Ali was sent to jail, but the ED that probes money-laundering cases found out from the Swiss authorities that Ali's accounts had been emptied.

The multi-billion dollar question then is: how many of the 627 whose names exist in a sealed cover would have done the same?

Mushrooming Companies Mystery

Over a two-week period in March 2012, thousands of shell companies are believed to have been formed all over the country, and before the beginning of the new financial year on April 1, 2012 thousands of small companies were incorporated across the country. It was estimated that the number of private limited companies formed in Kolkata alone, between March 16 and March 31, 2012, was around 3,173 (possibly more). The financial year which was to end two weeks after that budget speech was to set a record of sorts, with more companies being incorporated during that year than any other across India.

The Registrar of Companies (RoC) in West Bengal, under which companies domiciled in that State are incorporated, reported that 16,477 private limited, non-government owned companies were incorporated that year. Thus, a fifth of those were incorporated in just the last two weeks of March in Kolkata. On March 29 alone, around 416 companies were registered in Kolkata.

Start-up tax has been criticised. The government had tightened income tax laws that affect the way investors put money into new private limited companies. Any investments in those companies at a share price above what the law called 'fair market value' was to be treated as the income of the company and taxed. Little wonder then, that start-ups and entrepreneurs were nervous as it was seen as hurting the flow of venture funding into new companies (however, the law did exempt investments by recognised venture funds).

In that respect the burst of new companies being formed seems perfectly understandable. Entrepreneurs rushed to incorporate new companies before April 1 to avoid being affected by the new law which would kick in on that date.

Kolkata city, known more for industries such as coal and steel, was hardly a thriving hub of start-up culture. And then there were other oddities. Of the 3,173 companies formed in those two weeks, around 294 were located in just one building, on one street in the city.

As an income tax officer later termed it, those companies were a form of 'inventory' for an industry that is largely unknown, unless you happen to be an accountant, or a lawyer, or an executive well-versed in the ways that corporate India manages money, especially black money.

The Shell Company Business

The 'accommodation entry' business, or, to give it its colloquial Kolkata name, the 'jamakharchi' business has been around in one form or the other for decades, but began to get organized and streamlined into what in management-speak would be called a 'scalable' business in Kolkata in the '80s. Since then it has spread to other cities. However, Kolkata, at least till a couple of years ago, was its epicentre.

The jamakharchi business exists for one big reason—to help its 'customers' convert black money into white, or vice versa.

Given that, unaccounted-for money is a part and parcel of how Corporate India operates, it raises the very immediate problem of how that black money is to be created and converted. On the one hand, large listed companies with foreign investors have to report audited accounts and ostensibly account for each rupee spent. On the other, while the companies may run perfectly legitimate businesses, they often have to deal with entities that aren't very transparent and which would prefer to be paid, or pay, in cash. And this is just those companies which don't want to evade any tax at all.

The 'jamakharchi' business exists to make such transactions happen by the tens, or even hundreds or thousands of crores. It's important to point out that the jamakharchi business is, strictly speaking, not a money-laundering business, though they share similar aspect. While money-laundering aims to convert money earned from criminal activity into legitimate income, the jamakharchi business may deal in unaccounted-for money earned as part of a perfectly legal business.

One of the more common ways to do this, till the change in tax law in 2012, was as follows. If a company had black money, which it wanted to channel as seemingly legitimate investments back into itself or group companies, it would get in touch with one of many 'accommodation entry' operators in the country. Some of the largest ones manage a portfolio of thousands of companies, either on their own, or through 'sub-operators' whom they habitually do business with.

When the deal is struck (often through a broker rather than with the operator directly), the 'customer' buys shares at face value in one of the operators' companies. This can be worth just a few rupees. He hands over the black money to the operator, who has it deposited into bank accounts he controls (with the help of amenable bank managers). The money is invested and re-invested in dozens of other companies controlled by that operator, and into the target company, now owned by the 'customer', at a hefty premium to the share price. This can be shown on the balance sheet of the customers' company as a legitimate investment. The black money has been laundered. If tax authorities try to trace the antecedents of investors who put money into a company (which does no business at all) at a steep premium to the book value of the company, they will likely find other shell companies behind those investors, and still other behind them. It's a bit like peeling of an onion. This layering not only makes it difficult to trace the original source of funds, it acts as a way for the 'customer' to deny any knowledge of where the money comes from.

Directors in such shell companies are often just employees, or even the drivers and servants of the operator who for a few hundred rupees will sign their name on company papers. In Kolkata and elsewhere, say tax officials, there are those who actually act as 'freelance' professional directors of such companies. That too for a meagre ₹1,000 or so. Operators actually prefer such people since that puts even more distance between themselves and the 'directors' who eventually get hauled up by law-enforcement.

A striking feature behind many of the high-profile scams in recent years has been the involvement of Kolkata-based shell companies. In the 2G scam, for instance, part of the money trail went through Kolkata.

It was these kinds of transactions that the new tax law aimed at. Any investment at a substantial premium to book value would now lead to the very effect that the customer wanted to avoid—to be taxed on that money. In the process, though, genuine entrepreneurs and start-ups ended up being collateral damage, though the tax authorities have said that they will not target legitimate businesses. The companies set up in the last few days of March 2012, say tax officials, are essentially an inventory of companies to be used in future years and for future customers.

But the battle continues. And one of the tools the tax authorities plan to use is in response to an unusual and counter-intuitive tactic adopted by many jamakharchi operators. That instead of seeking to avoid the taxman, they actively seek to get their shell companies selected for scrutiny by tax authorities.

Shell companies that have had their books scrutinized by a tax officer and pronounced to be clean are more highly valued by 'customers' than a brand new company which has never been looked at closely by the tax-man. The value of an older company that has been given a clean chit is higher than a new company. Commission rates charged by a jamakharchi operator (as a percentage of the equity capital of the shell company that a customer buys) are 2-3% in Kolkata for a company that has undergone such scrutiny, as compared with 0.3% for a brand new company. The tax official says,

> "Kolkata's operators did well because they were relatively cheaper than in other places like Mumbai where commission rates were as high as 5-6%."
>
> "Also, they tended to be more 'honest' in their dealings than similar operators in Delhi who would probably cheat by offering you an untested company but try and pass it off as one that was investigated and pronounced clean by the tax authorities."

Another reason why Kolkata was preferred even by companies located in Mumbai or Delhi was simply because routing money through a company located in a different city than the customer made it all that harder for investigations to be pursued.

But given that nowadays tax returns are picked for scrutiny by a computer algorithm located at a data centre in Delhi, rather than by local tax authorities. How did operators ensure that their companies got picked? What operators did after filing a shell company's return was to file another application stating that they had omitted to disclose some income in the original return—often a small sum of a few thousand rupees and offering that money up to be taxed.

If the application came to an assessing officer who was pliable enough, and bribable enough, he would certify as well that the share capital of the company was in the clear and appeared to come from legitimate sources. In any further tax proceeding, which might come up as a result of that shell company being used to route black money, this would be valuable testimony.

Tax authorities in Kolkata have compiled a database of shell companies known or suspected to be used by well-established accommodation entry operators to route funds. They are aiming to ensure that as and when such companies come up for scrutiny before them (including those companies set up in March 2012), they will be declared as shell companies by the assessing officer, thus rendering them worthless in the eyes of customers. The tax official says,

> "Further, we want to ensure that any 'customer' who deals with shell companies on that database will automatically face scrutiny."

Tax authorities claim that because of the 2012 law and other measures, the 'jamakharchi' business in Kolkata has been dealt a body blow. Certainly, new company registrations in Kolkata are sharply down, to half of what they were in 2012. But in other cities such as Mumbai or Delhi, new registrations have actually risen since then, though no estimate exists of how many of these new companies are legitimate businesses and how many are used for accommodation entries.

Others are sceptical. People have already found a way around the legal provision. The law itself had specifically exempted investments by registered venture capital firms. The government, under its FDI policy, also allows the 'fair' valuation of shares issued by unlisted companies to foreign investors to be done in such a way as to take into account future expected cash flows—a method which while widely used and accepted, allows for a fair amount of leeway in determining a company's valuation. Further, valuing other aspects of a company's balance sheet such as intellectual property rights is also very subjective. A CA can easily certify a certain value of IPR. And other methods, such as the use of listed penny stocks to convert black money to white, still exist. Moreover, even if the 2012 law does reduce the ability of corporates to use shell companies and fictitious transactions to bulk up their balance sheets (and that's a big if), the damage is done. Using fairly simple yardsticks and basic assumptions, several tens of thousand crores of black money are estimated to have been moved through Kolkata alone in any given year, according to Income Tax investigators.

Further, shell companies are still being used for other purposes than simply evading tax or converting unaccounted for money. Companies for instance still use shell entities to bulk up their balance sheets through fictitious sales for purposes such as taking out bank loans.

Around half of all jamakharchi transactions are now done with the aim of faking accounts to take bank loans. As per tax officials, "The NPA levels that we see now are only the tip of the iceberg."

While no firm numbers exist income tax investigators say it is possible to work out a guesstimate, by making assumptions about the proportion of shell companies and the valuation at which money was invested in them. However, no one knows what the actual data is, so treat these numbers with caution.

Working of Shell Companies

Bogus Sale or Purchase

Shell companies are used to show fictitious sales or purchases of goods and services with 'customers'. These are often used to inflate balance sheets and profit and loss accounts to avail of bank loans.

One Time Entry of Share

Get bogus investors in to invest at a premium used by a customer to inflate company valuation.

Outright Sale of Company

The company is sold at a commission of up to 2-3% of share capital and is used to route black money into a company, to be converted to white.

Bogus Long-Term Capital Gains

By investing in listed penny stocks, customers can book bogus capital gains or losses by coordinating buy and sell orders with stock operators who control the trade in such stocks.

Corporate Ethics

One of the unique features of the Indian constitution is that, notwithstanding the adoption of a federal system and the existence of Central and State acts in their respective spheres, it has generally provided for a single integrated system of courts to administer the laws of both the Union and the States. The Supreme Court of India is at the apex of the entire judicial system. Below it are the High Courts in each State, below which lies a vast hierarchy of subordinate courts. The Indian Supreme Court has settled the disputed question of criminal liability of a corporation. The Standard Chartered Bank decision overrules prior decisions to the contrary and holds that corporations are liable for criminal offences and can be prosecuted and punished, at least with fines.

Fraud can be devastating for a company. The Chinese government has accused a company and its executives, including the former head of funnelling hundreds of millions of dollars in bribes to doctors and health officials. This has forced the company to terminate a number of senior executives.

This is hardly the only company battling corruption. Last year, Walmart India suspended several executives at its joint venture with Bharti including its CFO and CEO as it examined potential violations of US anti-bribery laws. Cadbury India is being investigated for alleged bribery by US authorities. Adidas India terminated and pressed criminal charges against its country manager and other senior executives accusing them of defrauding the company of over $150 million.

These are not shabby companies. They had implemented all the basics: a code of conduct, written policies, tight controls et al. Yet, they fell victim to fraud by their own senior leaders.

Increasingly, the biggest corruption risk companies may face is not that they will have to pay bribes or speed money to government officials but that many of their own employees may be on, the take. Partly that's because of the rising pressure on financial performance; the temptation to cook the books, stuff the channel with inventory, and make side agreements with customers and partners is great.

Greed is also driving more management fraud. Accepting kickbacks from vendors and advertising agencies, commissions on real estate transactions or machinery purchases, a deposit in an overseas bank on the successful acquisition or sale of a company; these are becoming routine.

It's not just multinational companies that are victims of employee fraud. Indian companies too are being victims. It's just that MNCs have home country anti-bribery laws that are more stringently enforced. Companies must take multiple precautions to inoculate themselves against the risk of employee fraud.

To start with, ensure that the basics are in place. Have you instituted a formal code of conduct with mandatory training for every employee and annual re-certification? How is the company's code of conduct communicated to customers, dealers, and vendors? Do vendors know the entertainment and travel reimbursement policies of the company? Does the company have a strong internal audit team and a competent fraud investigation unit? How does the company deal with a problem? Is investigation swift and punishment decisive and fair? Clear policies, procedures with approval processes and stringent controls, regular internal audits of high-risk areas, and so on are all necessary measures, but what really matters is strong leadership and a culture of compliance. The tone set by local leadership is critical, especially in our hierarchical culture. A zero-tolerance policy is vital. Few companies discuss the character of leaders during hiring or performance appraisal; hitting the numbers is almost all that really matters.

However, companies must pay attention to the small things, like segregation of personal phone calls, appropriateness of business expenses, lifestyle and addiction to status symbols and the personal use of company assets. A sense of entitlement in small things is often a predictor of bigger problems. An open and non-hierarchical culture is also important. In most cases, employees are aware of suspicious conduct long before it is officially discovered but they won't blow the whistle if they don't feel safe in coming forward or if they don't believe that top management is serious about punishing wrongdoing or the wrongdoers.

When it comes to ethics and compliance, culture and leadership really matter. The CEO has to ensure that in every part of the world, every employee is utterly clear about what conduct is acceptable and what is not. In many companies, when fraud is discovered, the response is shock and dismay; middle managers and front line employees are conveniently made scapegoats. Life goes on as usual.

Globalization today is fundamentally about expanding into emerging markets. Whilst these markets are dynamic and filled with talent and opportunity, many are also unfortunately very corrupt societies. Dealing with corruption is a new core competency that no global company can afford to do without.

There's a shadow that lurks in Indian organisations. It blends in nicely but systematically drills a hole in the company's finances. Unmask it, and this is what it's typically like: Male, 36-45 years of age, extrovert, respected in his role. Has been with the organisation for 1-4 years and is employed at the staff or managerial level. Possibly an engineer and plays a role in operations or procurement.

This, according to 'Profiles of a Fraudster', a KPMG International report, is the most prevalent profile of a fraudster, without generalizing the age or details.

At least 29 of the 596 fraudsters across 78 countries analysed for this study were from India. Fraud is becoming more sophisticated and one major change is the growing use of technology and access to much more information of previous generations, India.

A strong technology enabled platform to provide early warning signs; adoption of an ethical code of conduct amongst employees and stakeholders; technology-driven controls and a robust whistleblower mechanism are some ways in which organisations can mitigate the risk of fraud. (*The Economics Times*, 7th January 2014)

Gurgaon police have booked the former Managing Director (MD) and Chief Operating Operator (COO) of the India chapter of global sports goods firm Reebok on charges of forgery, cheating and criminal breach of trust and causing a loss to the tune of over ₹8,700 crore. The FIR charged one Subhinder Singh Prem, former MD, and COO Vishnu Bhagat, of misappropriating funds during their tenure. Their employment contract was terminated on March 26, 2012. The duo, employed with the company for 16 years, has been accused of operating four secret warehouses in Delhi to keep clandestinely diverted and stolen stocks. The company claimed that this fraudulent act had put at risk the jobs of around 40,000 people involved directly and indirectly in the business of Reebok and Adidas group in India. The complaint stated that in January 2012, company had identified fraudulent activities and conducted an internal inquiry. It was found the duo had been indulging in fraudulent activities over several years and was involved in systematically cheating and defrauding the company of hundreds of crores of rupees. The company also claimed that Reebok and Adidas Group had suffered irreparable damage to its reputation.

The FIR was registered under Sections 406/408 (Criminal Breach of Trust), Section 418 (cheating with knowledge), Section 467 (forgery of valuable security), Section 468 (forgery for cheating), Section 477A (falsification of accounts) and Section 120B (criminal conspiracy).

Adidas, the world's second largest sports goods makers, was hit by a crores' massive commercial fraud in its Indian unit. The German giant has already booked a negative impact of £125 million and suffered a further £70 million loss barely a month after replacing the local leadership team in India. This makes it one of the worst financial irregularities to surface in the Indian arm of any MNC, and comes amid mounting concerns over corporate governance issues in the country. It was first reported on March 27, 2012 that Managing Director Subhinder Singh Prem and chief operating officer Vishnu Bhagat had exited the local unit of Adidas, which also owns Reebok, after it plunged into the red due to financial irregularities.

In March 2012 the Adidas group had remained silent on specific queries whether the top-level changes were linked to financial mismanagement. The 13-billion euro group had replaced the top management in India with Claus Heckerott taking charge as MD and Frederic Serrant assuming the role of Sales Director.

> "We discovered commercial irregularities at our Reebok business in India. These irregularities will likely affect the prior-year consolidated financial statements of the Adidas group. In total, we are talking about a negative impact of up to a pre-tax amount of 125 million Euros. Additional onetime charges in the remaining quarters of 2012 amounting to an estimated 70 million Euros could also occur."

Said Herbert Hainer, CEO of the group, in the internal communication sent across to employees, and reviewed by the press. He said the company may take legal action if necessary.

Allegations of financial discrepancies and losses swirled at the group's India unit following the merger of Reebok's operations. Adidas and Reebok merged in India, even though a $3.8-billion global buyout of the latter happened in 2005. Reebok India had a turnover of about ₹600 crore, while Adidas clocked a revenue of ₹480 crore in 2011. The company on a combined level had debts to the tune of ₹600 crore and had registered a loss of about ₹90 crore with the Registrar of Companies. The former MD Prem and COO Bhagat came into the Adidas fold through the Reebok merger. Prem, who denied any wrongdoing while he was at the helm of the India operations, had joined Reebok in 1995 when it entered the country and rose up the ranks to become the MD in 2003. The alleged financial irregularities at Adidas India pointed to inflated performance figures. When the Germans appointed Prem as the MD of the group, they did that due to huge success that Reebok had achieved in India. They thought he must have done something outstanding. But it did not turn out to be that. Those close to the earlier management say, differences arose when Adidas wanted the management under Prem to push the Adidas brand and re-focus on it rather than Reebok. Adidas group has a clear multi brand strategy whereas the Adidas brand is the multi sport specialist. Reebok focus on fitness and training. Their intention is to grow business of both brands as part of their Route 2015.

Here's a fascinating and instructive story of how an executive's ambition collided with corporate due diligence and how a global brand didn't catch on till it was faced with a ₹870 crore loss. German sporting goods and apparel powerhouse Adidas has since long preferred to tiptoe in the Indian market. Many global retail giants believe that this is a market where pots of money can be made, but Adidas has largely been cool to India. As early as 2011, the group identified North America, Greater China, Russia/CIS, Latin America, Japan and the UK as key growth markets. India managed to find mention in the annual report, but as an emerging market. Adidas thought India was important. Adidas devoted considerable time and emphasis on India while announcing its first-quarter results in March, 2012. Only, it wasn't for reasons it would have preferred or imagined, Adidas global boss Herbert Hainer said: 'commercial irregularities' at its Reebok unit in India had wiped out €125 million (about ₹870 crore) from its global profits. The problems, limited to India, could lead to further charges of around €70 million (₹488.39 crore)', he said.

These are indeed big numbers, but it is not for nothing that the first-quarter earnings beat expectations on sales of €3.8 billion and operating profit of €409 million. Annual sales from soccer alone are expected to top €1.5 billion. Cast against these numbers, €195 million is not quite as damaging as it seems. What could be worrying Adidas is the nature of the losses. Reebok has been a constant underachiever in many global markets since Adidas bought its smaller US rival for $3.8 billion in August 2005. A notable exception was India. It was a market where Reebok enjoyed a head-start over rivals and even Adidas itself. A month before it lifted the lid on the irregularities, Adidas sacked Subhinder Singh Prem, its India head until then. Prem is credited with Reebok's breakneck expansion in India.

Prem has denied wrongdoing. He responded to the defamation and termination of services by launching legal action against the company. For its part, Adidas had replaced the management at Reebok India—COO Vishnu Bhagat also got the boot and said it would cut the number of Reebok stores in India by about one-third (nearly 900). The situation in India, although unfortunate, allowed him to now accelerate plans to improve a specific underperforming part of their business.

From star performer to an underperforming business, Reebok India's fall from grace has been as astonishing as its rise has been rapid. The Reebok story in India is replete with instances of strategic blunders, corporate mismanagement and financial mischief, according to three people with knowledge of the matter. One of the persons, a high-ranking Adidas official, left the company after a nearly five-year stint. Rather than an underperforming asset, Reebok India's problems are much bigger, they said. More on that later. To understand the Reebok mess, one must first turn to how Adidas and Reebok were run in India. Adidas bought Reebok in 2005, but the process of melting the two Indian offshoots began only in May 2011 when Prem was made the head of the combined entity. He took over from the then Adidas India Managing Director Andreas Gellner, who was named Managing Director, South-East Europe. Prem's appointment raised few eyebrows because Reebok appeared to be the bigger division then. He was also an old hand, having joined the company in 1995. What received less attention was how Prem landed the job. The integration of the two Indian offshoots was only a formality. But the candidate for the head of the combined entity was undecided. Around 2008, Prem began gunning for the job, according to the former Adidas official. His single-minded agenda was to become India MD, no matter what. Though Prem had the credentials, he knew he faced tough competition from Gellner. Adidas India began slowly, but was fast catching up with its Indian counterpart. Prem feared this might work against him, because Reebok boss decided that he must 'deliver' at any cost. What he did next played a major role in landing the company in its mess. Prem launched a massive expansion in India. This was done at the cost of profitability and margins. In no time, the number of Reebok stores shot up to more than 800. Reebok had only around 100 in 2003. Prem next turned his attention to volumes, according to the Adidas official. Franchises were billed goods beyond their selling capacity. They were assured that the company would manage leftover stocks. To the Germans, Reebok India was always a star asset. And here was this company throwing up even better numbers.

Gellner and his team raised red flags. They pointed out the increasing number of complaints from partners and the disputes regarding redeeming stocks. But the HQ looked the other way in the belief that the allegations were an upshot of a corporate contest. Prem was finally elevated, but matters began to unravel quickly. Franchises stopped payments, demanding that their leftover stocks be addressed first. "Partners could not buy fresh stock because they first had to deal with the past season's merchandise. Disputes with distributors and franchises became rampant, according to the probing person. To cite an example, there, was a distributor who claimed that Reebok owed him money while the company's books showed the opposite. There were also instances of raising the selling prices of merchandise to cover shortfall of receivables. The game plan to expand was about to backfire. Every time the issue of unsold stocks arose, franchises were promised they would be sold at retrospective prices. The promises remained promises. Reebok was unable to pay its vendors. Receivables of money to be recovered from partners were accumulating as were inventories. All things depicted as good were actually bad.

The crisis had precipitated. Reebok India now had the full attention of the German headquarters. The Germans finally knew they had made a blunder in appointing Prem. As first step towards fact-finding, they named Shahin Padath as CFO of the combined entity. Padath is an Adidas veteran, but more importantly he was from outside the Reebok India system—someone who Prem had no control over. His mandate was clear to investigate the true state of affairs at Reebok India.

Padath soon spotted gross irregularities and alerted the global office. Prem got the marching orders soon after. Prem ran Reebok as his personal fiefdom. His plan was to dean up the mess after taking over. But Germany got wind of the mess before that. The Germans had seemingly erred by delaying action. They should have acted much earlier. They did not even act on audit reports. The reason for the delay, besides their assumption that the charges stemmed from competition, was that India was still a crumb in the overall Adidas structure, contributing to about 1% of global revenues. Prem was essentially a Reebok man, having served the company for long. "There was no way he was going to play second fiddle in the combined operations."

To pursue breakneck growth, Prem relied on what in retail is known as the minimum guarantee (MG) model. The model is a potential magnet for franchises. There are different versions, but in all cases, the risks are zilch for a franchise. A fixed amount, a minimum guarantee is paid to a franchise to make up for losses or a deficit in turnover. Even the leftover stock is returned to the company.

Normally, the MG model is effective in an evolving market. Time lines are fixed after which companies switch to the alternate buy-and-sell model, where franchises gain better margins, but have to deal with left-over stock. Even the staunchest supporters of the MG model insist turnover from a store must be at least three times the money paid. The loss-making stores are shut. In Reebok's case, none of these checks were followed because Prem's intent was to show the big numbers. In his legal notice, Prem noted that Adidas was aware how the company was run, adding that the company was not a one-man show and all its finances and accounts were approved and checked by officials and auditors.

A Reebok store at a Ghaziabad mall offers some clues on the flaws in Reebok's strategy. The store wears a deserted look. The store attracts about 8-10 shoppers on a good day, but only two end up buying. Many of the stocks belong to the 2010 season, pointing to a row of T-shirts in which the small and medium sizes were missing. He questioned the logic of opening a store 50 metres away from a Reebok factory outlet. It is only after the controversy broke that Reebok officials visited. The manager was aware of Reebok's plans to downsize. He believed his store would be among the first to go. The nearby Adidas store was doing well, he said. "They have a better distribution setup, stocks are constantly renewed."

Same is the case with the Puma and Nike stores in the mall, according to their managers. The Puma store followed what is called a consignment model, where the store's margins were lower, but was offset by the company repossessing unsold stock. It has since embraced the buy-and-sell model where margins are higher due to the risk of managing inventories. The Nike store never encounters the problem of unsold stock. Those would be sold on discount. As Nike rarely offers discounts, this merchandise sells quickly. These retail chains are all doing well because they are following the buy-and-sell model, according to a retail analyst who is familiar with Reebok's operations. In this model, a company flags the performance of a franchise, guides it on trends and provides marketing support. It is a dean model. With others, there is scope to muddle. Reebok is a very good example of this.

The analyst cited the example of Italian apparel major Benetton in India. Reebok has three times the number of Benetton stores in Delhi, but Benetton racks up three times the turnover of all Reebok stores, according to him. The Reebok story is one of mindless expansion, but in the case of Benetton, a store would open only if company officials saw its potential to make profits. The Italian company works with only large partners who are experienced and who understand retail. It keeps out those who won't visit stores, the so-called armchair investors.

Less than a year after he was elevated as Adidas India head, Subhinder Singh Prem has been shown the door. Prem said he is in the middle of a battle, a reference to the legal suit he has launched against his former employers. The parent management had a convoluted thinking of pushing brand Adidas even if that meant at the cost of Reebok. There was no credit given to the Indian team for having built a robust brand Reebok. For its part, the German brass contests the argument of some observers that the Reebok controversy was an upshot of cultural differences with the Indian team. Chief Corporate Communication Officer Jan Runau said the group is a truly international company with 173 subsidiaries in all regions of the world. The same goes for their employees at the corporate headquarters in Herzogenaurach, Germany, where people of more than 60 different nationalities work. The executive board consists of three nationalities: German, American and New Zealanders. The financial picture of Adidas India is better than Reebok India is not correct. The share capital of Reebok is just ₹23 crore while that of Adidas is ₹55 crore, which is further supported by an interest-free loan of ₹44 crore from the parent company. In other words, the equity base of Reebok is one fourth that of Adidas (₹23 crore Vs ₹99 crore). Reebok therefore, had to rely more on bank borrowings to fund its expansion leading to higher interest payments as compared with Adidas, according to the analyst person. Reebok also pays royalty at 5% on sales to its parent whereas there are no royalty payments in case of Adidas. Until 2010, Reebok had paid close to ₹110 crore as royalty to Adidas AG. Citing another example, accumulated profits at

Reebok as of December 31, 2010 were ₹52 crore (after royalty) while Adidas showed accumulated losses of ₹137 crore (no royalty). If the accumulated profits at Reebok are adjusted for royalty of ₹110 crore, the accumulated profits at Reebok stood at ₹162 crore against accumulated losses of ₹137 crore at Adidas. In other words, Reebok was significantly more profitable than Adidas.

In Reebok's case, the company lured people who sell electronics or ran food stalls. They were promised a quick buck. The other attraction was the status elevation due to the association with a well-known brand. In retail, rentals are a huge challenge, but a bigger challenge is the selling itself. A franchise has the big problem of leftover stocks to tackle after a poor season. Franchises have to refresh stocks every season because customers are quick to spot old goods. The Reebok case is an example of how not to do retail in India, according to the analyst. Reebok should have perhaps borrowed a page from Adidas' rulebook. The India team's aim was to top turnovers carefully. They focused on distributors, key accounts, e-commerce, B2B partners and even sales to armed forces. This strategy paid off. Not only did Adidas make giant strides in expansion today, it is also in shipshape. Although the management hasn't revealed the irregularities in India, the ₹870 crore write-off could be a result of the wrongdoings of the past, according to the former Adidas official and retail analyst.

Now, Adidas India appears to be in much better financial shape than its Reebok counterpart. The financial statements of the two off-shoots are a study in contrast. Reebok has posted losses while Adidas has turned profits in 2010, suggesting that the former's operations have turned volatile while the latter's have stabilised. That wasn't always the case. Reebok's total current liabilities as a percentage of total Income rose to nearly 95% in 2009 and 102% in 2010 from 20% in 2005. Adidas India's total current liabilities, which were about 21% of income in 2005, rose to nearly 39% in 2009 but fell to around 38% the next year. For now, the Adidas brass is busy cleaning up the mess. Plans are afoot to restructure operations. Germany is using this opportunity to clean up the entire India operations. But the task at hand is not easy. The Germans have to shut stores, develop new ones, settle disputes, address receivables and inventories. With Reebok, it is as good as starting from scratch. The consolation is that Adidas is on a comfortable perch.

Several Reebok India employees could be under the scanner, as investigation agencies fear more employees being involved in the alleged scam that may set back its parent company by ₹870 crore. A senior Gurgaon police official told that the alleged fraud as in the complaint registered by the parent company Adidas, cannot be the handiwork of just two people. Adidas had only named Reebok's former Managing Director Subhinder Singh Prem and former Chief Operating Officer Vishnu Bhagat in its FIR registered with Gurgaon police for the alleged fraud.

Prima facie, the FIR indicated that either a loophole in the system was exploited to the hilt and there was no accountability or, there was a whole team involved. Gurgaon police has already set up a special investigative team, or SIT, of four people headed by an assistant commissioner of police for further investigation. Police have asked Adidas to provide substantiating documents for the allegations made in the FIR. Concerns on the affairs started arising way back in 2010 within the Adidas group due to huge account receivables (outstanding dues) and excess inventories that were later discovered by CFO Shahin Padath. Adidas has claimed that they will now have to incur a restructuring cost of over ₹487 crore while the parent company has suffered irreparable damage to Reebok and Adidas' reputation. Adidas was forced to file a criminal complaint against Prem and Bhagat after the issue came to light through media reports. After all, the company is answerable to its stakeholders back in Germany.

In its complaint, Adidas India has said that there was misappropriation of funds, inventory diversion, padding sales for incentives, which also led to increase in taxes. The FIR itself admits at various places that the receipts were received in the company's bank accounts and all payments were made to genuine parties through banking channels. Indeed, the FIR also admits that all goods of the company were physically with the company, Singh said, refuting most of the charges levelled against him. He also added that the allegations are very strange because all the decisions of the accused persons were approved by the complainant himself i e Shahin Padath, Claus Heckerott and the German parent entity. The company has alleged that the both the former officials stole products worth ₹62.99 crore and kept them in four secret warehouses as well as engaged in fictitious sales for several years. The copy of report also mentioned that a Franchisee Referral Programme (FRP) was started by the accused where amounts were collected on the pretext of opening of stores despite instructions from the Adidas group headquarters in October 2010 to not expand the store-base further. However, almost no franchisee stores were opened under the scheme despite ₹114.26 crore being collected from various investors, which incurred another ₹14.82 crore in interest charged at the rate of 24-33%. The company later posted ₹98.51 crore from the total funds as amount received from customers towards outstanding payments. The company has also accused the two former executives of raising invoices of ₹86 crores on customers for products already invoiced and delivered in the last two calendar years to claim bonus and incentives. As per the accused, the company did not pay them any bonus for years 2010 and 2011. They were paid a long term incentive only which was payable under a Global Incentive Scheme, and not because of local business performance. In addition, both executives were accused of cheating and fraud through maintenance of hidden accounting records including giving extra margins to the tune of over ₹530 crore. During the last two calendar years, invoices were raised against customers to the tune of ₹85.61 crore as artificial and retrospective price increases.

The international tax division, a wing of the Central Board of Direct Taxes (CBDT), has asked the Adidas company to file income tax returns in India as it reckons that Adidas is generating some of its income from the country, but not paying taxes. The profits that the tax authorities are seeking to tax are independent of the income that the company earns from its two subsidiaries in India—Adidas India Marketing Pvt Ltd and Reebok India Company. A notice has been sent calling for returns for the financial year 2010-11 (or assessment year 2011-12) and a letter has been sent seeking information for previous years. The move is the outcome of surveys conducted a few years ago where the department found some evidence of the global parent generating income in India, independent of its subsidiary, according to the Income Tax department. The notice was sent a few weeks before Adidas revealed that irregularities at its Reebok India business had shaved off ₹870 crore of its global profits. The disclosure forced Adidas to replace its top management in India and shut down 300 Reebok stores.

Adidas India files Income Tax returns in India and is also covered by transfer pricing audit meant to ensure that the company does not shift profits out of India. The Indian subsidiary recorded revenues of ₹455 crore and a profit of ₹9.11 crore for the 12 months ended December 2010. PE refers to a legal entity set up by a company to manage its operations. An alternative definition of PE is that of an agent who has the authority to conclude contracts. The existence of a PE is a fact based assessment. If the subsidiary is a PE, arm's length profit should subsume attribution. However, if a PE exists on a stand-alone basis, one needs to attribute additional profits to tax. The Adidas group posted an 11% rise in revenue to 13.4 billion euros (₹92,764.3 crore) and 18% increase in profit of 670 million euros (₹638.67 crore) for the year ended 2011. However, Adidas India's financial performance during 2011 was not available on the website of the Registrar of Companies.

The two former executives of Reebok India, in the centre of an alleged ₹870 crore alleged fraud, have accused German sports goods maker Adidas of attempting to hammer down the valuation of the Indian unit, as part of its strategy to reduce its payout to the minority shareholder in the company. Subhinder Singh Prem and Vishnu Bhagat have in separate suits filed in the Delhi High Court, said they were asked to "carry out certain illegal and unethical actions" by the Adidas group such as manipulating accounts, booking irrelevant expenses, and cancelling large distributorships to ensure that the market value of Reebok India fell significantly so that a significantly lower amount becomes payable to the existing Indian joint venture partner. Reebok India is a subsidiary of Adidas. While the petitions do not mention the names of the joint venture partner, Focus Energy Ltd, a group company of Ajay Kalsi's Phoenix International owns 6.85% in Reebok India. According to the shareholder's agreement, Adidas has a 'call option' or the right to purchase the shares of the Indian partner but the two have been locked in a legal dispute over the price at which Focus Energy will sell its shares. While Adidas does not want to pay more than ₹25 crore for Focus India's 6.85% stake against which the Indian partner was demanding as much as ₹550 crore. Both Adidas and Focus Energy declined to comment on these figures.

According to an internal e-mail of July 2010, Adidas and Reebok India executives have discussed several strategies to keep their payout to a minimum. One of the options considered then was to wind down the operation of Reebok India and remove the distribution rights to reduce market valuation. Adidas AG had also explored the option to transfer its stake in Reebok India to Adidas India based on Controller of Capital Issues (CCI) valuation that values a company based on past performance and the valuation based on this method is usually conservative.

In April 2010, the RBI changed this guideline and said the transfer value of the shares should be decided only through discounted cash flow (DCF) method, which takes into account the projected cash flow in the next five years and not on past performance. Under the present guidelines, the valuation of Reebok India would be much more than what it would have been under the CCI method. Adidas had sacked Prem and Bhagat in March 2010, and has accused them of commercial irregularities and financial embezzlement, adding up to ₹870 crore. In an FIR lodged with the Gurgaon police on May 2010, it has charged them with misappropriation of funds, inventory diversion, and fictitious inflation of sales revenue. Adidas had framed these charges against them to show exceptional losses of a much larger magnitude, thus bringing down the valuation of Reebok India. But the suits filed by the two former executives claiming unpaid dues from Reebok India, before the FIR was lodged, do not contain this specific allegation. The suits say that the refusal of the executives to carry out unethical and illegitimate requests aimed at bringing down the valuation of the company led to further bitterness between Adidas and the executives.

Adidas, through its wholly owned Reebok (Mauritius) Company Ltd owns 93.15% stake in Reebok India Company. Focus Energy Ltd, a group firm Phoenix International of Ajay Kalsi, owns the balance 6.85% or 1.56, 750 equity shares of ₹100 each.

Expat CEOs

Claus Heckerott had been called here with single-point agenda to save an international brand in India. When Adidas Germany-based HQ thought a mess was building up, it didn't hire a local to do damage control. Instead, the company sent Heckerott, for the job. Lending him a hand was Frederic Serrant, an expat from

France. It is an old MNC strategy at crunch hour, to get in one of your own or someone from outside India. Experience and familiarity with complex situations often drive the decision to look for global talent. Cultural differences play a role too. For instance, Americans are most open about scouting for local talent. As you move east, companies become more conservative about CEO appointments. So the Europeans experiment less than Americans and the Japanese less than the Europeans. The Koreans are one of the most conservative and maintain a very Koreanised top management in most of their companies. The type of business also influences choice of leadership. Complex technology-driven MNCs are more likely to have expats at the top as the local talent pool is often poor. But consumer-oriented companies lean on local managers as an understanding of a specific market is critical for success. Where companies are going also matters. For instance, in China, most MNCs are headed by expats due to a paucity of world-class talent. India, with plenty of global managers, is better off. But expats now look at India with different eyes. India is no longer the hardship posting where MNCs doled out hardship allowances and other fancy perks like US dollar salaries in India, paying mortgages back home, etc. The growth in the economy has made it a one-of-a-kind learning ground for ambitious managers.

This is one thing that hasn't changed about MNCs. Whenever there is a fraud or an irregularity, they want one of their own men on top. It is a move that companies across the spectrum follow, and is completely understandable. In a faraway subsidiary where things have gone wrong, the first thing that the headquarters would want is to be in control and get to the heart of the fraud. The best way to achieve this is by putting veterans in charge of the subsidiary as they can understand the extent of irregularity, get the right picture and clean up the mess to get the subsidiary back on track. In such situations, MNCs often draft in two-three senior executives as sort of crack team to take control. Adidas is a good example of the strategy. The company has eased out the CEO and COO and brought in a new MD, Heckerott, who is an old hand in the company, having spent 14 years with it. Adidas has also brought in Frederic Serrant from France who has been appointed as the Sales Director reporting to Heckerott.

Many MNCs follow this strategy when they are entering a new country. At the inception stage, it is critical to get the basics right and in some sense replicate the HQ template in the far-flung subsidiary. As most of the building blocks are put in place at this stage—from processes to organisational structure to hiring—expat CEOs prove to be one of the best options for the job. This is also the stage when the MNC is wetting its feet in the country, understanding the scope of business, cultural nuances and challenges. An expat at this stage can communicate lot better with the HQ.

Gary Bennett's mandate was clear when he came to India as the head of Max New York Life—to establish the company, set up the processes and find a local successor in 3-5 years before moving on. "I saw my role as an expat to develop an India strategy, groom local managers, build expertise, transfer knowledge and once that was done, to ensure there is recognition for the local people and move on. Groom it, grow it and then give it away," he once said in an interview. Bennett took up the top job in 2005 and in 2008, anointed his Indian successor Rajesh Sood whom he had groomed for the role.

In 2007, when Jagdish Khattar retired, after a 20-year stint, Maruti Suzuki brought in Shinzo Nakanishi, a Japanese, to take over the reins. Khattar was once the government's nominee at MUL when it was a joint venture between Suzuki and the Indian government. The Suzuki example buttresses a well-known fact—that Japanese, Koreans and some European companies are often closed culturally and prefer to appoint their own as subsidiary heads in different parts of the world instead of locals.

Almost all the Japanese companies in India, from Toyota to Honda to Nikon, are headed by Japanese, irrespective of the firm's familiarity with the Indian environment. They typically occupy the top two-three positions. Koreans take this a step further. Believing in total control, they follow the expat CEO model more intensely. Not just the top one-two positions but almost all critical functions are often headed by Koreans. Our own Indian MNCs too seem culturally closed and their global operations are often headed by Indian managers. To be fair though, alongside culture, language and other barriers, limited global experience of some of these MNCs also plays a role in deputing expat CEOs. This strategy evolves with time as the MNC become more comfortable with the new market. Last year, Deutsche Bank crossed a cultural barrier when it appointed Anshu Jain as its co-CEO. Globalization and shifting playfields is pushing the change.

This trend is fairly recent and is mostly linked to the rise of the BRICS. India and other emerging markets have become critical for global MNCs. As a result, top positions in markets like India are seen as part of the grooming strategy for top talent at MNCs. Egon Zehnder's Vasudeva says,

> "The normal in business world is shifting. It is increasingly becoming important for global leadership to have emerging market experience."

This has nothing to do with any of the other business reasons. MNCs work hard to provide crucial exposures to their top talent. India figures high on the list. Thus many expats are being deputed into India as country heads. Often they go on to occupy critical global positions.

Doug Baillie at HUL is a good example. When he took over the top job at HUL India in 2006, it was the first time that HUL appointed/an expat head in nearly 50 years. Baillie is now serving stints at the HQ as Chief HR Officer and is also a part of the Unilever Executive Committee. More and more MNCs see India contributing a bigger share of their future revenue and profits and more important, to their future growth.

For long, India remained a small outpost for the global $147-billion giant GE (General Electric). In 2009, it suddenly shifted gears and brought in John Flannery to replace Tejpreet Chopra as the India head. The change of guard was more than just that. It was also about GE waking up to India's potential and setting ambitious targets for the Indian business. As a result, Flannery, much higher in the GE hierarchy, was brought in and now reports directly to the global vice-chairman of GE. Under Flannery, GE has undergone a major organisational revamp to suit its new India ambitions. When an MNC is shifting gears in a country, it needs to substantially increase the heft of its top management. Not all MNCs have the comfort to have a senior local at their HQs who can be drafted in for the job. Appointing an expat—higher in the HQ hierarchy helps accord the subsidiary the new status that the MNC wants it to have. Such an appointment also often signals new reporting structures in the organisation. For example, in the case of GE, with multiple businesses in India, each business head was reporting to his global counterpart. But with the appointment of Flannery, vertical heads now report to him. The importance of India head has increased.

Those were difficult years at Coca-Cola India. Around 2005, the Atlanta-headquartered company was making headlines for all the wrong reasons. First it was the pesticide issue that hit the Cola major hard. Soon after, sludge contamination and depletion of ground water in Kerala gave it a bad name. Amid all this, lacklustre sales and poor financial performance was worrying the HQ. The company thrashed out a big restructuring plan shaking up the top deck, bringing in an expat CEO and re-organising its Indian bottling and marketing operations to infuse some energy and vigour. John Ustas was deputed from its Norwegian operations to take charge and ease out Coke India President Sanjiv Gupta. Priya Chetty of Stanton Chase, an executive search firm, says:

> "Whenever things go wrong, the first instinctive reaction of an MNC is to bring in an expat CEO to fix things."

Such a wholesale shake-up serves two critical purposes. One, it affords enormous flexibility to change things, question the status quo and restructure the organisation. It also helps an old MNC subsidiary to start on a clean slate. Drafting a new expat CEO helps align the subsidiary better to the parent. Also, it sends a signal that the subsidiary is under close HQ watch.

Fall of an Icon—Rajat Gupta

Rajat Kumar Gupta (born 2 December 1948) is an Indian-American businessman and philanthropist who is currently serving a two-year term in US federal prison for insider trading. He was the first foreign-born Managing Director (Chief Executive) of management consultancy firm McKinsey & Company from 1994 to 2003. He was also a Board member of corporations including Goldman Sachs, Procter & Gamble and American Airlines, as well as an advisor to non-profit bodies such as The Bill & Melinda Gates Foundation and The Global Fund to Fight AIDS, Tuberculosis and Malaria. Additionally, he is the co-founder of the Indian School of Business, American India Foundation, New Silk Route and Scandent Solutions.

He was convicted in June 2012 on insider trading charges of four criminal felony counts of conspiracy and securities fraud. He was sentenced in October 2012 to two years in prison, an additional year on supervised release and ordered to pay $5 million in fines. His conviction was upheld by a Federal Appeals Court on March 25, 2014. He then lodged an appeal with the US Supreme Court. An application to remain free until the court determined whether it would hear the appeal was denied on

June 11, 2014 leaving Gupta having to commence his two year prison term on June 17, 2014.

Insider Trading Conviction

On March 1, 2011, the SEC filed an administrative civil complaint against Gupta for insider trading with billionaire and Galleon Group hedge fund founder Rajaratnam. Coverage of the event noted that Anil Kumar—who, like Gupta, had graduated from IIT, was a highly regarded senior partner at McKinsey, and had also co-founded the Indian School of Business—had already pleaded guilty to charges in the same case. Gupta, Kumar, and Rajaratnam were all close friends and business partners. Gupta counter-sued and both sides eventually dropped charges.

On October 26, 2010 the United States Attorney's Office filed criminal charges against Gupta. He was arrested in New York City by the FBI and pleaded not guilty. He was released on $10 million bail on the same day. Gupta's lawyer wrote,

> "Any allegation that Rajat Gupta engaged in any unlawful conduct is totally baseless.... He did not trade in any securities, did not tip Mr Rajaratnam so he could trade, and did not share in any profits as part of any *quid pro quo*."

The SEC alleged, "The tips generated 'illicit profits and loss avoidance' of more than $23 million."

Manhattan US Attorney Preet Bharara said,

> "Rajat Gupta was entrusted by some of the premier institutions of American business, to sit inside their boardrooms, among their executives and directors, and receive their confidential information so that he could give advice and counsel."

Details of wiretap recordings and trading activity related to the charges were analysed at length in the media, assessing the strengths and weaknesses of the prosecution's and defence's cases.

The current case is focusing on the relationship between Raj Rajaratnam, Anil Kumar and Rajat Gupta. Gupta, Rajaratnam, and Kumar were all involved to varying degrees as founding partners of private equity firms Taj Capital and New Silk Route, though Rajaratnam and Kumar left before they began operation. Rajat Gupta remained as Chairman of New Silk Route, and Rajaratnam eventually invested $50 million in the fund.

Rajat Gupta's trial began on May 22, 2012. On June 15, 2012, Gupta was found guilty on three counts of securities fraud and one count of conspiracy. He was found not guilty on two other securities fraud charges. At the time, his lawyer told reporters,

> "We will be moving to set aside the verdict and will, if necessary, appeal the conviction."

The maximum sentence for securities fraud is 20 years and the maximum sentence for conspiracy is five years. In arguments in mid-October, prosecutors favoured prison time of up to 10 years while defence attorneys favoured probation and community service. As one service option, the latter suggested Gupta "work on health care and agriculture in rural Rwanda." Prosecutors based their recommendation in part on $11.2 million profits, or losses avoided by Rajaratnam based on the tips. The defence argued that Gupta "never profited on the alleged trading" per one news account.

On October 24, 2012, Gupta was sentenced to two years in prison by Judge Jed Rakoff of the United States District Court in Manhattan for leaking boardroom secrets to former hedge fund manager Raj Rajaratnam. His conviction was upheld by a Federal Appeals Court on March 25, 2014. His prison sentence will begin on June 17. On June 11, 2014, US Supreme Court rejected Gupta's bail plea, a week before his prison term commences.

The indictment of Rajat Gupta for insider trading by a tearful 12-member jury comprising eight women and four men has shocked the entire three-million strong Indian-American community. His life story, before the trial, has been, a perfect fairy tale of fulfilment of an American dream. He was the brain behind, and one of the founding fathers of ISB Hyderabad; he contributed significantly to make it a world-class institution. When the government instituted the Pravasi Bharatiya Samman Award, he was the first Indian-American to be honoured. Gupta, at the peak of his career, could do no wrong; he was wining and dining with the likes of Bill Clinton, Bill Gates and Kofi Annan.

It is rare for a jury to feel sorry while convicting an accused; Rajat Gupta's was such a case. Jury foreman confessed, I wanted to believe the allegations weren't true. Another jury member Ronnie Sesso was more emotional,

> "We wanted him to walk, go home to his family and live a prosperous life."

But in the end, the circumstantial evidence against him was found to be 'too overwhelming'. Everybody is asking why did he do it? Some sum up in four letters—more. R Rajaratnam, whom Gupta is accused of helping, was believed to have said in a conversation—taped secretly by the agencies—that the latter wanted to earn $50-100 million without doing much. There is speculation that Gupta wanted Rajaratnam to help his equity fund, New Silk Route. The jury felt that he was driven by his greed. Preet Bharara, Indian origin Federal Prosecutor who eventually nailed him, also felt sorry for him,

> "Gupta achieved remarkable success and stature, but he threw it all away."

To US prosecutors, former Goldman Sachs Group Inc director Rajat Gupta is a Wall Street insider who fed secret tips to his business partner Raj Rajaratnam so the fund manager could reap millions in illicit profits. According to 'www.friendsofrajat.com', Gupta, who is on trial in Manhattan Federal Court for securities fraud, is a man of 'great integrity', a philanthropist and a victim of prosecutorial overreach. Author Deepak Chopra and Mukesh Ambani, India's richest man, are among those who have taken to the website to praise him.

> "I have known Rajat Gupta for 25 years and am pleased to call him my friend."

Chopra, the best-selling author of *The Seven Spiritual Laws of Success* who is also on Gupta's witness list, said in an e-mail,

> "Rajat has devoted many hours working infields that are close to my heart—particularly in promoting global health through the eradication of infectious diseases."

The site 'Friends of Rajat' is different from sites for defendants like Martha Stewart or Rajaratnam because it was created by Gupta's bold-face-name friends and associates, some of them billionaires. The roster of endorsers reads like a guest list from the World Economic Forum's annual meeting in Davos, Switzerland, which Gupta once frequented. And they're speaking out. Those who have signed up on 'Friends of Rajat' also include billionaire Adi Godrej, Chairman of the Mumbai-based Godrej Consumer Products; billionaire Kushal Pal Singh, Chairman of DLF; Yogesh Chander Deveshwar, owner of ITC; Analjit Singh of Max India; and Rajendra Singh Pawar, Chairman of NIIT. Atul Kanagat, a former McKinsey & Co principal, who manages the website, said:

> "He's like a dolphin caught up in a tuna net."
>
> "The government refuses to admit it's a dolphin and not a big fat tuna, and they're not going to give up. That's what my website is trying to do, tell the story about the other Rajat."

Gupta is accused of leaking information about Goldman Sachs and Procter & Gamble, where he was also a Director. He is charged with one count of conspiracy and five counts of securities fraud, which carries a maximum term of 20 years in prison.

The website offers a glimpse into Gupta's world, where his supporters—some plutocrats, some lifelong friends—point to the millions of dollars he has raised for education and healthcare. In interviews, they said they know Gupta from the Indian School of Business in Hyderabad, which he co-founded, or from his fund-raising efforts for victims of an earthquake that struck Gujarat in 2001. Others know him from his time as Chairman of the Global Fund, an initiative to fight AIDS, tuberculosis and malaria. KD Godrej of Godrej Consumer Products, who has known Gupta for about 20 years, wrote on the website,

> "Rajat has done a lot for India—he went out of his way, and it's unfortunate he's got into this imbroglio."
>
> "Rajat has always been a person of great integrity and clarity of purpose."

A posting on the website attributed to Mukesh Ambani, praised Gupta's ethics. He always followed a Hindu creed, according to the posting:

> "You are only entitled to do your duty, not to the fruits of that duty."

Gupta came to the US as a student at Harvard Business School in 1971 and became a US citizen in 1984. Kanagat, 57, said he has known Gupta since 1987, when they were both at McKinsey. Gupta went on to lead the consulting firm for nine years.

Kanagat said the idea for the site 'Friends of Rajat' arose when a group of South Asian friends gathered at a party soon after Gupta was charged in October. Gupta, free on $10-million bond, wasn't present. Stewart, founder of Martha Stewart Living Omnimedia, started 'MarthaTalks.com' after she was charged with obstructing justice. Stewart, who was convicted in

2004 and served five months in prison, used the site to keep fans and journalists updated on her case. 'MarthaTalks.com' now directs visitors to Martha Stewart *Living* magazine's website and offers a free tote bag with a subscription.

Fighting back is exactly what Gupta's friends and associates are doing, online and in interviews. They scoff at the prosecutors' allegation that Gupta tipped Rajaratnam to enhance the holdings of a fund the two had invested in.

Analjit Singh, Max India Chairman and founder, said in an interview:

> "Rajat is too smart—he's not stupid to do something foolish, as what has been alleged."

For younger men like Sabeer Bhatia, 43, co-founder of the e-mail service 'Hot Mail' and Chairman of Sabse Technologies; Gupta is a mentor. "Everybody looked up to him," Bhatia said in an interview. Gupta advised Bhatia when he wanted to start a school in India and on a later business venture, the Hotmail co-founder said. Never once did Gupta seek personal gain, said Bhatia. He actually followed through, said Bhatia, who has known Gupta for 14 years.

> "He is a very gentle-mannered person, a man of integrity who, lived up to his word."

There's a chance that some of these plaudits will make it, into the courtroom. While jurors are instructed to not research cases on the web, many do, said Andrew Stoltmann, a Chicago securities lawyer who represents investors and isn't involved in the Gupta case. This is a fascinating, low-cost and effective means to influence the jury, the press, the public and the judge Stoltmann said. For Gupta, his greatest strength going into the trial is his background and his reputation. It will have appeal to jurors during the trial. How much the jury will hear in court about Gupta's philanthropy was a topic of debate at a May, 16, 2012 hearing. While the US has fought to block such testimony,

Gupta's lawyer Gary Naftalis argued that it was crucial to the defence. Naftalis said,

> "Here you have a man by everybody's lights who has lived a wonderful, blameless life and then one day, out of the blue sky, he decides to become a criminal the seventh decade of his life."

US District Judge Jed Rakoff, who's presiding over the case, expressed scepticism about the relevance of such evidence. "If Mother Teresa were here charged with bank robbery, what the jury would still have to determine is whether the evidence showed that she had committed bank robbery," he said. Rakoff ruled that Naftalis could give jurors a 'quick' sense of Gupta's good works and background. If Gupta testifies, the information can be amplified, the judge said. Naftalis declined to say whether his client will take the stand. "If he's convicted, Judge Rakoff will be taking these things into account," Stoltmann said. He said judges can consider a defendant's good works when passing sentence. "That's when Gupta's good deeds and stellar reputation will come in the most handy," he said. Kanagat meanwhile blames Gupta's woes on Anil Kumar; the former McKinsey MD who pleaded guilty and who testified against Rajaratnam last year. Kumar introduced Gupta to the Galleon co-founder Kanagat. "That's what got him into trouble with this Galleon thing," Kanagat said. "He looks past people's faults." I asked him, "How could you hobnob with these guys?" And he said, "I thought they were respectable."

Rajat Kumar Gupta (born 2 December 1948) is an Indian-American businessman who was the Managing Director (Chief Executive) of management consultancy McKinsey & Company from 1994 to 2003 and a business leader in India and the United States. He was arrested in late 2011 by the FBI on insider trading charges stemming from the Raj Rajaratnam Galleon Group case and is on criminal trial as of May 2012. In his capacity at McKinsey, Gupta was recognized as the first Indian-born CEO of a global corporation. After retiring from active practice, while maintaining an affiliation at McKinsey, Gupta served as Corporate Chairman, Board Director or Strategic Advisor to a variety of large and notable organizations corporations including Goldman Sachs, Procter & Gamble and American Airlines, and non-profits including The Gates Foundation, The Global Fund and the International Chamber of Commerce. Rajat Gupta is additionally the co-founder of four different organizations—Indian School of Business with Anil Kumar, American India Foundation with Victor Menezes and Lata Krishnan, New Silk Route with Parag Saxena and Victor Menezes, and Scandent with Ramesh Vangal.

Everyman is born with fault's, no matter how great his position is in the society from president to ordinary man. Corporate crime is more complex than crime against individual. Corporate law is invented daily to suit their need by the government in West. This is not a crime. In USA and UK if you cross the authority, then they will invent something to throw you in jail. Corporate crime is like getting parking ticket, it's legal but not moral. As said it's a body without soul. There are more law books on corporate law in west then religious books in entire world put together. This is a fact. Whenever there is a successful organization/company in west and they don't have connection in the government or with political party, they will be cut down to size by the current government and their PC thinkers. This is also true. If have right and powerful friends then you will get away with murder in west. President Nixon is prime example of this in USA. Integrity means nothing in western world. It's only a word to label and describe individual when it suits them, it is as important as virginity to a prostitute. Rajat Gupta guilty or not, one thing is certain, the destruction of his character and career.

Rajat Gupta was born in Kolkata, India to Pran Kumari Gupta and Ashwini Kumar Gupta. His father was a journalist for Ananda Publishers. His father was a prominent freedom fighter and had been jailed by the British for his efforts. His mother taught at a montessori school. Gupta had three siblings. When Gupta was five the family moved to New Delhi, where his father went to start the newspaper *Hindustan Standard*. Gupta's father died when Gupta was sixteen; Gupta's mother died two years later. Now an orphan, Gupta and his siblings decided to live by themselves. It was pretty unusual in those days. He was a student at Modern School in New Delhi. After high school, Gupta ranked 15th in the nation in the entrance exam for the Indian Institutes of Technology. He received a Bachelor of Technology degree in Mechanical Engineering from the Indian Institute of Technology, Delhi (IIT-D) in 1971. Declining a job from the prestigious domestic firm ITC Limited, he received an MBA from Harvard Business School (HBS) in 1973, where he was named a Baker Scholar. Gupta remarked that the first time he saw an aeroplane was when he flew to ITC to inform them he would be attending HBS.

McKinsey & Company

Gupta joined McKinsey & Company in 1973 as one of the earliest Indian-Americans at the consultancy. He was initially rejected because of inadequate work experience, a decision that was overturned after his Harvard Business School Professor Walter J Salmon called Ron Daniel, then head of the New York office and later also the Managing Director of McKinsey, on Gupta's behalf.

Gupta began his career in New York before moving to Scandinavia to became the head of McKinsey offices there in 1981. He did well in what was then considered a 'backwater' area; this is where he first made his mark. Elected senior partner in 1984, he became head of the Chicago office in 1990. In 1994 he was elected the firm's first managing director (chief executive) born outside of the US, and re-elected twice in 1997 and 2000. In this capacity, he was considered the first Indian-born CEO of a multinational organization.

During Gupta's time as head of McKinsey, the firm opened offices in 23 new countries and doubled its consultant base. His successor Ian Davis was elected by "emphasizing the need for a return to the McKinsey heritage". This was seen as a reaction against Gupta's aggressive firm expansion. It was also a time of perceived shifting of standards. Enron, closely identified with McKinsey, collapsed during Gupta's tenure. During the dot-com bubble he and Anil Kumar created a programme for McKinsey to accept payment from its clients in stock. Gupta's accountability for the shifting of standards was weighed differently by different observers. After completing three full terms (the maximum allowed, by a rule he had himself initiated) and nearly a decade as head of the firm, Gupta became senior partner again in 2003 and senior partner emeritus in 2007. Gupta is widely regarded as one of the first Indians to successfully break through the glass ceiling, as the first Indian-born CEO of a multinational corporation. Gupta's mentors at McKinsey included Ron Daniel, the former Managing Director who as senior partner first hired Gupta into the New York office, and Anupam (Tino) Puri, the first Indian at the Firm and eventual senior partner. He, in turn, mentored Anil Kumar as another early Indian-American at the consultancy. Gupta and Kumar were the face of McKinsey in India. According to *The Financial Times* the two operated as a forceful double-act to secure business for McKinsey, win access in Washington and build a brotherhood of donors around the Hyderabad-based ISB and a handful of social initiatives.

Gupta maintained an office, executive assistant, e-mail and phone at McKinsey & Company after 2007, and maintains the title 'Senior Partner Emeritus' of the firm. He also continued to receive a salary from McKinsey as senior partner emeritus, totalling $6 million in 2008 and $2.5 million for each of the following three years. However, in the wake of subsequent scandals a McKinsey spokesperson was quoted as saying,

> "Our firm no longer has a professional relationship with Rajat Gupta. Sources tell us that the firm dropped Mr Gupta from its alumni database, and called clients worldwide to say that they would have nothing to do with him going forward."

The manner in which the firm severed ties with its former head attracted some controversy.

Outside McKinsey & Company

In 1997 Gupta co-founded the Indian School of Business (ISB) with friend and fellow senior partner Anil Kumar. The school was ranked number 13 in the world by *The Financial Times* in its 'Global MBA Rankings 2011'. Gupta and Kumar have both since resigned as Chairman and Executive Board Director respectively. Before stepping down as managing director he co-founded Scandent Solutions with Ramesh Vangal and the American India Foundation with Victor Menezes and Lata Krishnan. After McKinsey Gupta co-founded and chaired the private equity firm New Silk Route, formerly named Taj Capital Partners, with Parag Saxena and Victor Menezes. He served on the corporate board of directors of Goldman Sachs, Procter & Gamble, American Airlines parent AMR, Harman International, and Sberbank. He was also senior advisor to KKR (formerly Kohlberg, Kravis, Roberts & Co), Chairman of Galleon International, and advisor to other financial institutions such as the Qatar Financial Centre. Gupta's philanthropic efforts focus on the areas of education, global health, and global business. His activities within the field of education include co-founding and chairing the Indian School of Business with Anil Kumar and serving on the Board of Directors of many business schools including Harvard Business School, Northwestern's Kellogg School of Management, MIT Sloan School of Management, Tsinghua University School of Economics and Management, Skolkovo and the Lauder Institute at Wharton. In addition, he served on the Yale President's Council, founded and chaired the

IIT Alumni Association, and was a member of the board of trustees of the University of Chicago. He was additionally on the board of Millennium Promise and the Pratham India Education Initiative.

Gupta's activities in global health include serving as a founding Board member and then Chairman of the Board for The Global Fund to Fight AIDS, Tuberculosis and Malaria and as the co-founder and founding Chairman of the Public Health Foundation of India. He was also on the board of the Emergency Management and Research Institute, Health Management Research Institute, and International Partnership for Microbicides. He was also Chairman of the advisory board and the India AIDS initiative of The Gates Foundation as well as its Global Health Initiative. He was a member of the board of the Global Health Council and the Harvard School of Public Health, as well as the Weill Cornell Medical College.

Gupta is also a supporter of global business through his work as Chairman of the International Chamber of Commerce, a founding Board member of the World Economic Forum, a Board member and Executive Committee member of the US-India Business Council, and member of the Advisory Council to the Prime Minister of India. Gupta was also appointed as special advisor on management reform to UN Secretary-General Kofi Annan. He additionally served on the UN Commission on the Private Sector and Development and was co-chairman of the United Nations Association of America. In addition, Gupta was a trustee on the board of The Rockefeller Foundation and was elected in 2009 to the American Academy of Arts and Sciences.

Controversy

The notion of company growth has been controversial from the 1970s as the firm began its global expansion; McKinsey opened many new offices under Rajat Gupta's tenure in the late 1990s.

The election of British-born Ian Davis as Gupta's successor was seen as "a return to McKinsey's heritage". Additionally, though a McKinsey spokesman said,

> "It has always been a clear violation of our values and professional standards for any firm member to provide consulting or advisory services outside of McKinsey for personal monetary gain."

Gupta was an advisory director from 2005-2007, for which he was granted 81,405 stock options, valued at 93 cents each then, according to Genpact's 2008 proxy statement. During this period, while as an active senior partner at McKinsey, he also set up New Silk Route and worked with InfoUSA for mind spirit. Gupta was paid nearly five times as much as the next corporate director for his board seat at Sberbank, prompting a watchdog group to vote against his re election.

Rajat Gupta, a former Goldman Sachs Director and senior figure in corporate America, has been charged with conspiracy and security fraud offences, making him the most high-ranking executive to become embroiled in a wide-ranging Wall Street insider dealing inquiry. Prosecutors said Mr Gupta had provided disgraced trader Raj Rajaratnam with an 'instant messaging' service from inside some of America's most esteemed boardrooms. The indictment accuses Mr Gupta of entering into an insider arrangement with Rajaratnam, founder of the hedge fund Galleon Group.

Rajaratnam was sentenced to 11 years in jail for insider dealing offences. During his trial, Mr Gupta's name came up on several occasions, suggesting it was only a matter of time before the authorities called him in. Mr Gupta's lawyer told the charges are totally baseless and are based entirely on circumstantial evidence. The indictment includes two episodes at the height of the banking crisis where Mr Gupta allegedly went from a Goldman Sachs boardroom conference call and, within seconds, called up Rajaratnam with insider information. Best known as the former head of consultancy group McKinsey, where he worked for 34 years, Mr Gupta was in the upper echelons of the corporate establishment in America, courted as a non-executive director by some of the biggest companies in the world. As well as Goldman Sachs, past directorships include Procter & Gamble and the parent company of American Airlines.

The charges against Mr Gupta carry a maximum sentence of 105 years imprisonment and are part of a crackdown on Wall Street. In the last years, federal prosecutors have secured 51 convictions. A key to the convictions was the extensive use of wiretaps, which were allegedly able to identify Mr Gupta as a source of Rajaratnam's information. One prosecutor said:

> "His eagerness to pass along inside information to Rajaratnam is nowhere more starkly evident than instances where seconds elapsed between his learning crucial Goldman Sachs information and lavishing it on his good friend. It could be termed instant messaging."

Harvard-educated Mr Gupta, allegedly helped his friend to trade in the knowledge that Warren Buffett's Berkshire Hathaway was to inject $5 billion into Goldman Sachs, the court was told. A call from Mr Gupta's office allegedly connected with Rajaratnam 16 seconds after he put the phone down on the rest of the Goldman Sachs board on 23 September 2008. Four minutes later—two minutes before the markets closed—Galleon bought $27 million of Goldman shares. A sale of the investment the following day, after news of Berkshire Hathaway's capital injection broke, generated a profit of about $8,40,000.

On 26 October 2011 the United States Attorney's Office filed criminal charges against Gupta. He was arrested in New York City by the FBI and pleaded not guilty. He was released on $10 million bail on the same day. Gupta's lawyer wrote,

> "Any allegation that Rajat Gupta engaged in any unlawful conduct is totally baseless.... He did not trade in any securities, did not tip Mr Rajaratnam so he could trade, and did not share in any profits as part of any *quid pro quo*."

The tips generated 'illicit profits and loss avoidance' of more than $23 million, the SEC alleged in the lawsuit. Rajat Gupta was entrusted by some of the premier institutions of American business to sit inside their boardrooms, among their executives and directors, and receive their confidential information so that he could give advice and counsel said Manhattan US Attorney Preet Bharara whose office is prosecuting the case.

In April 2012, another charge relating to passing P&G information was added by the prosecution. Gupta's lawyers countered that,

> "newly added charges—like the ones brought last year—are not based on any direct evidence, but rely on supposed circumstantial evidence."

More new charges based on new information may follow. The defence has maintained that 'the wrong person is on trial'.

In early May 2012, a pre-trial defence motion for access to SEC settlement-negotiation documents was denied by Judge Rakoff. Also in early May, the prosecution made a motion to play in trial three FBI wiretaps of two Rajaratnam "conversations with his principal trader and another with Galleon's then portfolio manager" related to the Goldman Sachs information. As well, details of wiretap recordings and trading activity related to the charges were analysed at length in the media, assessing the strengths and weaknesses of the prosecution's and defence's cases.

According to a prosecution witness, former Indian-American Director of Goldman Sachs Rajat Gupta was once on 'important people' list of Raj Rajaratnam, convicted hedge fund billionaire. On the second day of the insider-trading trial of

Gupta in Manhattan federal court, Rajaratnam's executive assistant Caryn Eisenberg said that her former boss was very particular about not being disturbed at the beginning and end of the trading day. But he made an exception for those listed as 'important people' in Eisenberg's notebook. Among them were Gupta and three other Indian-Americans. Rajiv, then an Intel Corporation Managing Director, Anil Kumar, a partner then at McKinsey and Parag Saxena, CEO of New Silk Rout LLC, an investment firm co-founded by Gupta, she said. Kumar and Goel—who was nicknamed 'Peter Pan' on the 'important people' list—both later pleaded guilty to insider trading and testified against Rajaratnam at his trial last year. Someone on that list, Eisenberg said, called urgently just before the market closed on September 23, 2008, the day Goldman board got word of Warren Buffett's $5 billion investment. Although she said she couldn't identify the voice, Eisenberg recognized it as one of the important ones and told Rajaratnam. According to phone records, Gupta called him at 3.54 PM that day. After the call, Eisenberg heard Galleon trader Gary Rosenbach say "buy Goldman Sachs". When, she said, Rajaratnam 'was smiling more'. Eisenberg, though, didn't hear about the Buffett business until the next day: "I went shopping at Bloomingdale's," she said. Former Galleon trader Ananth Muniyappa testifying about the minutes before the market closed the same day said that "Raj was either still on the phone or just getting off the phone" when he instructed him to buy 1,00,000 Goldman Sachs shares.

Gupta's lawyers acknowledge that Gupta and Rajaratnam were friends. But the relationship soured after Rajaratnam lost $10 million that Gupta invested in an entity called Voyager Capital Partners. In questioning Eisenberg, defence lawyer David Frankel brought out that Gupta was not the only person associated with Goldman Sachs on the 'important people' list. Part of the defence strategy is to show that Rajaratnam had other potential sources of inside information about Goldman other than Rajat Gupta.

A federal grand jury in Manhattan charged Rajat Gupta, one of the most prominent Indian-Americans in the financial sector, with one count of conspiracy to commit securities fraud and five counts of securities fraud, all related to Goldman tips in 2008.

Preet Bharara, the Manhattan US attorney, said in a statement,

> "Rajat Gupta was entrusted by some of the premier institutions of American business to sit inside their boardrooms, among their executives and directors, and receive their confidential information so that he could give advice and counsel for the benefit of their shareholders."

The statement said,

> "As alleged, he broke that trust and instead became the illegal eyes and ears in the boardroom for his friend and business associate, Raj Rajaratnam, who reaped enormous profits from Mr Gupta's breach of duty."

The charges carry a potential penalty of 105 years in prison. Gupta, 62, a former Director of Goldman Sachs and Procter & Gamble and head of McKinsey & Company, came under the scanner after prosecutors charged the Sri Lanka born Rajaratnam on insider trading charges. Rajaratnam was sentenced earlier to 11 years in prison. Indian Corporate Poster Boy fail the litmus test. The saying goes that corruption of the best makes the worst. Rajat Gupta after finishing his engineering from IIT-Delhi, went to Harvard Business School for his MBA. At 45, he was made the chief of McKinsey, the first non-US-born executive to run it, considered then the most influential consultancy firm. Clearly there was no holding him back. At the same time he seemed never to lose his focus on India, trying to give back to his homeland in diverse ways. "Try to make other people successful. If you work on making other people successful, they will in turn make you successful beyond your dreams." This was the advice that Gupta gave to students at the Indian School of Business, Hyderabad, the B-school that he helped start. Figures such as Gupta have become stories of achieving success the old-fashioned way, through sheer grit and determination, through relentless hard work.

However, if found guilty of charges of insider trading, this prominent global Indian could face 20 years or more in federal prison. Detractors argue that much of the evidence against him is circumstantial, that wiretapping as a means of gathering evidence is justifiable only in the absence of other reasonable means, etc. But public opinion is fast to form around an issue. The common man on the street feels vindicated if wrongdoings by the bigwigs are brought within the purview of justice. It takes years to build a reputation that a few moments' frailties, a crucial error of judgment, the smallest slip can undo.

The success stories such as those of Rajat Gupta do a volte-face and turn into murky tales of corporate greed and scandalous conduct. What is it in the human mind that suddenly blurs the sense of right and wrong. Is it what the ancient Greeks called 'hubris' by definition, a loss of contact with reality and an overestimation of one's own competence or capabilities, especially when the person exhibiting it is in a position of power. In classical literatures of almost all cultures, and especially of Western culture, the notion of a tragic hero has in it the seeds or germs of corruption even when its essence is made up of exalted qualities such as a penchant for excellence, the vision of things greater than what is allowed by one's immediate reality, the zeal to push the envelope, so to speak. Such an individual inspires us, holds our attention in awe. Then when he falls from grace we experience a vicarious fear laced with thrill and finally a cathartic relief that the ill fate has befallen that individual whom we were putting on a pedestal a while ago and that we have been spared of its ramifications.

Some important questions to be considered are—

1. What qualities did they admire in a professional.
2. What were some of their own uplifting experiences in dealing with other professionals.
3. What were their recollections of unprofessional conduct.

These men and women, from a diverse set of fields, indicated a list of qualities.... He then goes on to collate a list, which interestingly is topped by 'integrity', the one quality that is most prominent amongst all leaders and all professionals.

Integrity is a pre-requisite for any professional. There is no scope for any debate for it. Intelligence without integrity is like a body without a soul. However, to pass judgment on an erring individual from the comforts of one's couch is perhaps a fallacy. All of us watch news-clips on television but perhaps these are also occasions that warrant us to look into the deep abyss of our own souls. What we see on television are facts. But facts cannot and should not be confused with truth. The truth is shrouded in mystery. Visible, tangible facts are that the Guptas have failed at the altar of integrity. The truth to uncover is whether we as individuals would have passed the same test of temptation. Black, white or shades of grey.

Story of Rajat Gupta is an example for parents who want their sons to become investment bankers and their daughters to marry one. This story comes across as the striking story of neo-liberal greed that has inundated India, particularly so because Mr Gupta has been the poster child of success in the Indian landscape, depicting the markers of success along the lines that middle class parents desire for their children to model into. These markers of success are carried out in India by the trajectory of the IITs and IIMs, ultimately ending up with the ultimate job of an investment banker on Wall Street. The value of the investment banker for his parents lies in the markers of materialism he has achieved. This story furthermore gets gendered as we move ahead to complete the story: the parents of Indian girls in the marriage market desiring for their daughters to marry a hot-shot investment banker with all the material resources. This is of course then framed within the framework of desiring a comfortable life for one's daughter, which seems to be a fairly normal and perhaps the only dream of most middle class Indian parents. Amidst these dreams, the backside of the story goes something like this. As Indian parents spend their invaluable resources bringing up their child and training them for the competitive exams (spending loads of money on coaching centres), they also ensure that the child grows up with a tremendous sense of entitlement. One that tells him that he is somehow special. He is different, smart, intelligent, cut out from the rest of the population by his brilliance, separate from the teeming masses of the country. He is after all an IITian with an MBA. He is special. This sense of entitlement then becomes the fulcrum of choices that are made by the son who then goes on to use this brilliance to make money. This money then becomes the ticket to the Armani, LV, Channel, Burberry and the world of luxury. The cushy flats in the suburbs, the destination vacations in tropical places, the fancy meals in fancy restaurants ... these become the material markers of having arrived, of having accomplished something and of having succeeded in the world. The parents now are really proud of their son and his achievements. Where entitlement gets in the way however, is that it also pushes one to use whatever means that are available to make this money, because in the market, making the money is the marker of intelligence. So if he is able to figure out some loophole in regulations and make money, this is a sign of his brilliance, and he is entitled to the money. If he cheats specific regulations and makes the money, he is entitled to it because he is smart enough to cheat the system. If he is able to fool some people, that is of course a product of mind.

Unless the person concerned in overseeing any financial transactions especially security, the public will lose their confidence in the system and once people lose confidence there will be none to transact any business, it means collapse of the whole.

He's not an insider trader. He never defrauded anybody. He never cheated anybody, lawyer said in the Court for Rajat K Gupta, once one of America's most-prominent businessmen. "This is a straightforward case of insider trading," said Reed Brodsky the prosecutor, speaking to the jury. The government depicted Gupta as the ultimate insider who, after running the elite consulting firm McKinsey & Co, joined the boards of Goldman and P&G. As a director, he was privy to these companies' most closely-guarded secrets. "Gupta threw away his duties, threw away his responsibilities and broke the law." Brodsky emphasized the ties between Gupta and Rajaratnam, who began doing business together during the middle of the last decade. Gupta invested in Galleon's funds and the two helped start a $1 billion private equity fund together. "Together they offered each other far more than they could achieve individually," said Brodsky. Getting tips from Gupta was like knowing the outcome of a game before it ends or getting tomorrow's business news today. Specifically, he pointed to an emergency Goldman board meeting via phone that Gupta participated in during the financial crisis. On the call, Gupta and his fellow directors approved a $5 billion investment from Berkshire Hathaway. Brodsky said that immediately after the meeting ended, Gupta called Rajaratnam, who bought $43 million of Goldman shares in the company just before the market closed. The last-minute purchase earned the hedge fund manager $1 million.

Gary P Naftalis, Gupta's lead lawyer, accused the government of giving the jury a 'cropped photograph' instead of the entire picture. He emphasised that the government had no wiretapped recordings of Gupta's providing secret information to Rajaratnam. And on the few tapes in which Rajaratnam suggests to colleagues that he received tips about Goldman.

The Man Who Nailed Rajat Gupta

The desire for 'to have more' is probably the only reason for Rajat Gupta's fall. At 63, Rajat Gupta has a successful life to look back upon. The tragedy is that when he looks ahead, he will see a jail term that could go up to 25 years. There has been speculation that Gupta's stint on the Goldman board—when he saw the extraordinary amounts being made by far younger people—may have caused him discontentment. In August 2008, when Gupta was considering a position with private equity firm Kohlberg Kravis Roberts, Rajaratnam poked fun at his greed. In a phone chat with fellow conspirator Anil Kumar, Rajaratnam said, "He (Gupta) sees an opportunity to make a hundred million dollars over the next five or ten years, without doing a lot of work." Gupta's lawyer, Gary Naftalis, insists his client is innocent. Jurors were quoted as saying that Gupta seemed to have tipped off Rajaratnam because he wanted the latter's help in building his private equity fund, New Silk Route. Unfortunately, the new route he chose to take in what should have been his golden years is now set to lead him to a jail cell. Preetinder 'Preet' S Bharara, 43, US attorney for the Southern District of New York—widely believed to be the most high-profile and powerful attorney's job in the entire country—has unleashed an offensive against white-collar crime on Wall Street that has already earned him prestige. No one can say for sure what that tempestuous lady named Fate might have in store for any man. But if one were to heed the saying that the best way to predict someone's future is to look at his past, then Bharara is unlikely to ever be caught up in the kind of misdemeanour that saw Spitzer being prematurely ejaculated from public office. All his life, he seems to have been the classic squeaky clean, all-American kid—apart from the fact that he was born in India. Bharara was born in Ferozepur (Punjab) in 1968 to a Sikh father and a Hindu mother (he's married to the daughter of a Muslim father and a Jewish mother; the religious affiliation of their three young children is not known). In 1970, his family migrated to the US. Years later, after becoming the first Indian-American to feature on the cover of *Time*, Bharara told the magazine,

> "My dad is among the most principled people I know, and he didn't like some of the ways business was done in India, including how corrupt parts of it were."

Bharara's father, a paediatrician, seems to have passed on his sense of probity to his elder son. Preet's younger brother Vinit, 40, practised law before turning entrepreneur and selling his company Quidsi, that sold diapers over the internet, for $540 million to 'Amazon.com' in 2010. Bharara grew up in Monmouth County, New Jersey and still lives there. His neighbours include Bruce Springsteen, whose rasping vocals can often be heard playing in Bharara's office when he's working late into the night. Not unusually for Indian-Americans, his parents pushed him to excel—"The Tiger Mom actually made my dad look good," he's been known to joke. But even as a teenager, Bharara was willing to stick his neck out against perceived injustice. In 1986, when he was studying in New Jersey's Ranney School, Barbara Tomlinson, who taught history and literature there, got fired. Bharara—valedictorian of his high school class—had already been accepted at Harvard. He insisted on leading students into the headmaster's class. It was one of the few fights he lost, but it showed his willingness to battle for the underdog. Having graduated from Harvard and Columbia Law School, he got his wish in 2000, when he was appointed prosecutor in the Southern District of New York. Assigned to the organized-crime unit, he took on New York's top mafia families. It was during this stint that Bharara first used wiretaps—something he was to repeat against Wall Street. "When you're trying to make a racketeering case that involves charges of extortion, which by definition include threats of violence, and you have a guy saying, like you might see on The Sopranos, 'I'm going to staple your eyeball,' that's pretty good evidence," Bharara told *Time*. "There's no reason why you can't use appropriate street crime tactics to fight white-collar crime." In 2005, Bharara became chief counsel to New York Senator Charles Schumer in 2005. In that capacity, he helped lead the investigation into the firings of eight US attorneys under President George W Bush, which led to the ouster of US attorney general Alberto Gonzales. The probe could have degenerated into political partisanship, but didn't because as a Bush administration official admitted, "So many people have respect for him (Bharara). He's a political person, but foremost, he's a prosecutor." In August 2009, Schumer lobbied with newly elected President Barack Obama to make Bharara the new US Attorney for the southern district of New York. It was an appointment that was hailed. In an interview to *The New York Times*, New Jersey attorney general Anne Milgram said of Bharara,

> "He never carries himself like he's the smartest guy in the room, even though he often is."

As part of his job, Bharara oversees over 200 lawyers handling terrorism, organized crime, drug-trafficking, financial fraud and public corruption. His team has convicted Times Square bomber Faisal Shahzad; crippled international criminal networks run by Russian arms dealer Viktor Bout, Jamaican drug trafficker Christopher Coke and Colombian rebel group FARC. But his biggest claim to fame is as the man who's busting Wall Street, with his convictions including hedge fund manager Raj Rajaratnam, who was convicted. Bharara has taken on 58 cases of insider trading. He's yet to lose one. He's a registered Democrat, and certainly a big enough name. *Time* has named him "one of the 100 most influential people in the world" and CNN declared him one of the "most fascinating people". There's been speculation that Obama might tap him to serve as US attorney general if he's re-elected and incumbent Eric Holder decides to leave. For now, Bharara is dismissive of all such talk, insisting he has the best job in the world and he intends to keep it. Still, if his career continues on its present trajectory, the smart money wouldn't bet against his eyeing a political career. And you don't need any inside information to figure that out.

A decade ago, one of the top IT company heads was voted the best businessman of the year; he was hailed for his vision and leadership qualities, and considered a pioneer and a role model. Little did the distinguished jury know that he had committed a massive fraud on his shareholders and siphoned off crores of rupees. His name was Ramalinga Raju founder of Satyam Computers—who possessed an MBA from Ohio University (US). Rest is history; he is being prosecuted for cheating, embezzlement and insider trading. Not long ago, there was a Houston-based energy company looming like a colossal, Enron; at one time, it was estimated worth $110 billion. Thanks to its CFO and other senior executives who misled the board and pressured audit firm Arthur Andersen to ignore the issues, Enron was forced to declare bankruptcy, the biggest in the US corporate history. Some of its executives are serving jail term. We have the Joshi couple, IAS officers, in Madhya Pradesh who amassed more than ₹350 crore in a short span of service. Another smart, intelligent and gizmo-savvy IAS officer in Maharashtra, in his coded messages, used to call bribes as hardware and call girls software. A Secretary in the Ministry of External Affairs, who was responsible for promoting economic relations, was removed from his post and chargesheeted for aiding and abetting illegal emigration. He comes from a well-to-do family and could have lived comfortably without a government salary.

In 1994, Gupta was quoted in the *Chicago Tribune* to have said that McKinsey stood for meritocracy. But a stage came in his many life when he wasn't content with what he had; he wanted more, he wanted to join the billionaires' club.

Why do highly-intelligent, successful and meritorious individuals earning relatively high salaries or profits and living a comfortable life take such risks and throwaway all the achievements, kudos and laurels? Are they consumed by ambition? Is it their insatiable desire to get rich and richer? Don't their academic brilliance and meritorious record shield them against such temptations. If the top executives have not inculcated moral and ethical values in corporate management, mega frauds can't be ruled out from time to time. Self-discipline (cut your coat according to your length), contentment (to shun insatiable desire to acquire more), foolproof checks and balances in financial transactions and moral and ethical values adhered to by a company do help in avoiding cases of fraud and corruption. But the basic reason why the seemingly successful people resort to frauds and corrupt practices is that they have deleted the *Lakshman Rekha* of the right and wrong from their mental disc. Once an individual stops asking the question what he is doing is right or wrong, that individual can do anything without any compunction or remorse.

Eventually, it is the choice between two contrasting concepts of success underlined long ago by Mahatma Gandhi and Chinese leader Deng Xiaoping. Gandhi stressed that noble goals must be reached through noble means. On the other hand, Deng, who is the father of economic transformation of China, maintained, "So long as the cat caught the rat, it didn't matter whether it was white or black." Whether it is 2G scam or CWG scam or mining scam or allocation of coal mining rights, those who perpetrated the scams had not drawn *Lakshman Rekha* for themselves.

Whether it is Rajat Gupta or Raju or Raja or Suresh Kalmadi, they all seemed to be following the dictum of the Chinese helmsman Deng Xiaoping rather than the father of our nation. It is high time we go back to Mahatma and embrace his moral and ethical values and discriminate between right and wrong. That is the bedrock of a just, fair, equitable, successful and caring and sharing society.

Radia Tapes Controversy

The Radia tapes controversy relates to the telephonic conversations between Nira Radia, a political lobbyist and an acquaintance of the (then) Indian Telecom Minister A Raja, and with senior journalists, politicians, and corporate houses, taped by the Indian Income Tax Department in 2008-09. The tapes led to accusations of misconduct by many of these people. Nira Radia used to run a public relations firm named Vaishnavi Communications, whose clients include the Tata Teleservices and Mukesh Ambani's Reliance Industries.

After getting authorization from the Home Ministry, the Indian Income Tax department tapped Radia's phone lines for 300 days in 2008-09 as part of their investigations into possible money-laundering, restricted financial practices, and tax evasion. In November 2010, *OPEN (magazine)* carried a story which reported transcripts of some of the telephone conversations of Nira Radia with senior journalists, politicians, and corporate houses, many of whom have denied the allegations. The Central Bureau of Investigation has announced that they have 5,851 recordings of phone conversations by Radia, some of which outline Radia's attempts to broker deals in relation to the 2G spectrum sale. The tapes appear to demonstrate how Radia attempted to use some media persons to influence the decision to appoint A Raja as Telecom Minister. In the recorded conversations between Nira Radia and prominent figures, referred to as the Radia Tapes, several prominent figures are heard in conversation with Radia:

Politicians

- A Raja, Telecom Minister at that time
- Kanimozhi, Rajya Sabha MP, DMK
- Achari

Journalists

- Barkha Dutt, Group Editor, English News, NDTV
- MK Venu, Senior Business Journalist
- Prabhu Chawla, Editor of *India Today* magazine
- Rajdeep Sardesai
- Shankar Aiyar, then with India Today Group
- Vir Sanghvi, HT Advisory Editorial Director

Industry Heads

- Tarun Das, former CII Head

Others

- Ranjan Bhattacharya (foster son-in-law of former Prime Minister Atal Bihari Vajpayee)
- Suhel Seth, Brand Manager
- Balaji MS alias Balaji Subhash (controversial lobbyist from Bangalore involved in Madhu Koda Scam)

Political Lobbying

According to the transcripts of the tapes, Radia lobbied against the reappointment of Dayanidhi Maran to the post of Union IT and Communications Minister.

- Radia spoke with Ms Barkha Dutt at 0948 IST.

Dutt: 'The stalemate (between Congress and DMK) continues, ya.'

Radia: 'my honest advice is that you tell them (Congress) that they need to tell him (Karunanidhi) directly.'

Dutt: 'OK, let me talk to them.'

In a later conversation at 1047 IST, Barkha says that it (conveying the message to Congress) was 'not a problem' and that she would talk to Ghulam (Ghulam Nabi Azad).

- Radia, in a later conversation with Ranjan Bhattacharya, who also appears to be acting as a conduit to the Congress, mentions the above conversation, where she says, 'I made Barkha call up Congress, and get a statement from Congress whether the Prime Minister has actually said that he doesn't want Baalu, which she carried that he had never said it'. She also mentions to Bhattacharya, that 'your friend Sunil Mittal, has been lobbying against Raja (for Maran).'

The news gained prominence following sustained pressure on social networking sites Twitter and Facebookhttp://en.wikipedia.org/wiki/Radia_tapes_controversy-cite_note-24 against an attempted blackout orchestrated by many prominent Indian TV channels and newspapers. Barkhagate was a trending number one topic on Twitter in India for more than a week, since the breakout of the news. According to the *Washington Post*,

> "Twitter has played an important role in launching what has become an international conversation on the issue, with the Indian diaspora weighing in".

Initially, only a handful of the mainstream newspapers in India, like *The Deccan Herald, Indian Express* had openly written about the tapes. Some newspapers like *Mint* (the business newspaper also owned by HT media) and NDTV said "the authenticity of these transcripts cannot be ascertained." CNN-IBN's Sagarika Ghose discussed with a panel of experts, if the corporate lobbying is undermining democracy, on the 'Face the Nation' programme on the channel. The Radia tapes is seen to have also made a dent in the image of the media in the country.

G Sampath, the Deputy Editor of the *Daily News and Analysis (DNA)* newspaper, wrote:

> "The complete blackout of the Nira Radia tapes by the entire broadcast media and most of the major English newspapers paints a truer picture of corruption in the country,"

After it became an international news, more and more media houses covered the story. *The Deccan Chronicle* commented,

> "The 'Radia tapes' may have torn the veil off the nexus between information hungry journalists, lobbyists and industrialists, and opened everyone's eyes to what has long been suspected—the ability of a small but powerful group to use their connections to influence policy."

The largest circulated English newspaper in India and the world, *The Times of India* finally opened up on November 25, 2010, and commented:

> The people are showing who the boss is. The weapon in their hands is the internet, ... has seen frantic activism against 'power brokering' by journalists in collusion with corporate groups and top government politicians...."

Barkha Dutt, Vir Sanghvi, and others have refuted the allegations. *OPEN (magazine)* maintained that the conversations were carried as they appeared in the recordings. Dutt defended her reputation through her Twitter account. "Struck by the bizarre irony of being accused of favouring a man I have never met (Raja) and have always attacked in print and on TV. Gnite!", she said via one of her tweets on Twitter.

New Delhi Television Limited posted a strong rebuttal on its website terming the insinuation that Barkha lobbied for A Raja as "unsubstantiated, baseless and defamatory" and threatened action against *OPEN (magazine)*. *Hindustan Times* cited Sanghvi's clarifications on his website, and stated that the authenticity of these transcripts cannot be ascertained. On 26 November 2010, Barkha Dutt released a detailed statement, addressing questions raised by the tapes, which she claims were edited. On 27 November 2010, Vir Sanghvi released a detailed statement, clarifying his role.

Nira Radia has served a legal notice on *The Pioneer*, on the report titled 'Tapped and Trapped' published by the newspaper.

The notice asserted that *The Pioneer*'s report regarding corruption and manipulation in the allotment of 2G spectrum to telecom operators, in so far as it referred to Radia's connections with Telecom Minister A Raja, are "absolutely false, baseless and malicious and constitute gross defamation." The original tapes are now annexures in a Supreme Court petition seeking Raja's prosecution. The opposition parties in India have demanded a Joint Parliamentary Committee (JPC) probe into the 2G spectrum scam, which could also to be extended to include a probe into the Radia tapes to ascertain the media's role in the controversy. The government is also accused of selectively releasing merely 10 hours of the 2,000 hours recorded of the Radia tapes.

The CBI in its affidavit in the Supreme Court in the 2G spectrum allocation case, on November 22, 2010, had stated that Radia will be approached for investigation at an appropriate time, and that the probe would be completed latest by March 2011. On 24 November 2010, Nira Radia was questioned by the Enforcement Directorate (ED) officials and they recorded her statements in relation to the 2G scam probe.

Nira Radia—Her Life and Tapes

Nira was born in 1959 in Nairobi, Kenya, where her parents of Indian origin Iqbal Narain Menon had settled. Her adopted name Nira Radia or before marriage Nira Menon suggests that she is a Keralite but she is daughter of Punjabi parents and had contact with a Gujarati after her family had shifted to London. She married that Gujarati young entrepreneur Janda Radia and come to be known as Nira Radia and worked with her husband initially but, being more ambitious than Janda, she entered into airline business as an adviser. She made quite a success, while her husband had got a bad name by liquidating or dissolving eight trade companies. In 1994, she came to India where her father had negotiated a job for her in SAHARA Airlines. That was the turning point in her life. Though she had three children from marriage with Janda Radia, she abandoned them and after a few years had illicit relations with Dhiraj Singh with whom she remained close from 1994 to 2002. When both went to open a bank account in a Swiss bank, she had become so close to Singh that she was Mrs Singh when both went to USA. But despite such closeness for almost a decade when they were living together as a family, she broke up with Singh and changed living for kidnapping her 16 year old son, for which Dhiraj Singh spent two years in jail. This was the character of Nira Radia that she could be close to one for her selfish business purpose and dump him when she no longer needed his help or association.

As Nira Radia had assets of more than ₹300 crore in short span of a decade, Income Tax authorities as well as Finance Ministry got suspicious about her clandestine, even anti-national activities, as she had been called a foreign agent, though not substantiated. From 2007, because of her contacts particularly with Ratan Tata and Mukesh Ambani, her conduct, movements and association with business tycoons, IAS officers and Ministers of States and Centre, her 14 telephone lines were taped on the direction of Finance Minister. However, it took almost a year to find out the truth. Though allegations against her came to light only after the Nira Radia tapes when on November 2009 it was decided by CBI and Income Tax authorities to depute someone to collect her tapes.

Now, in brief, names of persons and organizations in business and government follow hereinafter who were using the influence of Nira Radia for their personal purposes of collecting wealth and with influence and association of Nira Radia, knowingly or unknowingly. First of all comes Ratan Tata, almost the richest and most talked about and influential business tycoon. How he got close to Nira Radia and what he gained for some years and what he lost (status and respect as the most intelligent entrepreneur). Nira Radia had met Ratan Tata in

2001 which was the most significant year of her life when she was working for Tata Airlines and Singapore Airlines, a joint venture. She impressed Ratan Tata so much that within a couple of years she was handling public relations of 14 Tata companies and by 2009 she had so much influence on Ratan Tata that she was controlling public relations of about 90 Tata companies.

Because of Radia's closeness to Tata and her influence in 2008, the business tycoon, richest Indian, Mukesh Ambani thought of similar rise with the influence of Radia with publication and bureaucrats. Thus, Mukesh Ambani gave to Nira Radia virtually entire control of Reliance Industries. This sudden rise of Nira Radia also disturbed the central government. UPA-II whose Communication Minister A Raja was also in close contact of Nira Radia and through her was indulging in more corruption as he was till then unchallenged. But Nira Radia-Raja alliance had also tainted the image of Prime Minister and UPA-II government in general. This led a year or so to investigate the activities of Nira Radia and finally the Nira Radia tapes disclosures. Nira Radia was expecting to get hold of right men to achieve her objective both in industry and the government, without being herself in front line. So she had, what is called a 'Fixer' for this purpose. She chose Tarun Das who, as eminent organizer of Indian industry, was not only in good books of the government but had untold influence even on Prime Minister Dr Manmohan Singh, on whose recommendation he had been awarded Padma Bhushan in 2006. Nira Radia's conversation with Das virtually shows that Das was willing to influence the government to get what she wanted, of course at a price to Das. Besides many fixing done by Das, Nira Radia got two important approvals made by the government viz, appointment of Kamal Nath as Minister of Surface Transport, to support A Raja and appoint Sunil Arora as Chairman of Indian Airlines. To all these suggestions by Das, the fixer, PM agreed and lost his prestige, particularly by defending Raja for long and also by opposing JPC, so that Raja, whom he defended for a long time could not be exposed.

Nira Radia, educated in London, was very intelligent and particularly impressive in conversation. As a result, she could impress business stalwarts like Ratan Tata in first meeting, but she being over ambitious and determined to achieve her objective by fair or foul means. Her conversation on tapes and her almost a dozen telephone numbers, when got in possession of government and got publicity in media people all over India, many bureaucrats and ministers and even UPA-II got into trouble along with Nira Radia. Her rise and fall during two decades proves that no one, whether businessmen, politician, bureaucrat or even common man or woman, should never adopt foul means to attain their object, howsoever right it may be.

Cadbury: Nigeria's Fraud

Cadbury Nigeria sacked its Managing Director, Mr Bunmi Oni and Mr Ayo Akadiri, the company's Finance Director which was a fallout of the financial book padding scandal and corruption, that rocked the company. The bold actions of the Board of Directors led by Dr Uduimo Itsueli should be commended. The Board commissioned the firm of PricewaterhouseCoopers to review and investigate the company's financials. The outcome of the investigation had confirmed a deliberate overstatement of the company's financial position over a number of years to the tune of between ₦13 and ₦15 billion. This was Nigeria's version of the Enron Corporation scandal in the United States.

Corporate ethics has gone to the dogs, or, better put, has been in the pouch of the dogs all along in Nigeria. It is noteworthy to mention here that the Bunmi Oni management at Cadbury for years packaged itself as the best example of a professional establishment, its best practice with strong ethical clout and rectitude. It was sad to suddenly discover that this had been a ruse and a huge deception all along; the unsuspecting

Nigerian public had been fooled and misled by Mr Bunmi Oni and Mr Ayo Akadiri over the years.

Cadbury Nigeria had to adjust it accounts to reflect an operating loss of between ₦1 and ₦2 billion. The company's Public Affairs Manager, Mr Kufre Ekanem told newsmen that,

> "Over the number of years, Cadbury Nigeria had assigned itself an ambitious growth target. To achieve these targets, several systems abuses occurred. The overstatements are directly traceable to those systems abuses."

Mr Ekanem referred to "deliberate breaches of our accounting systems and controls," and cooking up numbers became an obsession with the central focus of maintaining a mirage.

It is a shame that Messrs Oni and Akadiri ended their long years of service at Cadbury in disgrace with their reputation in tatters. Both men should be in the custody of the Economic and Financial Crimes Commission (EFCC) to explain their roles in the overstatement of accounts and the deliberate manipulation of finances at Cadbury. Enron Corporation founder, Kenneth Lay was convicted on all six counts of fraud and conspiracy while Enron Chief Executive Jeffrey Skilling was found guilty on 19 of the 28 charges brought against him. The case of Messrs Bunmi Oni and Ayo Akadiri should not be different, and the EFCC should not fail in its duty to protect investors and serve a warning to corporate looters and crooks still in several companies in Nigeria.

The attitude to reap off and to loot in the private sector in Nigeria has not been given the attention it deserves, yet there are lots of abuses and number juggling going on in most companies in Nigeria. Corruption is so rife in the private sector in Nigeria that most foreign companies find it difficult to appoint Nigerians as helmsmen to run their Nigerian offices. Lever Brothers Nigeria suffered a similar setback a few years back when it suddenly removed Chief Rufus Giwa after a careful review of its finances discovered abuses and irreconcilable figures. The average Nigerian executive considers the funds of his/her company just another piggy bank from where all sorts of personal expenses are taken care of and every imaginable purchase is made. In Cadbury Nigeria's case this included the provision of generators, fuel and maintenance services to the home of one of the company's former Chief Executives.

Several accounts in Cadbury Nigeria are coded so well and there are many headings that meant far more than they ordinarily present at a casual look. Many Cadbury staff confirmed the existence of a mafia headed by a former Chief Executive holding on to the company, and only this former executive's sidekicks cum anointed candidates have risen to executive cadres in more than 15 years. The average Nigerian company and banks are run like this. In such an environment, honest, hardworking and straightforward folks have no place; they are hounded, sidelined and eventually pushed out. There were several such cases at many of the now defunct new generation and the not-so-new generation banks and manufacturing companies.

In Nigeria, corporate governance and responsibility has been sacrificed at the altar of nepotism and corruption. It is no news to declare that more than 60% of the existing banks in Nigeria today are padded up and their financial statements heavily suspect. Many of them are not worth placing funds with and their leaderships continue to carry on business as usual. The era of forex magic and round tripping may not be over yet at these banks. It was forex that provided opportunities to many crooks in Nigerian banks some years back to embezzle funds. Many of such crooks are scattered around Europe and North America with their loot, not anxious to return to Nigeria anytime soon. They have for company those one-room apartment finance house magicians who promised unimaginable returns on investment to unwary and sometimes greedy people only to run away and leave their victims in tears.

Many medical doctors and professors met their untimely death at the hands of these lowlifes who took their money and gave nothing back in return—no interest, no deposit, nothing. After several years of medical labour and hard work, the doctors returned from Saudi Arabia and placed their hard earned money in these finance companies. But when the bubble busted and the funds juggling could no longer be maintained any longer, the finance house wizards made for Europe and America, their loots in tow. Cadbury Nigeria must come clean and take every step necessary to clean up the books in the interest of its shareholders; good corporate responsibility, and integrity once touted by Mr Bunmi Oni as a cornerstone of the firm's way of doing business.

Another similar case to Cadbury's is that of Afribank Nigeria Pic. Afribank's financial statement woes and accusation by its former Managing Director that the Board of Directors colluded with its auditors to cook the books came more than a month before Cadbury's, but while Cadbury took quick and necessary steps to put the records straight, Afribank is still at work. It is surprising what is delaying the review and what the Central Bank of Nigeria is doing to ensure that nothing but the true position of Afribank's accounts is produced and presented to the shareholders.

Godrej in Trouble after Employee Fraud

An employee of consumer goods maker Godrej Consumer Products Ltd (GCPL), has embezzled gold worth crores of rupees, that has come under the radar of the Economic Offences Wing (EOW) of the Mumbai police, after some city based jewellers failed to receive dues, making it one of the biggest embezzlement cases involving an Indian company in recent times. Five city based jewellers and one from Kolkata, who used to supply gold coins to the company, said that GCPL is refusing to pay them their dues because a senior employee forged an order and embezzled the coins. The company used to buy gold coins to give it to retailers and distributors as an incentive for sales. City-based Orra Diamond Jewellery, Cygnus Jewellery, Asmi Jewellery, Basanti Gold Pvt Ltd, Hiralal Jain Enterprises and Kolkata based PC Chandra Jewellers together claim ₹25 crore from GCPL.

However, the company said the order was placed illegally without any authority by one of its former employees Amit Gaine. He falsely projected himself as acting on behalf of the company. Upon further investigation, it also came to their knowledge that he had forged signatures of some of their officials and created false purchase orders, e-mails etc. The company specifically disowns all such illegal ads committed by Amit Gaine and states that Amit Gaine is himself responsible for these purported transactions with outsider parties. The company is not liable for the claims arising out of the dispute between the outsider parties and the individual who has committed the fraud. The jewellers, however, said that Gaine was the Deputy General Manager of the company and orders were always officially placed by the company through him.

Sunil Jain, proprietor at Hiralal Jain Enterprises, a company which supplies corporate gifts said Godrej owes him ₹2.5 crore for gold coins supplied in January. He said,

> "I have been supplying coins to the company and there was no problem in payments. I am a registered vendor with the company. But in the last instance the payment did not come till the second week of February 2010."

Jain said the company called them for a meeting on 18 February 2010,

> "they also sent us a letter by their advocates on 19 February 2010 saying that they were looking into the matter."

But after sitting over the issue for a month they wrote to us on 15 March that they have nothing to do with purchases made by

Gaine. They also filed a complaint with EOW on 18 February, 2010 without telling us when we met them. "We are shocked at the way GCPL has treated us," he said.

The jewellers then approached the EOW of the Mumbai police against Godrej claiming their amount. GCPL has also filed a complaint against Gaine, who is now in judicial custody. "The company has already issued a notice to Basanti Gold Pvt Ltd and Harilal Jalan Enterprises for making incorrect, wrongful and defamatory statements against us," GCPL said. EOW confirmed that its department is investigating cases involving GCPL.

Two other jewellers Asmi and Basanti said they have been supplying coins to the company since 2008, with Gaine being their one point contact. Hitesh Sanghvi a lawyer representing Basanti said GCPL owes his client ₹8 crore. He is preparing to send the company a legal notice to recover his dues.

> "I have already drafted the notice and will send it to the company tomorrow or the day after. If they don't pay up with in a month, we will approach the Bombay High Court."

A similar case at software company Wipro Ltd came to light after some bankers alerted the company in December about the lack of funds in an account.

Anup Kumar Agarwal, a chartered accountant joined the company as an intern in 2006, and was later promoted as an assistant manager in a division of the finance department which had powers to authorize payments on behalf of Wipro. On 23 December 2010, Agarwal was found dead on a railway track in east Bangalore.

Chicago Furrier Pleads Guilty in Money-Laundering Case

The jingle is a staple of Chicago radio and TV commercials. "Andriana Furs..." sings the female vocalist. Now, the owner of the Chicago fur chain is singing a different tune. Sohrab

Tebyanian, 62, of Chicago, sang a plea of guilty Friday morning to a federal judge in a money-laundering conspiracy case. Far from the Boul Mich glamour depicted in Andriana's fur advertisements, Tebyanian's plea deal offers a look into a sordid tale of crack cocaine and ghost pay rolling ... with a small fortune being laundered through the famous furrier. The case was originally investigated and filed in Iowa, where three people who ran a cocaine trafficking ring for a decade already pleaded guilty in Davenport. The $3 million operation was run by Mario Murray and his mother Jeanette and a Chicago postal worker/ courier Tina Hollins.

Mario Murray first came to the attention of law enforcement in 1996, when Chicago police officers found crack cocaine and a gun in the home he shared with his parents. In 2000, an officer from the Illinois State Police stopped Murray on Interstate 80 near Geneseo, Ill. The officer found $35,000 in cash in Murray's back seat. He seized the cash, which Murray said he was planning to buy a car with. Murray did not dispute the seizure, however. About that time, Murray was working for Andriana Furs. The owner, Tebyanian, told federal authorities that Murray worked there for six months in 2000. However, W-2 forms were filed for Murray by Andriana Furs from 2000 onward. In the plea agreement Tebyanian admits that Murray did little, if any, work for the furrier and that it was part of a scheme to launder drug money. Judge Wayne Andersen set sentencing for Tebyanian on April 16, 2009. Assistant US Attorney T Markus Funk handled the plea agreement in Chicago. Defence attorney Mchael Monico represented Tebyanian.

Money-Laundering Case of Hasan Ali

The Enforcement Directorate chargesheeted Pune-based stud farm owner Hasan Ali Khan and his associate Kashinath Tapuriah in a case of alleged money-laundering.

Khan is alleged to have stashed huge amount of black

money abroad including over $8 billion in the Union Bank of Switzerland (UBS) in Zurich.

Khan was arrested in Mumbai in March 2011 after several hours of grilling in the wake of the Supreme Court's criticism of the government over its inaction against the black money hoarders, particularly him. The arrest of one Tapuriah, a Kolkata businessman, followed soon. Khan is also under the scanner for terror links as he is suspected to have laundered money of international arms trader Adnan Khashoggi, who is alleged to be associated with terrorist outfits. There have been allegations against Khan of money-laundering, engaging in hawala operations, transferring cash and valuable assets outside the country by unlawful means with the help of foreign nationals and forgery. He has been accused of obtaining passports from Mumbai and Patna using forged documents. Pondicherry governor Iqbal Singh has also been questioned by the ED for helping Khan in securing the travel document from Regional Passport Office in Patna through a Bihar Congress politician Amlendu Kumar Pandey, who is also under investigation. The statements of Singh and Khan are said to be part of the chargesheet. Khan, according to ED, has reportedly confessed to stealing antiques belonging to the family of Nizams, the erstwhile rulers of Hyderabad State, from the famous Salar Jung Museum and selling them to off-shore customers for ₹50 lakh.

Sani Abacha

General Sani Abacha (20 September 1943–8 June 1998) was a Nigerian military dictator and politician. A Kanuri from Borno by tribe, he was born and brought up in Kano, He was the *de facto* President of Nigeria from 1993 to 1998.

Abacha was commissioned in 1963, after he had attended the Mons Defence Officers Cadet Training College in Aldershot, England. Before then, he had attended the Nigerian Military Training College in Kaduna. He took part in the countercoup of July 1967, from the conceptual stage, and may have been a participant in the Lagos or Abeokuta phases of the January 1966 coup. He was also a prominent figure in three *coup d'etats* of later decades, the first two of which brought and removed General Muhammadu Buhari from power in 1983. When General Ibrahim Babangida was named President and Commander-in-Chief of the Armed Forces of the Federal Republic of Nigeria in 1985, Abacha was named Chief of Army Staff. He was later appointed Minister of Defence in 1990.

Abacha took over power from the caretaker government of Chief Ernest Shonekan, who was put into place by General Ibrahim Babangida after his annulment of the 12 June 1993 elections (won by Moshood Kashimawo Olawale Abiola), this caused a massive popular uproar, which in turn caused untold hardship for millions of Nigerians.

On 6 September 1994, Abacha declared that his regime had absolute power, placing his government above the jurisdiction of the courts. He did, however, promise to hand the government over to civilians in 1998.

Despite his stated commitment to returning the country to democracy, Abacha's government was accused of human rights abuses, especially after the hanging of Ogoni activist Ken Saro-Wiwa by the Oputa Commission (only one of several executions of Ogoni activists opposed to the exploitation of Nigerian resources by the multinational petroleum company, Royal Dutch Shell Group); Abiola and Olusegun Obasanjo were jailed for treason, and Wole Soyinka charged in absentia with treason. His regime suffered stiff opposition internally and externally by pro-democracy activists who made the regime unpopular, and responded by banning political activity in general and by controlling the press in particular; a significant fraction of the military was purged. Abacha surrounded himself with approximately 3,000 armed men loyal to him. His government compared to other Nigerian governments was characterised by an inconsistent foreign policy. He supported the Economic Community of West African States and sent Nigerian troops to Liberia and Sierra Leone to restore democracy to those countries while denying it at home. Abacha scoffed at the threat of economic sanctions on account of the world's dependence on petroleum, of which Nigeria is a major producer.

Despite being repeatedly condemned by the US State Department, Abacha did have a few ties to American politics. In 1997, Senator James Inhofe (R-Oklahoma) travelled to Nigeria to meet with Abacha as a representative of 'The Family', a group of evangelical Christian politicians and civic leaders. Abacha and 'The Family' had a business and political relationship from that point until his death.

Abacha also developed ties with other American political figures such as Senator Carol Mosley Braun, Rev Jessie Jackson and Minister Louis Farrakhan. Several African American political leaders visited Nigeria during his reign and Farrakhan supported the regime, while it was seen as an international pariah. Farrakhan also had a street in Nigeria named after him. The street name was changed back to its original name after Abacha's death.

During Abacha's regime, a total of £5 billion was reported siphoned out of the country's coffers by the head of State and members of his family. At that time Abacha was listed as the world's fourth most corrupt leader in recent history. Abacha's national security adviser, Alhaji Ismaila Gwarzo, played a crucial role in the looting and transfer of money to overseas accounts. His son Mohammed Abacha was also involved. A preliminary report published by the Abdulsalami Abubakar transitional government in November 1998 described the process. Sani Abacha told Ismaila Gwarzo to provide fake funding requests, which Abacha approved. The funds were usually sent in cash or travellers' cheques by the Central Bank of Nigeria to Gwarzo, who took them to Abacha's house. Mohammed Abacha then arranged to launder the money to offshore accounts. An estimated $1.4 billion in cash was delivered in this way.

In early 1998, Abacha announced that elections would be held on 1st August of that year. It soon became apparent, though, that Abacha had no intention of permitting an honest vote; during the spring he strong-armed the country's five parties into endorsing him as the sole presidential candidate.

Abacha died in June 1998 while at the presidential villa in Abuja. He was buried on the same day, according to Muslim tradition, without an autopsy. This fuelled speculation that foul-play was involved and that he may have been poisoned by political rivals via prostitutes. On the contrary, Nigerian military rulers cited his cause of death as a sudden heart attack. It is known that he was in the company of six teenage Indian prostitutes imported from Dubai. It is thought that these prostitutes laced his drink with a poisonous substance, making Abacha feel unwell around 4:30 AM. He retired to his bed and was dead by 6:15 AM.

After his death, Maj Gen Abdulsalami Abubakar, Nigeria's Defence Chief of Staff, was sworn in as the country's head of State. Abubakar had never before held public office and was quick to announce a transition to democracy, which led to the election of President Olusegun Obasanjo.

Abacha was married to Maryam Abacha and had seven sons and three daughters.

After Sani Abacha's death, the Obasanjo government implicated Abacha and his family in a wholesale looting of Nigeria's coffers. According to post-Abacha governmental sources, some $3 or $4 billion USD in foreign assets have been traced to Abacha, his family and their representatives, $2.1 billion of which the Nigerian government tentatively came to an agreement with the Abacha family to return, with the *quid pro quo* being that the Abachas would be allowed to keep the rest of the money. Although this proposal caused a massive outcry at that time for seeming to reward the theft of public funds, it was subsequently rejected by the late dictator's son, Mohammed Abacha, who continues to maintain that all the assets in question were legitimately acquired. In 2002, Abacha's family agreed to return $1.2 billion that was taken from the central bank.

The names of Sani Abacha, his wife Maryam, and son Mohammed are often used in advance fee fraud (419) scams; he is 'identified' in scam letters as the source for 'money' that does not exist. One website that is dedicated to exposing Nigerian 419 (advance fee) scammers and similar schemes, 'ebolamonkeyman.com', famously exposed one use of the Abacha family name, resulting in a wider exposure and awareness of these type of scams in general.

A bus bombing two decades ago and a New Jersey father's quest for justice—inadvertently set off a chain of events that led American Prosecutors to accuse some of the world's biggest banks of transferring money for nations like Iran. The trail that ultimately led to BNP began in 2006, when the Manhattan district attorney's office came upon a lawsuit filed by the father; who blamed Iran for financing the Gaza bus bombing that killed his 20-year-old daughter. Buried in the court files, prosecutors found a stunning accusation, a charity that owned a gleaming office tower on Fifth Avenue was actually a 'front' for the Iranian government, a claim that the prosecutors ultimately verified.

The prosecutors soon discovered that Credit Suisse and Lloyds, two of the world's most prestigious banks, had acted as Iran's portal to the United States financial system. To disguise the illicit transactions—the United States is closed for business to Iran—Credit Suisse and Lloyds stripped out the Iranian clients' names from wire transfers to the Fifth Avenue charity and affiliated entities. The findings led the Manhattan prosecutors and the Justice Washington to announce criminal cases against both banks.

The twists and turns leading to the BNP case open a window into the interconnected yet shadowy world of global finance. It is a cautionary tale of how European banks, spotting a lucrative business opportunity that American rivals shunned, opened their doors to countries under sanctions and ultimately exposed their reputations to the stain of criminal cases. The interviews with prosecutors, some who spoke freely and others anonymously, also tell a story of how a local prosecutor's office in New York, known for crack downs on drugs and organized crime, landed in the middle of an international investigation into terrorist bombings and foreign banks.

The district attorney's role in the case, which began under Mr Vance's predecessor; Robert M Morgenthau, was not always clear. Adam Kaufmann, a prosecutor who helped lead the investigations, once travelled to Washington to meet with officials from the Treasury Department's Office of Foreign Assets Control, the primary enforcer of American sanctions against Iran. The Treasury Department, was baffled as to why a Manhattan prosecutor was investigating the case at all.

The investigation, explained, began in earnest back in January 2006. At the time, in a cramped office cubicle in lower Manhattan, a 32-year-old analyst for the Manhattan district attorney's office pored over the New Jersey father's lawsuit against Iran. The father; Stephen Flatow of West Orange, NJ, accused Iran of funding the terrorist group responsible for the suicide bombing in Gaza that killed his daughter; Ailsa, in 1995.

A federal judge awarded Mr Flatow, a lawyer at a title company, $250 million in damages. Iran never paid. And so Mr Flatow sought to collect from the Alavi Foundation, the charity that he claimed was a front for the Iranian government. The analyst at the district attorney's office, Eitan Arusy, took a keen interest in the father's accusations. Before joining the office, he was an Israeli soldier who happened to have responded to the scene of that very same bus bombing. And the Alavi Foundation, it turned out, was in the heart of the district attorney's jurisdiction. It held an ownership stake in a Fifth Avenue sky scraper just steps from Rockefeller Center and the Museum of Modern Art. The 36-story tower, formerly known as the Piaget Building, was built in the late 1970s by a non-profit set-up tied to the Shah of Iran.

One day in 2006, Laura Billings, a prosecutor in the district attorney's office who helped lead the Alavi Foundation investigation, visited the tower to see for herself whether anything suspicious was unfolding inside. But the building, which has housed the offices of Ivan F Boesky, the famed Wall Street speculator who was convicted as part of the 1980s insider trading scandal, and is currently home to Godiva, the chocolate maker; was an ordinary office tower.

The prosecutors reached a breakthrough, however; during a visit to a Persian rug shop owner who had ties to Iran. Gathered around a table, picking at watermelon and pistachios, the shop owner and prosecutors discussed politics and family. At the end of the conversation came a revelation: the Alavi Foundation, the shop owner declared, was completely under the control of Iran.

Another confidential informant provided additional clues, specifically that the Alavi Foundation had received millions of dollars from Bank Melli, an Iranian State-owned bank. Get the payment records, the informant explained, and prosecutors would find the trail to Iran. But when the prosecutors and the FBI pulled the charity's bank records, Bank Melli was nowhere to be found. Credit Suisse and Lloyds were there instead.

The evidence against the Alavi Foundation was extensive, former prosecutors say; but pointed to a federal case rather than a local one. The district attorney's office ceded its Alavi investigation to the United States attorney's office in Manhattan. Under United States attorney Preet Bharara, federal prosecutors filed a civil complaint accusing the Alavi Foundation of "providing numerous services to the Iranian government."

That action led to Mr. Bharara announcing a settlement agreement that forced the Alavi Foundation to forfeit its holdings in the office tower. When the government sells the building, the proceeds will flow to the families and estates of victims of terrorism. With the Alavi Foundation case off its plate, the district attorney's office turned its focus to Credit Suisse and Lloyds. The prosecutors offered the banks a choice: turn over records related to Iranian banks or face a criminal case.

The Banks chose to cooperate, producing reams of records that laid bare a scheme to disguise how Bank Melli was funnelling money into the United States. To avoid detection, the records showed, Credit Suisse and Lloyds falsified money-transfer paperwork, replacing Bank Melli's name with their own. "Please do not mention our name to any bank in the USA," Bank Melli wrote to Lloyds in one of the documents obtained.

Not known to the prosecutors in Manhattan, the Justice Department's criminal division in Washington had its own investigation into Credit Suisse. The inquiry from the division's asset forfeiture and money-laundering section, now led by Jaikumar Ramaswamy, began with a tip from an IRS agent who had spotted a suspicious transaction. The parallel investigations merged at a legal conference in 2007, when Mr Kaufmann from the district attorney's office lunched with a Justice Department official. Out of the meeting came a plan to pursue not only Credit Suisse and Lloyds, but other foreign banks suspected of flouting United States sanctions. The cases benefited from a trove of internal emails from Credit Suisse that showed how bank executives strategized ways to capture business from Iran once Lloyds left the market. If Credit Suisse did not act fast, the emails warned, it might lose out to other European banks.

In 2009, prosecutors kicked off a string of cases, first taking aim at Lloyds and then Credit Suisse. Barclays settled in 2010, laying the groundwork for ING, Standard Chartered and HSBC to strike their own deals in 2012.

As the deals were being negotiated, a whistleblower approached a rank and file prosecutor at the Manhattan district attorney's office about BNP's ties to Iran. BNP was also doing business with Sudan at a time that the nation was operating a genocidal regime. The whistleblower is not expected to receive any compensation for assisting the case.

The case-a collaboration among the Justice Department in Washington, the US attorney's office and the district attorney's office in Manhattan, as well as the Federal Reserve, Treasury Department and Benjamin M Lawsky, New York State's financial regulator-stood apart from the others. The volume of transactions reached tens of billions of dollars. And the $8.9 billion penalty is more than triple the amount that the six other banks collectively paid to resolve sanctions cases. For Mr Flatow, who ultimately received $25 million, the actions are vindicating.

Corruption in Bank

A very senior public sector bank person was accused of taking a bribe on a loan he sanctioned. But the nature of this rather odd kind of bribe-one taken for just doing your job—has brilliant comedic possibilities. A bank should give loans. That's why it is there. There is a person paid by an organisation just to do that. You go in and see that person and she says, "Sure I will, but it will cost you." You say, "I know. It is costing me 10.5%." And the person says, "But what about my cost?" "Um, but your cost is borne by your employer. This is your job. Why do I have to add my cost to your cost?" "Well, because you want me to do my job." But what if, you say, you won't pay her and want a loan? "Well, then," the person says, "I'll just sit here, do nothing, play solitaire, till someone comes along to take the loan and bribe me." "You can't do that! You essentially exist 9 to 5 to activate loans." "Who says? I exist from 9 to 5 but 1 am only activated when I'm bribed." You walk away from the meeting with a thought. This is not a person. This is one of those toys in a fair that starts only when you put in a coin. When one thinks of this. If enough employees start asking for bribes to do their job, companies can change their HR policies and have everyone as independent contractor. Then we are essentially looking at an entire country of entrepreneurs of freelance salesmen. The notion of the salary won't need to exist.

The message under this satire is, of course that don't take bribes to do your job. The complex economic message could be: perhaps we need to look at pay structures, from constables to CEOs, to understand what would drive reasonably timid-salaried people to seek bribes.

The philosophical message depends on what kind of a person you are. If you think people are inherently good, you'd think, "Oh, he's made a mistake." If you think people are inherently deceitful, you'd say,

> "We're all corrupt and greedy and there's no hope. India's changed a lot. The entire system of middlemen and suitcases and someone shady in Europe being a contact and that nefarious undertone of the parallel economy seems to be dwindling with everything becoming more transparent and electronic. People are realising it is more of a hassle to bribe than not bribe, Employees are realising that the guilt and illegality of the bribe—not to mention the early heart attack you'd get worrying about if you'd be caught is not worth the honesty of the company bonus: an all-expense paid business-class trip to Australia. In 21st-century Indian Inc, the perks have replaced the secret briefcase. Which is probably why when cases like these pop up, they seem like a throwback to the olden days, when middlemen were important. When someone who used the term, 'He is known to me', was considered as a qualification. When deceit, not venture funding, was a skill."

Is the bribery charge against the Syndicate Bank Chairman and Managing Director Sudhir Kumar Jain a trailer of what's in store for perceived standard operating procedure at State-owned banks that are vulnerable to pressure from political bosses? Or is it a one-off incident? Investment revival in the Indian economy in the short run rides on the answer to that question. If Jain's arrest leads to a freeze in lending or loan-restructuring decisions across banks, projects will remain stalled. Which first-generation promoter in India has deep-enough pockets to bring in the equity needed for any large project? It is common practice to mobilise the promoter's equity contribution also from the loan raised from the bank for the project by inflating the project cost.

If the promoters are honest, the gold-plating is 30%. A project actually worth ₹100 crore would be implemented for ₹130 crore and banks give a ₹90 crore loan from which the promoters take out ₹40 crore to bring the amount back as their equity contribution. And this is probably the best case scenario.

In some cases, this gold plating goes up 50%. And bankers are kept in the loop, obviously for a consideration. Or, at the behest of political masters, across party lines.

Such projects are unviable from day one. But the promoters and bankers work together to defer the impending problem by delaying the completion of the project to reap two gains. A company is allowed to capitalise the interest during the construction period, which means interest payment is part of the project cost. After commissioning, the project needs to generate enough resources to meet interest obligations, which is often difficult. The longer the period of implementation, the easier it is to take out the money from the project and convert it as equity. It also helps in justifying the rise in project cost that further helps the nexus. Once you reach closer to commissioning and the interest meter is about to start ticking, such promoters start another project. This helps the bank to give a new loan that is diverted to repay the old loan. The cycle continues and the promoters become bigger and bigger till they become a systemic, multi-billion-dollar problem. And the bankers involved, having already made crores, gracefully retire, passing on the headache to the next boss.

The majority of Indian banks have a top-down approach to loan clearance, justified on the grounds of speed and improving market share. In case a branch manager does not approve the loan, promoters go directly to zonal or regional managers. In case they are reluctant, they go to the general manager, executive director or the chairman-managing director. And every superior justifies the decision on the ground of business growth but without any transparency or accountability. No wonder Percy Mistry, who chaired a government panel on financial sector reforms, chose to call Indian public sector bankers 'zombie bankers'.

Let loan decisions come through a strengthened decision-making process with a committee structure at branch, zonal and headquarter levels. And everyone should be empowered to give his or her rationale for supporting or opposing any financing proposal in a time-bound manner. Senior officials are entitled to overrule the decisions of their subordinates. But they should record detailed justifications.

Banks must monitor the implementation of a project regularly and the end-use of funds. Why not make the branch manager or zonal officer responsible to ensure that the money disbursed goes into stated purposes and is not left at the mercy of the promoters? And someone should be held accountable for this before any fresh disbursal of loan is made.

Most importantly, there should be a complete ban on executing projects through an in-house company, unless a discount to third-party executions at an arm's length can be demonstrated. Finally, let promoters pony up the committed equity contribution upfront or provide a detailed mechanism for the purpose, such as how they will raise the equity for each project and what their back-up plan would be in case of any eventuality.

The Hidden Watch Dog

Bank's losses due to crimes at Automated Teller Machines (ATMs) may be a drop in the ocean as compared with corporate fraud-generated losses. Nevertheless, banks are responding with sophisticated monitoring systems to prevent it from getting out of hand.

With crimes at ATMs on the rise, banks are beginning to replace the previous decade's approach of 'physical guarding or monitoring' with 'alert-based surveillance'.

Having a camera inside the ATM and a security guard posted at the premises has not helped much—especially in preventing crimes—as in the case of a bank employee being attacked a few months ago in Bangalore. "The alert-based system, however, aims to prevent crimes, especially where criminals have perfected the art of concealing their identity. One such system at Axis Bank recently helped to catch criminals in the act. Last year, inspector Devendra Shinde from a police station in a Pune suburb got an unusual call at 1.30 AM. Someone was alerting him that two criminals were at work to break open an ATM machine. It was unusual in the sense that it was not from someone passing by the ATM, but from a distant Navi Mumbai-based centralised control room operated by Securens Systems, a private service provider that was monitoring its client ATMs.

"We had fun operating in a live environment," says Shinde, on how the police team were able to prevent the burglary and arrest the duo. "All banks should have a mechanism like this."

Integrated surveillance systems are being put in place to help banks receive alerts from ATMs across the country, be it someone breaking into an ATM in Palakkad or Ludhiana.

All the monitoring happens from one point, depending on the company that sets up the system based on the bank's needs.

The alert-based monitoring system is a software that buzzes an alarm for about 30 different kinds of activities inside the ATM, barring a normal withdrawal or other transactions. It detects attempts to tamper with the cash vending machine and any unusual movement inside an ATM such as a person staying inside for more than a few minutes-and throws up alerts at the control room. This helps someone or the control room operator to ask a customer through a microphone what he or she is looking for, giving them the idea that someone is watching them live.

In most cases, the warning through a speaker drives miscreants out, but if it does not, follow the process alerting our quick response teams and then the local police. The technological solution not only detects crime on a real-time basis, but also attempts to prevent it immediately.

Although there is no data with regard to ATM crimes, industry interaction shows it is on the rise. According to the latest available Reserve Bank of India data, ATM/debit/credit card related complaints rose by 25% to 17,867 during 2012-13, some of which may be just related to poor internet connectivity. RBI too has been in favour of stricter ATM security, although it stopped short of specifying what banks should do. There are 1,60,055 ATMs in India, as on March 31, 2014. A meagre 1% of them already have or have proposed to install alert-based surveillance.

While private sector banks are already installing alert-based surveillance and are expanding, public sector lenders are following them. Four large to mid-size State-owned banks including the Punjab National Bank, State Bank of India, Central Bank of India and Bank of Maharashtra collectively floated tenders for about 10,000 ATMs in the past month.

SBI is planning to finalise tenders for nearly 3,000 ATMs. SBI and its associate banks, it together have 53,107 ATMs. PNB has floated the largest tender so far, with plans to bring 6,000 ATMs under the more 'cost-effective' e-surveillance. After a few incidents of robbery and attack on customers at ATMs last year, there is a demand for physical guarding of all ATMs on the back of perceived risks but, if banks do that, the economic viability of ATMs will come under severe stress. Adoption of alert-based surveillance could actually bring down the costs of maintaining ATMs. "E-surveillance is a reasonable option.

An industry estimate suggests the cost of deploying three private security personnel at an ATM for 24 hours at around ₹35,000 a month compared with e-surveillance, which may range between ₹7,000 and ₹12,000, depending on services.

Although its sellers may be marketing the concept hard in an attempt to expand their market, there are questions on whether they can be effective in a country as vast as India with poor infrastructure. For all the alerts, if there is no immediate physical presence in the form of policemen, or someone from a private sector quick response team personnel at the ATM, the alerts are of little help.

Given that most police stations are thinly staffed and are far from many ATM locations, it is impossible to expect to police to react within a few minutes to reach the location. Besides, with ATMs being located in remote villages where there are no police stations either, alerts will be meaningless. The fact that it is more economical is accepted. Whether e-surveillance will replace the entire physical guarding system depends on how it proves to be effective in the 24 × 7 format. The biggest challenge for e-surveillance comes from internet connectivity. If the network is poor, it is as good as not having it. E-surveillance will expand but is not the be-all and end-all for bank security or their ATMs.

Bank of Credit and Commerce International

The Bank of Credit and Commerce International (BCCI) was a major international bank founded in 1972 by Agha Hasan Abedi, a Pakistani financier. The Bank was registered in Luxembourg with head offices in Karachi and London. Within a decade BCCI touched its peak. It operated in 78 countries, had over 400 branches, and had assets in excess of US $20 billion, making it the 7th largest private bank in the world by assets.

BCCI came under the scrutiny of numerous financial regulators and intelligence agencies in the 1980s due to concerns that it was poorly regulated. Subsequent investigations revealed that it was involved in massive money-laundering and other financial crimes, and illegally gained controlling interest in a major American bank. BCCI became the focus of a massive regulatory battle in 1991 and on July 5 of that year customs and bank regulators in seven countries raided and locked down records of its branch offices.

Investigators in the US and UK revealed that the BCCI had been,

> "Set up deliberately to avoid centralized regulatory review, and operated extensively in bank secrecy jurisdictions. Its affairs were extraordinarily complex. Its officers were sophisticated international bankers whose apparent objective was to keep their affairs secret, to commit fraud on a massive scale, and to avoid detection."

The liquidators, Deloitte & Touche, filed a lawsuit against PricewaterhouseCoopers and Ernst & Young—the bank's auditors—which was settled for $175 million in 1998. A further lawsuit against the ruling Sheikh of Abu Dhabi, a major shareholder, was launched in 1999 for approximately $400 million. BCCI creditors also instituted a $1 billion law-suit against the Bank of England as a regulatory body. After a nine-year struggle, due to the Bank's statutory immunity, the case went to trial in January 2004. However, in November 2005, Deloitte persuaded creditor Abu Dhabi to drop its claims against the Bank of England, except for a claim for return of its deposits, in that Abu Dhabi owned 77% of the bank shares at closing, and was therefore also facing a major lawsuit. To date liquidators have recovered about 75% of the creditors' lost money. A decade after its liquidation, its activities were still not completely understood.

BCCI's founder, Agha Hasan Abedi, started the bank in 1972. Abedi, a prolific banker, had previously set up the United Bank of Pakistan in 1959. Preceding the nationalization of United Bank in 1974, he sought to create a new supranational banking entity. Abedi was succeeded by Swaleh Naqvi as the bank's chief who, in the aftermath following controversy over BCCI, was replaced by Zafar Iqbal Chaudhry in the late 1990s. BCCI was created with capital from Sheikh Zayed bin Sultan Al Nahyan, the ruler of Abu Dhabi in the United Arab Emirates and Bank of America (25%).

BCCI expanded rapidly in the 1970s, pursuing long-term asset growth over profits, seeking high net-worth individuals and regular large deposits. The company itself divided into BCCI Holdings with the bank under that splitting into BCCI SA (Luxembourg) and BCCI Overseas (Grand Cayman). BCCI also acquired parallel banks through acquisitions: buying the Banque de Commerce et Placements (BCP) of Geneva in 1976, and creating KIFCO (Kuwait International Finance Company), Credit & Finance Corporation Ltd, and a series of Cayman-based companies held together as ICIC (International Credit and Investment Company Overseas), International Credit and Commerce (Overseas), etc. Overall, BCCI expanded from 19 branches in five countries in 1973 to 27 branches in 1974, to 108 branches in 1976, with assets growing from $200 million to $1.6 billion. This growth caused extensive underlying capital problems. *The Guardian* alleged that BCCI was using cash from deposits to fund operating expenses, rather than making investments. Investigative journalist and author Joseph J Trento has argued that the bank's transformation was guided by the head of Saudi intelligence with a view to enabling it to finance covert intelligence operations at a time, in the aftermath of Watergate, when the American intelligence agencies were defending themselves from investigations by domestic authorities. BCCI entered the African markets in 1979, and Asia in the early 1980s. BCCI was among the first foreign banks awarded a license to operate in the Chinese Special Economic Zone of Shenzhen which bore testament to Agha Hasan Abedi's public relations skills, a feat that had yet to be achieved by the likes of Citicorp and JP Morgan. Some of China's largest State banks were depositors in BCCI's Shenzhen branch.

There was rigid compartmentalization; the 248 managers and general managers reported directly to Abedi and the CEO Swaleh Naqvi. It was structured in such a way that no single country had overall regulatory supervision over it so as not to hinder potential growth and expansion opportunities. Its two holding companies were based in Luxembourg and the Cayman Islands—two jurisdictions where banking regulation was notoriously weak. It was also not regulated by a country that had a central bank. On several occasions, the Office of the Comptroller of the Currency told the Federal Reserve in no uncertain terms that BCCI must not be allowed to buy any American bank because it was poorly regulated.

By 1980, BCCI was reported to have assets of over $4 billion with over 150 branches in 46 countries. Bank of America was 'bewildered' by BCCI and reduced its holding in 1980, and the company came to be held by a number of groups, with ICIC owning 70%. By 1989, ICIC's shareholding was reduced to 11% with Abu Dhabi groups holding almost 40%. However, large numbers of shares were held by BCCI nominees. It was very common for Middle Eastern elites to use nominees to hold their stock, as they did not want the public to know the details of their holdings.

In 1982, 15 Middle Eastern investors bought Financial General Bankshares, a large bank holding company headquartered in Washington DC. All the investors were BCCI clients, but the Fed received assurances that BCCI would be in no way involved in the management of the company, which was renamed First American Bankshares. To alleviate regulators' concerns, Clark Clifford, an adviser to five presidents, was named First American's chairman. Clifford headed a board composed of himself and several other distinguished American citizens, including former United States Senator Stuart Symington. In truth, BCCI had been involved in the purchase of FGB/First American from the beginning. Abedi had been approached about buying it as early as 1977, but by this time BCCI's reputation in the United States was so poor that it could not hope to buy an American bank on its own (as mentioned above, the OCC was adamantly opposed to BCCI being allowed to buy its way into the American banking industry). Rather, it used the First American investors as nominees. Moreover, Clifford's law firm was retained as general counsel, and also handled most of BCCI's American legal work. BCCI was also heavily involved in First American personnel matters. The relationship between the two was so close that rumours spread BCCI was the real owner of First American. F Lee Bailey and Florida State prosecutor Richard Gerstein were the directors of Centrust Federal Savings Bank, a failed satellite of BCCI; this would eventually lead to Bailey's disbarment.

BCCI had an unusual annual auditing system: PricewaterhouseCoopers were the accountants for BCCI Overseas, while Ernst & Young audited BCCI and BCCI Holdings (London and Luxembourg). Other companies such as KIFCO and ICIC were audited by neither. In October 1985, the Bank of England and the Institute Monétaire Luxembourgeois

(Luxembourg's bank regulator) ordered BCCI to change to a single accountant, alarmed at reported BCCI losses on the commodities and financial markets. PricewaterhouseCoopers became the sole accountants in 1987.

In 1990, a PricewaterhouseCoopers audit of BCCI revealed an unaccountable loss of hundreds of millions of dollars. The bank approached Sheikh Zayed bin Sultan Al Nahyan, who made good the loss in exchange for an increased shareholding of 78%. Much of BCCI's documentation was also then transferred to Abu Dhabi. The audit also revealed numerous irregularities. Most seriously, BCCI had made a staggering $1.48 billion worth of loans to its own shareholders, who used BCCI stock as collateral.

The audit also confirmed what many Americans who watched BCCI long suspected—that BCCI secretly (and illegally) owned First American. When the Fed cleared the group of Arab investors to buy First American, it did so on condition that they supplement their personal funds with money borrowed from banks with no connection to BCCI. Contrary to that agreement, several stockholders had borrowed heavily from BCCI. Even more seriously, they pledged their First American stock as collateral. When they didn't make interest payments, BCCI took control of the shares. It was later estimated that in this manner, BCCI had ended up with 60% or more of First American's stock. Despite these problems, PricewaterhouseCoopers signed BCCI's 1989 annual report, largely due to Zayed's firm commitment to propping up the bank.

Lending Practices

BCCI's rapid growth alarmed the financial community, as well as regulators. When a bank grows rapidly, it is lending more and more money each year. BCCI contended that its growth was fuelled by the increasingly large number of deposits by oil-rich

States who owned stock in the bank as well as by sovereign developing nations. However, this claim failed to satisfy the regulators. For example, the Bank of England ordered BCCI to cap its branch network in the United Kingdom at 45 branches.

There was particular concern over BCCI's loan portfolio because of its roots in areas where modern banking was still an alien concept. For instance, a large number of its customers were devout Muslims who believed charging interest on loans—a major pillar of modern banking—was riba, or usury. In many Third World countries, a person's financial standing didn't matter as much as his relationship with his banker. One particularly notable example is the Gokal family, a prominent family of shipping magnates. They had a relationship with Abedi dating back to his days at United Bank. Abedi personally handled their loans, with little regard for details such as loan documents or creditworthiness. At one point, BCCI's loans to the Gokal companies were equivalent to US $1.5 billion, three times the bank's capital. Longstanding banking practice dictates that a bank not lend more than 10% of its capital to a single customer.

BCCI was not squeamish about dealing with disreputable clients. It frequently handled money for dictators such as Saddam Hussein, Manuel Noriega, Hussain Mohammad Ershad and Samuel Doe. Other account holders included the Medellin Cartel and Abu Nidal.

The US Central Intelligence Agency held numerous accounts at BCCI, according to William von Raab, former US Commissioner of Customs. Oliver North also used and held multiple accounts at BCCI. These bank accounts were used for a variety of illegal covert operations, including transfers of money and weapons related to the Iran-Contra scandal, according to *Time* magazine. The CIA also worked with BCCI in arming and financing the Afghan Mujahideen during the Afghan War against the Soviet Union, using BCCI to launder proceeds from trafficking heroin grown in the Pakistan-Afghanist an borderlands, boosting the flow of narcotics to European and US markets. The US intelligence agencies used BCCI to funnel drug money to Afghan Mujahideen in their fight against Soviet invasion and to insurgents such as Nicaraguan Contras.

BCCI's demise began in 1986, when a US Customs undercover operation led by Special Agent Robert Mazur infiltrated the bank's private client division and uncovered their active role soliciting deposits from drug traffickers and money-launderers. The so-called C-Chase investigation began when it was apparent that Soviet Union was weakening and Washington lost interest in funding the Mujahideen. This two year undercover operation concluded in 1988 with a fake wedding that was attended by BCCI officers and drug dealers from around the world who had established a personal friendship and working relationship with undercover agent Mazur. At the same time he was dealing undercover with BCCI executives, Mazur used his undercover operation to establish a relationship with the hierarchy of the Medellin Cartel as one of their sources for laundering drug proceeds. In 1988, the bank was implicated for being the centre of a major money-laundering scheme. After a six-month trial, BCCI, under immense pressure from US authorities, pleaded guilty in 1990, but only on the grounds of respondent superior. While federal regulators took no action, Florida regulators forced BCCI to pull out of the State.

The bank established the Third World Foundation in London, which published the widely circulated *Third World Quarterly* and paid special attention to the promotion of the Urdu language and literature through the Urdu Markaz located in London. BCCI also established the Infaq Foundation in Pakistan, which was instrumental in funding the establishment of some of the top universities of the region, such as BCCI FAST (Institute of Computer Sciences) and GIK (Institute of Science, Engineering and Technology), in addition to regular support for many other educational institutions.

BCCI also established the Cromwell Hospital (now owned by Bupa) in London. In addition to the above, BCCI helped revive hundreds of historical buildings and monuments throughout the developing world and contributed significantly to the arts, culture, sports, health, and education in many poor, Third World countries. A significant percentage of employee's salaries were regularly contributed through their consent to global charitable causes.

In March 1991, the Bank of England asked PricewaterhouseCoopers to carry out an inquiry. On June 24, 1991, using the code name 'Sandstorm' for BCCI, PricewaterhouseCoopers submitted the Sandstorm report showing that BCCI had engaged in 'widespread fraud and manipulation' that made it difficult, if not impossible, to reconstruct BCCI's financial history.

Apple Sidesteps Billions in Taxes

It is reported that the company has devised strategies that take advantage of gaps in the tax code. Apple, the world's most profitable technology company, doesn't design iPhones here. It doesn't run Apple Care customer service from California city. And it doesn't manufacture MacBooks or iPads anywhere nearby. Yet, with a handful of employees in a small office here in Reno in a company subsidiary named Braeburn Capital, Apple has done something central to its corporate strategy. It has avoided millions of dollars in taxes in California and 20 other States.

Apple's headquarters are in Cupertino, Calif. By putting an office to collect and invest the company's profits out of Reno, just 200 miles away, Apple sidesteps State income taxes on some of those gains. California's corporate tax rate is 8.84%, Nevada's zero. Setting up an office in Reno is just one of many legal methods Apple uses to reduce its worldwide tax bill by billions of dollars each year. As it has in Nevada, Apple has created subsidiaries in low-tax countries like Ireland, The Netherlands, Luxembourg and the British Virgin Islands—some little more than a letterbox in Luxembourg or an anonymous office here—that help cut the taxes it pays around the world. Almost every major corporation tries to minimize its taxes, of course. For Apple, the savings are especially alluring because the company's profits are so high. Wall Street analysts predict Apple could earn up to $45.6 billion in its current fiscal year which would be a record for any US business. Braeburn is a variety of apple that is simultaneously sweet and tart. When someone in the US buys an iPhone, iPad or other Apple product, a portion of the profits from that sale is often deposited into accounts controlled by Braeburn, and then invested in stocks, bonds or other financial instruments, say company executives. Some profits from those investments are shielded from California tax authorities by virtue of Braeburn's Nevada address.

Since founding Braeburn in 2006, Apple has earned more than $2.5 billion in interest and dividend income on its cash reserves and investments around the globe. What's more, Braeburn allows Apple to lower its taxes in other States because many of those jurisdictions use formulas that reduce what is owed when a company's financial management occurs elsewhere. While Apple's Reno office helps the company avoid State taxes, its international subsidiaries—particularly the company's assignment of sales and patent royalties to other nations—help reduce taxes owed to the US and other governments.

The Luxembourg subsidiary, named iTunes Sarl, has just a few dozen employees, according to corporate documents filed in that nation and a current executive. But when customers across Europe, Africa or the Middle East and potentially elsewhere download a song, television show or App, the sale is recorded in this small country, according to current and former executives.

The country has promised to tax the payments collected by Apple and numerous other tech corporations at low rates if they route transactions through Luxembourg. Taxes that would have otherwise gone to the governments of Britain, France, the US and dozens of other nations go to Luxembourg instead, at discounted rates. Without such tactics, Apple's federal tax bill in the US most likely would have been $2.4 billion higher last year, according to a recent study by a former Treasury Department economist, Martin A Sullivan. As it stands, the company paid cash taxes of $3.3 billion around the world on its reported profits of $34.2 billion last year, a tax rate of 9.8%. Apple does not disclose what portion of those payments were in the US, or what portion are assigned to previous or future year.

2. Detection of White-Collar Crime Through Audit

Looking back at Enron, perhaps the company best known for committing accounting fraud, we can see the many methods that were utilized in order to fraudulently improve the appearance of its financial statements. Through the use of off-balance sheet special purpose vehicles, the firm continued to hide its liabilities and inflate its earnings. In 1999, limited partnerships were created for the purpose of purchasing Enron shares as a mean of improving performance of its stock. That year, the company returned 56% to its shareholders, which was followed by another 87% appreciation at the onset of the new millennium. As Enron's aggressive accounting practices and financial statement manipulation began to spiral out of control, the scandal was eventually uncovered by the *Wall Street Journal*. Shortly after, on December 2, 2001, Enron filed for Chapter 11 in what was the largest US bankruptcy in history ... only to be surpassed by WorldCom less than a year later.

Complex accounting fraud such as that practised at Enron is usually extremely difficult for the average retail investor to discover. However, there are some basic red flags that help during the preliminary stages of the investigation. After all, the Enron fraud was not exposed by high paid Ivy League MBA holding Wall Street analysts, but by news reporters who used journal articles and public filings in their due diligence process. Despite passage of Sarbanes-Oxley, financial statement fraud remains too common an occurrence, often damaging people's retirement and educational savings. Being first on the scene to uncover a fraudulent company can be very lucrative from a short seller's perspective and can be rather beneficial to a sceptical investor who is weighing in the overall market sentiment.

What is Financial Statement Fraud?

According to a study conducted by the Association of Certified Fraud Examiners (ACFE), fraudulent financial statement accounts for approximately 10% of incidents concerning white-collar crime. Asset misappropriation and corruption tend to occur at a much greater frequency, yet the financial impact of these latter crimes is much less severe. ACFE defines fraud as,

> "Deception or misrepresentation that an individual or entity makes knowing that the misrepresentation could result in some unauthorized benefit to the individual or to the entity or some other party."

Greed and work pressure are the most common factors pushing management to deceive investors and creditors.

Financial statement fraud can surface in many different forms, although once deceptive accounting practices are initiated, various systems of manipulation will be utilized to maintain the appearance of sustainability. Common approaches to artificially improving the appearance of the financials include overstating revenues by recording future expected sales, understating expenses through such means as capitalizing operating expenses, inflating assets' net worth by knowingly failing to apply an appropriate depreciation schedule, hiding obligations off, of the company's balance sheet and incorrect disclosure of related party transactions and structured finance deals. Another alternative to financial statement fraud involves Cooki-Jar accounting practices, a procedure by which a firm will understate revenues in one accounting period and maintain them as a reserve for future periods with worse performance.

Such procedures remove the appearance of volatility from the operations.

Financial Statement Fraud Red Flags

Financial statement red flags provide a general overview of the warning signs investors should take note of. They do not necessarily indicate an undoubted occurrence of financial statement fraud, but merely signal that further in-depth research must be conducted to assess the validity of the corporate documents. Creditors would find such information useful to ensure that loans are not provided to firms operating with an elevated amount of risk. Investors, on the other hand, may want to take note of the following factors to discover new, shorting opportunities. Government regulators, however, aim to catch and punish fraud to ensure the transparency and reliability of the financial markets.

Five basic types of financial statement fraud exist:

- fictitious sales
- improper expense recognition
- incorrect asset valuation
- hidden liabilities and
- unsuitable disclosures

Effectively spotting these fraudulent disclosures involves keeping an open eye for the most common financial statement fraud red flags:

- Accounting anomalies, such as growing revenues without a corresponding growth in cash flows. Sales are much easier to manipulate than cash flow but the two should move more or less in tandem over time.
- Consistent sales growth while established competitors are experiencing periods of weak performance. Note that this may be due to efficient business operations rather than fraudulent activity.

- A rapid and unexplainable rise in the number of day's sales in receivables in addition to growing inventories. This suggests obsolete goods for which the firm records fictitious future sales.
- A significant surge in the company's performance within the final reporting period of fiscal year. The company may be under immense pressure to meet analysts' expectations.
- The company maintains consistent gross profit margins while its industry is facing pricing pressure. This can potentially indicate failure to recognize expenses or aggressive revenue recognition.
- A large buildup of fixed assets. An unexpected accumulation of fixed assets can flag the usage of operating expense capitalization, rather than expense recognition.
- Depreciation methods and estimates of assets' useful life that do not correspond to the overall industry. An overstated life of an asset will decrease the annual depreciation expense.
- A weak system of internal control. Strong corporate governance and internal controls processes minimize the likelihood that financial statement fraud will go unnoticed.
- Outsized frequency of complex related-party or third-party transactions, many of which do not add tangible value (can be used to conceal debt off the balance sheet).
- The firm is on the brink of breaching their debt covenants. To avoid technical default, management may be forced to fraudulently adjust its leverage ratios.
- The auditor was replaced, resulting in a missed accounting period. Auditor replacement can signal a dysfunctional relationship while missed accounting period provides extra time to 'fix' financials.
- A disproportionate amount of managements' compensation is derived from bonuses based on short term targets. This provides incentive to commit fraud.

- Something just feels off about the corporation's business model, financial statements or operations.

Financial Statement Fraud Detection Methods

Spotting red flags can be extremely challenging as firms that are engaged in fraudulent activities will attempt to portray the image of financial stability and normal business operations, vertical and horizontal financial statement analysis introduces a straight-forward approach to fraud detection. Vertical analysis involves taking every item in the income statement as a percentage of revenue and comparing the year-over-year trends that could be a potential flag cause of concern. A similar approach can also be applied to the balance sheet, using total assets as the comparison benchmark, to monitor significant deviations from normal activity. Horizontal analysis implements a similar approach whereby rather than having an account serve as the point of reference, financial information is represented as a percentage of the base years' figures. Likewise, unexplainable variations in percentages can serve as a red flag requiring further analysis.

Comparative ratio analysis also allows analysts and auditors to spot discrepancies within the firm's financial statements. By analysing ratios, information regarding day's sales in receivables, leverage multiples and other vital metrics can be determined and analysed for inconsistencies. A mathematical approach, known as the Beneish Model evaluates eight ratios to determine the likelihood of earnings manipulation. Asset quality, depreciation, gross margin, leverage and other variables are factored into the analysis. Combining the variables into the model, an M-score is calculated; a value greater than 2.22 warrants further investigation as the firm may be manipulating its earnings while an M-score less than –2.22 suggests that the company is not a manipulator Similar to most other ratio-related strategies, the full picture can only be accurately portrayed once the multiples are compared to the industry and to the specific firm's historical average.

The Bottom Line

In the spring of 2000 financial fraud investigator Harry Markopolos approached the SEC, claiming that the wealth management business of Bernard Madoff was fraudulent. After modelling Madoffs portfolio, Markopolos realized that the consistent returns achieved by Madoff were impossible. For example, according to an interview with the Certified Fraud Investigator, he "concluded that for Madoff to execute the trading strategy he said he was using, he would have had to buy more options on the Chicago Board Options Exchange than actually existed." Although, Markopolos' warnings went unnoticed, in 2009 Madoff was charged with operating a $65 billion Ponzi scheme.

Instances such as this are rare since fraudulent behaviour often caught before it has a chance to escalate to such levels. Having proper knowledge of the red flags to avoid companies indulging in unscrupulous accounting practices is a useful tool to ensure the safety of your investments.

Financial Fraud—Accounting for Criminals

When a suspect cooked the books for his company, generally he was a number of complicated accounting tricks to dupe auditors. But some tactics were simple. Like diverting auditors with attractive staff, accounting fraud is all about distraction, Antar said. It's like David Copperfield, it's an illusion. These auditors are usually single kids just a few years out of school. What do kids in their 20s think about all the time? Sex," said suspect, who was at the centre of a multi-million dollar fraud 20 years ago. So he would pair 'cute hot female' employees with male auditors as part of his distraction strategy. "In effect, he was a fraudster, matchmaker and pimp. Since the financial crisis struck, accounting scams—such as the multi-billion dollar Bernard Madoff scheme—have made regular headlines. A Hong Kong executive at Ernst & Young was detained by police and documents were seized after evidence of falsified audit documents came to light in a court case. Ernst settled a $1 billion negligence claim by the liquidators of Akai Holdings out of court for an undisclosed sum and the executive was suspended awaiting internal disciplinary action.

A London executive for accounting firm KPMG—another of the 'Big Four' accounting firms (along with Ernst, PricewaterhouseCoopers and Deloitte Touche Tohmatsu)—was sentenced to four years in jail for siphoning nearly $900,000 of company funds for personal use. While there are no international statistics charting white-collar crime arrests, the number of people being trained to detect accounting shenanigans has exploded since the financial crisis. There's always an uptick in fraud activity when the economy goes down. "It's like the ocean going out and you can see everything that was hidden under water."

The Fraud Triangle

If an employee is having an affair, exactly where he would look to find equivalent accounting chicanery. "Look at his or her company expense reports—they will almost always have false entries," an accountant who specializes in fraud. "No one budgets to have an affair."

Although there are millions of ways to commit fraud, there are always three common elements in any employee fraud case—incentive, opportunity and rationalization.

Although greed is an obvious incentive, it is not the only one—infidelity, gambling debts, drug use or simple ego can start the slide into accounting crime.

> "Look at the Société Générale incident where a single trader, Jerome (Kerviel), lost the company $7 billion

referring to the incident that nearly destroyed the French financial services company in 2008. He wanted to show what a smart securities trader he was.... He was looking for psychic income, not monetary income."

Opportunity is created when a culprit feels there is a relatively low likelihood of being caught—most often at private companies. They have less internal controls than publicly listed companies.

Rationalization is the conversation with the white-collar criminal has with him or herself to assuage their conscience—something that is much more likely to have during a downturn, when companies are downsizing and employees are asked to do more for less.

Catching a Crook with Crooks

But many accounting fraudsters don't operate within the bounds of right and wrong. Large-scale frauds such as Madoff or Enron are more pathological in nature. You have to take morality out of the equation to understand the criminal mind. This could still be going on today if they didn't get caught.

How to Read Financial Statements and Check Accounting Fraud

The Satyam accounting scam, one of the biggest in India, left millions of investors in the lurch, as the stock fell from ₹179 to ₹23 in one trading session. The inability of stock analysts to identify the 'gaps' in Satyam's books and ring warning bells proved costly for investors. Had investors known the basics of reading financial statements and techniques used by companies to report false numbers, they would have asked their advisors a few valid questions about Satyam's finances.

A report by a brokerage on Satyam Computers gives an 'accumulate' rating, which means it expects the stock to go up. The rating is based on the company's high cash/market cap ratio.

The information technology company had reported a cash balance of ₹4,500 crore at the end of the 2007-08 financial year. The report gives a one-year price target of ₹373 for the stock. The stock closes at ₹273 the day the report is written.

The same brokerage releases a hurriedly-compiled report suspending the previous rating. "Low market cap, high cash status no longer holds," it says. On 7 January 2009, the founder of Satyam Computers admits to inflating cash and bank balances by ₹5,040 crore, overstating debtors' position (money lent) of ₹2,650 crore as against the actual figure of ₹490 crore and non-disclosure or understatement of liabilities worth ₹1,230 crore.

The following are common forms of accounting frauds that companies indulge in and signs that may alert wrongdoings.

Financial Reports

A company's financial health can be gauged through three documents or statements—balance sheet, profit and loss account and cash flow accounts.

A balance sheet records a company's assets (land, machinery, inventory, cash balance, investments, loans given), liabilities (loans taken, Income Tax payable, tax liabilities) and owner's equity. It is generally prepared annually.

A profit and loss statement (or income statement) records a company's earnings and expenses. Any company whose shares are traded on exchanges is required to release its income statement every quarter.

A cash flow statement tells us where cash is coming from (inflow) and how it is being used (outflow). There are three types of cash flow-operating cash flow (sale of goods, revenue from services, interest/dividend received, payment for purchases, payment for operating expenses), investing cash flow (sale and purchase of assets, sale and purchase of debt/equity, loans advanced to others) and financial cash flow (issue of equity shares, borrowing, repayment of debt).

Indicators of Earning Quality

1. High debt reserves relative to past loan defaults. A debt reserve is money set aside to account for losses that may arise as a result of defaults on future loans.
2. Minimal use of off-balance sheet techniques. It's a form of financing in which large capital expenditures are kept off a company's balance sheet through various methods
3. Use of accelerated depreciation. It allows one to deduct far more in the first years after purchase. The straight-line method spreads the cost evenly over the life of the asset.
4. Showing shorter useful life of assets. Any changes on this front cause higher or lower depreciation write-offs.

Notes to accounts are important as they detail the accounting policies followed, pension and other post-employment benefits and potential liabilities/losses.

Manipulation of Statements

There are many items in financial statements for which companies use different policies. These are inventory valuation, investments and fixed assets, conversion of foreign currency and asset depreciation.

Companies often manipulate these to inflate revenue, assets, cash inflow and understate expense, liabilities and cash outflow in financial statements.

Inflating Earnings

1. **Lending to customers:** Sometimes companies lend money to customers to buy their goods. This way they can report high revenue in the income statement and high receivables (treated as an asset) in the balance sheet.

2. **Trade stuffing:** Companies use this usually just before the end of a reporting period. They ship goods to customers even though the latter may not need them immediately. This increases sales ahead of the reporting period.
3. **Understating provisions:** Companies often allow credit sales on generous terms, sometimes even to customers with a poor credit history. Ideally, in such sales, the company should set aside a higher amount for bad debt provisioning. This amount is recorded as a liability. Understating such liabilities is another way of 'enhancing' the financial statement.
4. **Round-tripping:** This means getting into fictitious transactions with related parties to inflate revenue. In round-tripping, a company sells unused assets to a party with the promise of buying back at a later date at the same price.

Understating Expenses

1. **Spreading out expenses:** According to accounting norms, if an expense has been made for acquiring an asset whose benefits the company will avail of over a long term, the expense is to be reported in the books in a spread-out manner over that period. The process is called capitalising. Companies often use this to delay recognition of short-term expenses.
2. **Cookie jar accounting:** Companies put aside money for possible loan defaults. Some companies, during periods of high revenue growth, increase the amount and release the same during periods of poor revenue, offsetting the impact of low sales growth. Among other common forms of financial statement manipulation are revaluation of assets, showing unrealised gains as profits and assigning higher values to fixed assets.

3. **Off-balance sheet items:** Some assets/liabilities or financing activities are not fully recognised in the balance sheet due to the complexity of transactions involved. These include pension assets and liabilities, assets and liabilities of joint ventures and unconsolidated subsidiaries and lease arrangements. These are recorded in footnotes of financial statements.

Many companies resort to off-balance sheet financing by way of entering into joint ventures, research and development partnerships and lease contracts. Floating special purpose entities or subsidiaries to expand business is another off-balance sheet arrangement.

As the liabilities/risk involved in such transactions are not reflected in the balance sheet, one may draw wrong conclusions about a company's financial health. It is, therefore, necessary to check the footnotes of financial statements.

Red Flags

Some manipulations mentioned earlier are difficult to detect even for finance professionals. Here are some indicators of rot in a company's financial books.

- **Continuous high level of cash, cash equivalents and current assets:** Satyam Computers showed high cash balance over the years. Later it turned out it had inflated cash and bank balances by as much as ₹5,040 crore.
- **Reported earnings consistently higher than cash flow:** If cash flow from operating activities of a company is consistently less than the reported net income, it is a warning sign. The investor must ask why operating earnings are not turning into cash.
- **Sudden increase in inventory/sales ratio:** This indicates the company may be inflating assets such as inventories.

Financial ratios not in line with industry peers could be due to inflated earnings, asset valuation or understating of expenses and liabilities.

- **Spurt in other income:** Revenue sources recorded under other income are non-recurring and may include earnings from asset sales and closure of debt or debt restructuring. However, sources of earnings are seldom disclosed under this head. A sudden spurt should raise eyebrows.
- **Frequent changes in policies:** Earnings and assets can be inflated by alternative accounting policies. If one sees frequent changes in these policies, there may be something fishy about the company's books.
- **Financial ratios not in line with industry peers:** This could be due to inflated earnings, asset valuation or understating of expenses and liabilities.
- **Too many off-balance sheet transactions:** If a company has been expanding by creating special purpose entities and has entered into many lease contracts, it is possible a lot of liabilities are not reflected in its balance sheet.

The Enron Game Plan

Enron, an energy trading company in the US, used various accounting methods for years to show high revenue and profit and understated debt.

Inflated Revenues

Enron was supposed to report trading and brokerage fees as revenue. However, it chose to report the entire value of transactions as revenue instead of just the fees. This led to a huge jump in sales figure. In four years between 1996 and 2000, Enron's revenue jumped from $13 billion to $100 billion, a compounded annual growth rate of 65%. It also started marking its revenue to the market, something unheard of, in a non-financial company. This allowed it to record revenue from long-term contracts by estimating the present value of future cash flow even before it actually made any income from the project. This method, approved by the US market regulator in 1992, helped Enron show inflated income.

Detection of White-Collar Crime through Audit

The main pillar of our capitalistic free market economic system, which is a cornerstone of democracy, is the integrity of financial information. Without reliable financial information, capitalism cannot and will not survive. However, the integrity of financial information can only be achieved through building blocks such as sound internal controls and independently verifiable financial information. The well-educated, skilled, and experienced accountant is the first line of defence for the capitalist system.

Cost and management accountants produce the chunks of information that allow companies to turn in performance that fetches their top management fat bonuses. Cost accountancy does the solid work of generating, assembling and making sense of the information that companies need about their own working to take intelligent decisions. As the Indian economy grows, forms more and more companies, and all of them compete with companies from around the world even for a share of the domestic market, the need for intelligent decisions based on thorough knowledge of their own internal working can only increase.

Time was when cost accountants were required as essential staff to meet compliance requirements. The government requires companies in eight sectors—telecom, electricity, fertilisers, cement, sugar, petroleum and chemicals including bulk drugs and formulations—to prepare cost audits. Companies hired cost accountants to prepare these statements. A vast majority of qualified cost accountants work in the finance wings of companies as employees. But the times are changing.

Increasingly cost audits are inputs to achieving excellence—in management practices, in financial results, in meeting rising shareholder and consumer expectations of respect for the environment and for corporate governance. Management accounting is gaining importance in the era of globalization. On the one hand, companies are increasingly accepting the need to demonstrate how they relate to society, the environment and governance, in addition to shareholder expectations on financial results on the other hand. Taking stock of a company's performance in creating and managing its carbon foot print or in determining how much water it consumes and recharges calls for accounting of a kind that cost and management accountants are trained to perform. Similar is the case with regard to the need to report corporate social responsibility. For a company to say confidently that it has reached a particular level in socially-responsible bebaviour it must have data to back up its claim.

It, in short, is the basic building blocks of corporate reputations, in the new era of heightened consumer and investor expectations going beyond utility and financial results, are made out of the diligent work of cost accountants. Another area of rising importance in which cost accountants play a critical role is transfer pricing. The standard way to judge whether more or less value is being charged in a transaction between one division of a company from one country with another in a different country is to see how such a transaction would be valued at arm's length, that is, between two unrelated parties. But there are cases when such an arms-length comparison is not possible. A classic example would be when a company transfers proprietary technology or parts that embody proprietary technology which it does not sell to any third party. In such cases, determination of fair value depends on the expertise of cost accountants.

A Powerful Punch 5 Ps to Combat White-Collar Crime

We require a comprehensive approach by law enforcement, the accounting profession, the education establishment, the government, and private industry to effectively deal with the issue of white-collar crime. To effectively combat the white-collar crime we require:

1. **Prevention:** Strong internal controls reviewed by competent and independent external auditors. Strong internal controls are barriers to crime for criminals. Internal controls help businesses operate more efficiently and effectively too.
2. **Power:** Legislation and standards issued by the Public Company Accounting Oversight Board and the Institute of Charted Accountants.
3. **Professionalism:** A better educated, skilled, trained, experienced and independent accounting profession. All efforts at prevention, any legislation, and any standards issued will not be fully effective unless the accounting profession addresses its educational issues.
4. **Prosecution:** Aggressive prosecution of white-collar criminals. Such criminals must know that they will be prosecuted for their actions.
5. **Prison:** Strong punishment and accountability for those convicted of white-collar crimes. Such criminals must be held fully accountable for their actions.

Reforms embodied under ICAI and other reforms relating to stock exchange do not go far enough. Even with any reforms, government cannot legislate competence on the part of management, external auditors, outside directors, audit committees, and others.

There is a movement today to weaken through legislation. One area relates to the reporting of internal controls. The first line of defence against financial fraud is strong internal controls. Fighting any weakening of such measures to reduce monitoring of internal controls by external independent auditors who are experienced, skilled, and competent may be recommended.

Critics complain about the increased costs associated with implementing tough legislation. The plain truth is that audit fees were preset at extra 'low ball' or low profit margin rates in efforts of drawing other business from audits clients by accounting firms. In addition, the cost of frauds is now approximately 10% of the average revenue of major accounting firms. A proper review of internal controls has always part of audit theory and practice. ICAI has only increased adherence to the ultimate goals of an adequate audit. Credible audit cannot be conducted on a company that does not have a good system of internal controls in place. Internal controls and good auditing are not mutually exclusive as some of the critics, who would have audit, relaxed for small companies, would have you believe, the cash was there, but how the cash got there was never examined. The auditors failed to detect any fraud. Other critics complain that permitting accounting firms to provide consulting services to the companies they audit increases their knowledge of the client and reduces errors. From experience it can be said that this point is absolutely untrue. Our auditors had major consulting agreements for work that exceeded the audit billing by over eight times. The audit firm at one point in time had staff round the year doing consulting work. Many others have argued that tough audit is causing many companies to seek capital in other markets not regulated by its requirements. We should compete with those capital markets on the greater transparency and quality of investor protections our system offers. Others have said that there will be more frauds to come despite the recent reforms under audit and other changes. However, to prevent such frauds, as enumerated, we need to further improve the effectiveness of audit and new accounting and auditing regulations and not weaken them. Now is not the time to retreat from progress.

Long prison sentences is not a substitute for strong internal controls in preventing fraud. Strong prison sentences for white-collar criminals would be more effective in deterring white-collar crime. Such policy would result in leaving us in a position of uncovering corporate crime only after it happens and the end result would be more of the same—the damage has already been done and billions of rupees lost. We cannot prevent white-collar crime by solely sentencing criminals to long prison sentences. You may ask any prison inmate and recently convicted corporate criminal if they ever planned on going to jail. While strong prison sentences for white-collar crime such a policy should be used as society's means of imposing responsibility on such criminals and not be considered a primary means of fraud prevention. Almost every criminal, upon learning about the recent convictions and long prison sentences imposed on recent corporate felons, will "wake up the next morning and begin life again reborn." No significant amounts of crimes contemplated and no crimes in progress are stopped by criminals being informed of very long prison sentences given to other criminals. Any criminologist about the same issues can be continued. The best tool to combat white-collar crime and increase the integrity of financial information is for companies to have strong internal controls which are reviewed by external, independent auditors who are properly educated, skilled, trained and experienced. Strong internal controls create barriers to crime and result in the increased integrity of financial information. We require effective monitoring of internal controls required by ICAI. However, in order to be effective we must solve the education problem in the accounting profession.

Accounting Education and the Accounting Profession

While we cannot legislate competence, it can be learned. Accounting students are not receiving the proper amount of fraud training and education they require to prepare themselves for today's audit environment. Most accounting students never take a separate college level course on fraud or internal controls.

The accounting profession is not adequately trained to deal with the likes of fraudsters of calibre. The current inadequate amount of fraud training provided to our future account managers must not be allowed to continue and must be immediately expanded as a matter of public policy. It is vital for their education, and it is vital for the integrity of capitalism. Without adequate fraud training, future generations of criminals similar to past calibre will continue to have an 'upper hand' in the escalating carnage caused by their economic crimes. In addition, accounting students must take separate college level courses in criminology, securities laws, internal controls, insurance/risk management and other vital 'real experience' area for the field work they will encounter on audits. In-depth detailed courses in audit techniques which include investigative techniques such as proper questioning of management are seriously lacking at most colleges. In fact, there are still many important subject areas covered in CPA review (cram) courses and on the CPA exams that are never taught to accounting students in college. For example courses such as securities law are almost never taught to accounting students in college. Such courses must be part of the basic 150 credit curriculum taught to accounting students and not taught as electives.

Collaring White-Collar Criminals

Even today with the increased emphasis required by the accounting profession to focus on areas of internal controls under ICAI, significantly, most accounting students today never take a single specific course on internal controls, white-collar fraud, criminology, or securities law. Many complaints related to reviews of internal controls by companies are due to the lack of deep understanding in internal controls by auditors. Many auditors are mostly filling out questionnaires and checking boxes in forms in their reviews of internal controls. Internal controls evaluations cannot be handled through a 'bean counter' approach. The very fact that most accounting students never take a separate college level course in specifically in accounting fraud, criminology, securities law, and internal controls in today's environment is equivalent to sending troops to battle without arms and body armour.

Reforms cannot be fully effective until the accounting profession has the requisite education, training, experience, and skills to implement them. In short, the whole accounting/audit curriculum requires a new overhaul to the real world. Even if it requires a law school type structure post-graduate education to enter the profession, so be it. The education required for this profession must evolve to keep up with the changing requirements of the financial world or it will continue to lose credibility and battles with criminals. If the profession does not adjust to the changing demands placed upon it by the changing environment it faces by properly educating its entry level accountants, it risks being deemed another licensed trade instead of a profession. The profession and licensing authorities are not adequately flushing out accountants who perform malpractice. Many accountants who, as partners and managers, presided over audits that went bad, have never been disciplined and have even gone on to higher positions in the profession. This cannot be a profession where incompetence rises to the top. The Securities and Exchange Commission should require minimum education, skills, and training standards for accountants. As they participate in public company audits. Such a requirement would push the profession and the educational community to wake up and adapt to the changing reality of the needs of professionals involved in audits concerning their education, training, experience, and overall competence.

Mumbai, a city with a big craze for fast cash every day, is fraught with the risk of people becoming victim to fraudulent investment schemes. Remember Aryarup Travel and Club Resort? Aurum Realty? Yes Cube Infrastructure? The owners of all three are under investigation for soliciting investors with promises of astronomical returns, paying off old investors with money from new ones, and ultimately reneging on their deals.

Such schemes seem to recur with regularity. To prevent this, the Economic Offences Wing (EOW) of the police is required to educate cops to investigate white-collar crime. Police personnel are taught to detect crime during their training (at the time of joining the force). But the trend in crime is changing, with new strategies emerging everyday. To prevent fraud and scam, we need to educate police personnel about the *modus operandi* of such crime and investigating them.

While the programme should focus on investment fraud, it should also touch upon bank, credit card and online transaction fraud, medical and jewellery scams, and education, housing and job rackets.

Most policemen don't know what an invoice, a bill or a hundi is. These are common terms, but they become a problem when complicated fraud is reported at police stations. Cops are used to cases like murder, dacoity and robbery. But when they are transferred from police stations to the EOW, they take three or four months to learn to investigate economic offences. If they are trained in advance, it will help save time, and help in the fast detection of crime and the filing of chargesheets.

The programme will also benefit cops not slated for an EOW posting. While the EOW investigates frauds where the amount is above ₹50 lakh, police stations handle frauds up to that limit. But to deal with the cases, cops at the police stations often approach the EOW since they do not know how to investigate white-collar crime.

The Economic Offences Wing (EOW) of the police has been provided with additional personnel to nab the directors of Aryarup Travel and Club Resort, suspected to have launched various fraudulent investment schemes. The EOW is on the lookout for Ravindra Deshmukh and his wife Vasuda. The fresh impetus in the case has been provided by the recent suicide of an Aryarup agent who had collected over ₹5 crore in Goa and was under pressure from investors to pay up. The fraud came to light when a Mumbai based businessman lodged a complaint with the EOW stating that Aryarup duped him of ₹81 lakh with promises of fast money and handsome profits. A police officer said,

> "Senior officers have provided additional manpower to the investigating team to nab the suspects. More victims who lost money in the investment scheme are coming forward to lodge complaints."
>
> "The agent who committed suicide belonged to Latur. He ended his life when he realized he couldn't pay the investors back. A case has been registered with the Goa police."

The Deshmukhs floated several schemes in Gujarat, Haryana, Rajasthan, Karnataka and Maharashtra. Through Aryarup, they would lure people with a promise of 86% return on investment and commission if others were brought in. For a while, they kept their promise, but all of a sudden stopped making payments. Aryarup could have more than one lakh investors in the country, 15,000 being in Maharashtra, where the Deshmukhs started schemes in Mumbai, Navi Mumbai, Thane, Buldana, Nasik, Nanded, Parbhani, Jalgaon, Bhusawal, Pune and Latur. In February, the EOW, acting on a court order, attached two Deshmukh-owned plots totalling 75 acres and worth ₹2 crore. One, measuring 50 acres, was near the Jaipur airport and the other in Murbad.

Company Whistleblower Systems: Detecting and Preventing White-Collar Crime

Whistleblower systems in businesses and administrative organizations can be used as an instrument to detect and prevent abuse and wrongdoings such as white-collar crime. In the past, whistleblowers—i e people who blow the whistle on perceived irregularities—have helped uncover inhumane treatment in care homes and rotten meat that had illegally re-entered the distribution chain. In the United States and UK, there are already laws in place to protect whistleblowers. This is not yet the case in Germany.

When allegations of white-collar crime become public knowledge, the damage to everyone involved can be serious, regardless of how true the allegations are. There is a loss of trust and respect among third parties, such as clients and suppliers, not to mention banks and stakeholders as well as investigators. It's also difficult to quantify the damage to a company's reputation. Many potential whistleblowers lose heart, worrying about the mental anguish and the work and legal implications if they are identified. Until now, whistleblowers in companies and public authorities have enjoyed little public recognition, personal support or legal protection. This may be because whistleblowers are seen as 'informers' who denounce companies for their own ends. It could also be due to the absence of a legal framework and the resulting lack of protection for whistleblowers. But introducing a whistleblower system in corporations is more than just a useful way to uncover and prevent white-collar crime. It can also be a reflection of professional management practice and promote corporate culture.

The United States has introduced a slew of laws to protect people who 'speak out'. The Sarbanes-Oxley Act (SOX) gives special protection to people at companies listed on the American stock exchange if they reveal wrongdoings in accounting or financial practices. Companies must have whistleblower systems and people in place to receive tip-offs and investigate allegations relating to accounting practices, accounting controls and auditing issues. It's forbidden by law to sack, demote, suspend, threaten, bully or in any way discriminate against whistleblowers. People are also allowed to contact the authorities, members of congress and superiors who have the authority to investigate and rectify abuse or wrongdoings. The Dodd-Frank Act, which came into effect in 2010, provides further incentives to whistleblowers in the form of rewards for uncovering abuse or wrongdoings. The law makes special provisions for the protection of anonymity.

In the UK, whistleblowers are protected by the Public Interest Disclosure Act. In July 2011, the Bribery Act also comes into power, and this will also affect German companies. This act lays down tight restrictions regarding compliance and corruption avoidance guidelines, although the law doesn't specifically mention whistleblowers. Nevertheless, companies are obliged to introduce compliance systems to avoid corruption. Indirectly, this means whistleblowers will have more protection, and guidelines for setting up the necessary anti-corruption procedures will need to be drawn up. These will have to include instructions, checklists and forms for specific scenarios, including guidelines covering the anonymous reporting of suspicions. Firms will face criminal action if corruption is uncovered or if they fail to implement suitable measures.

If employees choose to hand on company information, their freedom of expression is already subject to special restrictions due to clauses in their contract of employment. But even if there are no special contractual obligations, workers do have a loyalty and allegiance towards employers, which stems from their obligations as an employee. The integrity interests of an employer are easily affected. Confidentiality obligations, often the norm in employment contracts, frequently go beyond the statutory non-disclosure obligations. This relates to unfair competition, ie the protection of corporate and trade secrets. It also covers information declared confidential by the employer and any other issues worthy of protection, of a personal nature or relating to a business. It is not difficult for a would-be whistleblower to enter an area of legal uncertainty regarding who may be told what. Employees who disregard non-disclosure obligations can be dismissed instantly.

Companies can use Monitoring, a standard for compliance check to regularly inspect and evaluate their degree of compliance. The assessment is based on the current situation in the company, with the aim of ensuring the implementation of suitable and effective compliance standards. The assessment looks at individual measures to see if they are in place at all (ie their integrity) and whether they are effective and efficient (ie their quality). All of this is captured in a four-box model. The assessment also considers the elements that make up a whistleblower system and whether there are tools in place to ensure the system is sustainable.

Factors that affect the integrity and quality of systems include anonymity protection and the existence of whistle blowing channels, such as an ombudsman, help lines, electronic or web-based systems. The key issue is whether employees know who to turn to, and where, if they discover wrongdoings or abuse—and whether they can expect sanctions, or whether the whistle blowing system is accepted in all areas of a company, and can thus be considered an integrated and established part of the corporate culture.

Audits

The main pillar of our capitalist free market economic system which is corner stone of democracy, is the integrity of financial information. Without a reliable financial information a firm cannot grow. Regular audit automatically brings reliability in financial accounting. Today's overall audit model must be rethought in terms of the rapid growth of technologies that can circumvent internal controls without detection. The 'year-end audit model' is in many situations obsolete and must be replaced by continuous year-round audits. The CEO and CFO should not be the only persons in a company certifying financial information. Accounting and other corporate personnel throughout the entire accounting, financial, and internal control structure should sign off individually to the auditors about any information they control or represent to them. There must be full direct accountability throughout the corporate accounting structure for the information presented to auditors. Firms auditing a client should provide no other services to that client without exception during the audit relationship and for a certain period even after the audit relationship terminates. When an audit relationship terminates the reasons must be disclosed publicly and to the new auditors. The review committee should periodically and independently review audit work papers for public corporations similar to the way the IRS reviews tax returns.

We require people with the intelligence, background, and experience specific to the Board's they serve on and the functions they are responsible for. We do not need well-meaning, intelligent people, who in many cases make ineffective Board members serving in positions they are not suited for. The time for 'window dressing' must end.

Audit Committees

The external auditors are supposed to be monitored by the Audit Committee of the Board of Directors. In practice such Audit Committees are no better prepared (if not worse) to handle their responsibilities than the external auditors they oversee. Many Audit Committee members receive compensation in stock options or own company stock of the Board they serve on which provides a disincentive to effective independent oversight and can affect their objectivity and professional scepticism. In addition, many members of Audit Committees have no formal accounting, auditing, internal control, and fraud education or backgrounds. Their requisite education, skills, training, and experience to fulfil their responsibilities are lacking.

The Public Company Accounting Oversight Board (PCAOB) is wrong in not making public quality-control problems and structural deficiencies found during its inspections of audits of accounting firms. The reasoning that making such information public only if they are not fixed within twelve months creates any incentive for such firms to remedy such problems is simply flawed. The inspection process has found far too many problems in the quality of audits conducted by accounting firms. Many of these problems could be alleviated by better education and training that would increase competency in the profession. However, education and training needs to be focused in areas effecting risks affecting the public and the profession today such as fraud, interviewing skills, internal controls, etc.

Corporate directors, financial, and accounting personnel should not be compensated with stock options or any other compensation that would give them a direct beneficial interest from 'earnings management'. While there is plenty of debate about the proper accounting of stock options, there is little discussion as to the proper awarding of them. The awarding of stock options in such an unwise manner can induce otherwise honest people in key areas, like accounting and internal audit, to commit white-collar fraud.

There have been recommendations to reform ICAI to increase auditor reliance on management internal control representations and/or have management report on such controls. However, the people administering the internal controls structure within companies do not have enough independence for such reliance by auditors since their compensation and job position is determined by management.

Instead, there should be greater accountability by internal accountants and internal auditors for external audits. All work that they perform should be certified by the auditors as truthful and accurate to the best of their knowledge and understanding.

Internal Auditors

We must require professional accredited, licensed, trained, skilled, and adequately educated internal auditors. While their work is not a substitute for the external audit function, as licensed professionals their work can be invaluable in preventing fraud by increasing internal controls by the nature of their knowledge on their company. We need to strengthen this profession by requiring the licensing of internal auditors similar to the way of our State's licensed Certified Public Accountants. By requiring licensing of internal auditors they will have increased independence, responsibility, and accountability for the work they perform. The internal auditors should report directly to the Audit Committee of the Board of Directors. The CEO and CFO should have no authority over them. This legislation must be reformed. It has shifted the power of selection of the lead counsel in class action litigation to the large institutional investors. Many of these institutional investors are large public employee pension funds. The Trustees to the funds are either elected government officials or appointed by elected government officials. Some of the class action law firms have contributed huge sums of money directly and indirectly benefiting the politicians who control the public employee pension funds. Such political contributions create a conflict of interest when these funds are involved in the selection of lead counsel for class action law suits. This 'pay to play' practice must stop. In addition the Act has caused a concentration of power in the class action bar and has eliminated competition among rival qualified law firms seeking to protect investor interests at the least cost.

Stock Exchange

We should be concerned about the integrity, independence, and quality of internally generated research reports issued by stock exchange firms. We should also be concerned about the potential for opinion shopping for the outside research reports used in conjunction with IPOs. Analysts who write such reports should disclose what actual experience they have working in the specific area of the industry they are reporting on. Analysts must disclose their track records based on certain standards in easily understandable terms and uniform reporting criteria. Investment banking firms, brokerages, and banks should not issue research reports on companies. Such reports should be issued by completely independent firms subject to rigorous professional standards that are strictly enforced. We cannot realistically expect to have investment bankers issue objective research reports of companies which they have a relationship with. In too many instances such reports have become marketing tools.

Law Enforcement Resources

Top-notch, experienced CBI agents are leaving as soon as they qualify for retirement causing a problem becoming increasingly complex for our government, leaving the Bureau for higher paying, private industry jobs as brain drain within the CBI. As regards the white-collar crime, it would be well-advised to pay these agents fair market value. The CBI, the Securities and Exchange Commission, and other federal agencies responsible for white-collar crime do not have adequate legal, technological, and personnel resources to meet their responsibilities. Compensation levels do not compete with the private sector causing inadequate human resources to the government agencies.

With today's computer automation and the ability to move money across borders in seconds, and the fact that banks and financial institutions handle gross dollar value transactions on a single day many times their net worth, are today's controls and audit structure keeping up with the times? In addition, with these companies merging, there is often a period of flux where the various computer systems of each entity have not been made fully compatible with each other.

Cooking the Books

The deliberate distorting of a firm's financial accounts, often with the aim of avoiding the payment of tax is called cooking the books

Cooking seems a rather odd choice of word to convey fraud. *The Oxford English Dictionary* lists a dozen or so meanings of the verb 'to cook', ranging from 'prepare opium for use' to 'make the call of a cuckoo' and, of course, 'prepare food by the action of heat'. Tucked away at the bottom there is also the meaning 'present in a surreptitiously altered form' and it is that meaning of cook that was used in the coinage of the phrase 'cook the books'. The allusion appears to be the changing of one thing into another, as in the conversion of food ingredients into meals. This usage dates back to Stuart and possibly Tudor England and was used by the Earl of Strafford in his letters and dispatches, 1636:

> "The Proof was once clear, however they have cooked it since."

The verb was in common use by the 18th century and Tobias Smollett's *The Adventures of Peregrine Pickle*, 1751, made the link to finance explicit:

> "Some falsified printed accounts, artfully cooked up, on purpose to mislead and deceive."

Apart from the expression 'cooking the books' this use of 'cook' has become less common in the 19th and 20th centuries. The preferred euphemism for the manipulation of financial statements has come to be 'creative accounting'. This is first recorded in the 1960s and is attributed to the US comedian Irwin Corey, as in this example from the *Middlesboro Daily News*, May 1968:

> "Professor Irwin Corey claims his CPA (Certified Public Accountant) isn't exactly crooked—but the government's questioning him about his creative accounting."

The numerous corporate fraud cases of the 1990s turned public opinion against the semi-admiring tone of 'creative accounting' and journalists stopped using it. That, and the transformation of bookshops, which now seem to sell more coffee and cakes than they do books, has brought about a revival of the term 'cooking the books', which looks like staying with us for some years to come.

Financial Statement Fraud: Detecting the Red Flag

The red flags of financial statement fraud are distinctly different from those of asset misappropriation. Some of common general red flags of financial statement frauds are:

- Accounting anomalies.
- Unusually rapid revenue and/or profit growth.
- Readily noticeable internal control weaknesses.
- Noticeably 'aggressive' financial actions by senior management.
- Personality or character flaws of the CEO and/or other 'C-level' executives.

Personality Alert

Of these general indictors, top management personality and character are by far the most compelling with regard to financial statement fraud. Typically, a senior executive who is inclined to 'cook the books' possesses low ethical standards, though this trait may often be difficult to detect prior to the commissioning of a crime. However, most executives with ethical weaknesses also exhibit very noticeable signs of aggressiveness in almost everything they do-including making critical financial decisions. Examples:

- Overly domineering, disrespectful or abusive management style vis-a-vis subordinates.
- Actively 'steering' internal and external auditors away from financial reports that could reveal the fraud.
- Secretive or distinctly evasive attitude regarding critical financial information.

Detection Methods for General Financial Statement Frauds

- Internal audit is consistently engaged in substantive anti-fraud activities.
- Auditors aggressively apply standards of Institute of Chartered Accountant of India.
- Frequent and thorough fraud-oriented ratio analysis-focusing in particular on long-term trends and on comparisons between business units.
- Surprise audits and/or cash counts.
- Implementation of an anonymous, user-friendly tip hotline for use by employees, vendors and customers.
- Data mining using one of the common auditing software applications such as ACL or IDEA.

Specific Red Flags

As with asset misappropriation, there are also specific red flags of financial statement fraud that are present in many of the common varieties of such accounting violations. Examples:

- Complex or unstable organizational structure.
- Unusually intricate or confusing financial transactions with third-party entities.

- Sudden or gradual increase in gross margin compared with the company's prior performance, and with industry averages.
- Cash flows that are negative for the first three quarters and suddenly positive for the fourth quarter-not by just a little, but by more than all losses to date. (This scenario is exactly what happened at Enron. That is why Sherron Watkins said, after the company's demise, that if anyone had been paying attention to the cash flows they would have known that Enron's statements were suspicious and/or fraudulent.)
- Significant sales to companies or individuals whose identity and business track record are questionable.
- Sudden above-average profits for specific quarters.
- Executives or Board members have direct personal dependence on the company's performance.
- Conspicuously lax Board oversight of top management.

Fraud Categories

Also similar to asset misappropriation, financial statement fraud has distinct categories. Each has its unique red flags and detection methods.

Revenue Recognition or Timing Schemes

Also known as improper treatment of sales. This fraud category is possibly the most common form of financial statement fraud-usually employed when management seeks to conceal the real numbers for a weak quarter or two.

Red Flags

If a sale is legitimate, but is posted prematurely, the red flag would be a GAAP violation by early recording of the sale. Similarly, channel stuffing—where sales are recorded before they've actually been made-would be indicated by an excessive number of subsequent period returns of merchandise, accompanied by an unusual jump in credits.

Fictitious Revenue

One of the oldest financial statement schemes around—this involves posting sales that simply never occurred.

Red Flags

- Unusual increase in assets-the other side of the entry to mask fictitious revenues.
- 'Customer' records are missing key data such as physical address and phone number or ID proof.
- Unusual changes in ratio patterns—such as a spike in revenues with no commensurate increase in accounts receivable.

Concealed Liabilities (Improper or Under-Reporting of Expenses and Other Liabilities)

By shifting expenses from one entity to another or reclassifying liabilities as assets, which is what got WorldCom into trouble when it improperly reported $3.8 billion in expenses as capital expenditures, management can make the company's financial condition appear much rosier than it is.

Red Flags

- Use of different audit firms for different subsidiaries or business entities.
- Recurring negative cash flows from operations or an inability to generate cash flows from operations while reporting earnings growth.
- Invoices and other liabilities go unrecorded in the company's financial records.
- Writing off loans to executives or other parties.
- Failure to record warranty-related liabilities.

Inadequate Disclosures

This tactic is used after a financial statement fraud has occurred, in an attempt to cover it up. Red flags:

- Disclosure notes are so complex that it is impossible to determine the actual nature of the event or transaction.
- Discovery of undisclosed legal contingencies.

Improper Asset Valuation

Fraudulently inflating asset valuations is a common form of profit manipulation. Red flags:

- Unusual or unexplained increases in the book value of assets such as inventory, receivables, long term assets, etc.
- Odd patterns in relationships of assets to other components of the financial report, such as sudden changes in the ratio of receivables to revenues.
- GAAP violations in recording expenses as assets.

Detection Methods

To reduce the risk of having these frauds occur or continue, undetected auditors should use such practices as:

- Horizontally and vertically analysing all financial reports.
- Conducting frequent ratio analysis, including assessment of trends over a period of several years.
- Using Beneisch's Ratios which pinpoint anomalies in year-to-year measures of gross margins, sales growth, receivables levels and other key accounting ratios.
- Rigorously applying the guidance of ICAI to all audit exercises.

Accounting Theory for Investigators

A business expends considerable time compiling accounting data to produce a balance sheet. It remains for the investigator, however, to interpret the significance of the figures. The preliminary lines of a balance sheet can reveal a great deal about the financial health of a company.

One very important calculation available from the balance sheet figures is the net working capital. Net working capital is the difference between current assets and current liabilities. Net working capital often determines the ability of a company to meet its current obligations, expand its volume, and to take advantage of business opportunities.

The current ratio, or ratio of current assets to current liabilities, may also be a helpful calculation. Analysts generally agree that a business should maintain a 2 : 1 current ratio that is ₹2 in current assets for each ₹1 in current liabilities. This generalization, however, is subject to modification depending on the business. The investigator can find typical current ratios by comparing the ratios of similar other businesses.

Another important calculation from the balance sheet is the net book value of a company's securities. The book value represents the business's assets backing or protecting bonds or each share of common and preferred stock. To state this figure for bonds, subtract from the total assets the value of intangible assets and current liabilities. This yields the net tangible assets. The net asset value of the bond is the net tangible assets divided by the number of outstanding bonds.

Capital surplus is the amount over the par or legal value of each share the various shareholders pay. Accumulated retained earnings, sometimes called earned surplus, are the amounts of profit a corporation earns, less declared dividends.

Statement of Source and Application of Funds

The Statement of Source and Application of Funds identifies a business's sources and uses of cash over the reporting period. This statement is extremely useful for identifying how a company is funding operations, whether from owner investments, earnings or borrowings. It also shows what the company is doing with its money, whether it is being distributed to the owners, being used to make additional investments, or being used to operate the business.

In the Statement of Cash Flows, net income is usually converted to cash flow by allowing some adjustments. These adjustments are necessary because some accounts effect net income in the Income Statement, but they are not cash receipts or expenditures.

Depreciation is added to the net income because it is a non-cash expense that reduces net income, but does not reduce cash.

Although attribute and variables sampling may be useful to auditors to suggest areas of additional research, they may be of little use to the white-collar crime investigator. An investigator is seldom interested in proportions of errors. Financial auditors may allow a deviation rate of 2-3%, but the investigator must produce specific documents to prove embezzlement or fraud.

A special kind of attribute sampling that may be useful to investigators trying to find whether critical errors exist is discovery sampling. Discovery sampling is a technique that allows an investigator to conclude with a certain confidence level whether any problems or critical errors exist in a population. Discovery sampling is attribute sampling with an expected zero error rate. A discovery sample table is an attribute based on a 95% confidence level that no errors will be found in various items of the entire population. Following table contains an example of a simplified discovery sampling table.

Using the sampling table an investigator reviews 300 invoices from the population and finds no errors. From this table, the investigator will conclude with only a 26% certainty that errors will occur in no more than 0.1% of the population. He will decide with a 78% certainty that the errors will occur in no more than 0.5% of the population. He will decide with 99% plus certainty that the errors will occur in no more than 2% of the

Probability of Including at Least One Error in the Sample

Sample Size	*Rate of Occurrence in the Population*							
	.01	.05	.1	.2	.3	.5	1	2
50	2	5	9	14	22	39	64	
70	1	3	7	13	19	30	51	76
100	1	5	10	18	26	39	63	87
200	2	10	18	33	45	63	87	98
300	3	14	26	45	59	78	95	99
400	4	18	33	55	70	87	98	99
500	5	22	39	63	78	92	99	99

population. If however, the investigator reviews 300 invoices and finds an error, he will be 100% certain that a problem does exist, as he has found an example. He will know nothing about the occurrence rate or the rate of deviation, but he will know that an error exists, and that is what he wanted to know.

Discovery sampling table probabilities change, of course depending on the size of the entire population to be sampled. The larger the population, the larger the number of samples is required to assure a constant probability. Thus the investigator can know before the audit begins how many samples he must examine to reach a certain probability that no errors exist.

The use of statistical sampling in auditing, though not universal, is growing. Its main use today is in accounts receivable and inventory. As the demands for enforcement of white-collar criminal statutes increases, statistical sampling will begin to play a greater role for the investigator in near future.

3. Interrogation Techniques of Embezzlers and Financial Fraudsters

Embezzlement and financial fraud is a white-collar crime financially motivated, non-violent crime committed for illegal monetary gain. Lying, cheating and stealing—that's white-collar crime in a nutshell. This is now synonymous with the full range of frauds committed by business and government professionals. It is not a victimless crime. A single scam can destroy a company, devastate families by wiping out their life savings. Although white-collar crimes are quite varied, they have several characteristics in common. First, they involve the use of deceit and concealment, rather than the application of force or violence, for the illegitimate gain of money, property or services. A defendant convicted of making false statements in order to obtain a government contract for example, is considered a white-collar criminal. White-collar crimes typically involve abuse of position of trust and power. Public officials who solicit and accept bribes or corporate officers who fix prices to drive competitors out of business are engaging in such abuse of their position.

Within the field of criminology, white-collar crime initially was defined by sociologist Edwin Sutherland as "a crime committed by a person of respectability and high social status in the course of his occupation". Sutherland was a proponent of symbolic interactionism and believed that criminal behaviour was learned from interpersonal interactions. White-collar crime is similar to corporate crime because white-collar employees are more likely to commit fraud, bribery, ponzi schemes, insider trading, embezzlement, cyber crime, copyright infringement, money-laundering, identity theft, and forgery.

White-collar criminals attributed different characteristics and motives than typical street criminals. Mr Sutherland originally presented his theory in an address to the American Sociological Society in attempt to study two fields, crime and high society, which had no previous empirical correlation. He defined his idea as "Crime committed by a person of respectability and high social status in the course of his occupation. Many denote the invention the Sutherland's idiom to the explosion of US business in the years following the Great Depression. Sutherland noted that in the time, less than 2% of persons committed to prisons in a year belong to the upper-class. His goal was to prove a relation between money, social status, and likelihood of going to jail for a white-collar crime, compared to more visible, typical crimes. White-collar criminal exhibit narcissism in spades. Warning signs of work place violence include a sense of entitlement and egocentric behaviours. These offenders believe they are entitled to fraud and feel victimized when challenged. Although the percentage is a bit higher today, numbers still show a large majority of those in jail are poor, 'blue-collar' criminals, despite efforts to crack-down on white-collar and corporate crime. The introduction of white-collar crime was a relatively new issue to criminology at that time. The types of individuals who committed these crimes lived successfully and were respected by society in general because these criminals were held in such a high regard, these individuals were given a blind eye to the crimes they committed. Other fiscal laws were passed in the years prior to Sutherland's studies including anti-trust laws in the 1920s, and social welfare laws in the 1930s. After the Depression, people went to great lengths to rebuild their financial security and it is theorized that this led many hard workers, who felt they were under paid, to take advantage of their positions.

Much of Sutherland's work was to separate and define the differences in blue-collar street crimes, such as arson, burglary, theft, assault, rape, and vandalism, which are often blamed on psychological, associational, and structural factors vis-a-vis white-collar crimes. Contrarily, white-collar criminals are opportunists, who learn they can take advantage of their circumstances to accumulate financial gains. They are educated, intelligent, affluent and confident individuals who are qualified enough to get a job which allows them the unmonitored access to often large sums of money. Many also use their intelligence to con their victims into believing and trusting in their credentials. Many do not start out as criminals, and in many cases never see themselves as such.

Some ways that employees of a company can become victims of white-collar crime can be that workers are being exposed to the harms and risks of being involved in a crime. Even if the workers are unaware of the crimes his or her corporation is committing, this poses a threat to their job security. Essentially, if a company is charged with a white-collar crime, such as fraud or embezzlement, and loses copious amounts of money forcing the company to declare bankruptcy, the employees are at risk of losing their jobs. Another harm making employees victims of white-collar crime can be when employers are aware of a physical harm that can affect their employees. An example of this danger can be depicted with miners in coal field who were exposed to methane gas, which the company (and the Canadian government) were aware was a danger to people's health, yet there was nothing done to protect the employees. They believe in if you want to know what God thinks of money, just look at the people he gave it to. (Dorothy Parker)

White-collar crime is crime committed by a person of respectability and high social status in the course of his occupation. The colour of the collar doesn't mean anything. It could be blue-collar or pink-collar. It is generally accepted wisdom in criminology that although Sutherland's definition falls short in some ways, the underlying constructs of what he meant—deception and lack of physical force—remain true, even while forms of this crime evolve. The NW3C definition is considered a good 2005 update: "white-collar crimes are defined as illegal or unethical acts that violate fiduciary responsibility or public trust for personal or organizational gain," and the Edelhertz (1970) typology is the most frequently cited one, in this area, including:

1. crimes against government by public officials;
2. crimes against government by private citizens;
3. crimes against businesses;
4. crimes against investors;
5. crimes against consumers;
6. crimes against employees; and
7. crimes affecting public health.

Something called the Green (1990) typology includes:

1. crimes for the benefit of one's employer;
2. crimes by government officials;
3. crimes by professionals in the course of doing business; and
4. crimes by individuals in the course of their occupation. Some would add 'technocrime' to existing typologies.

Siegel (2004) defines white-collar crime as "illegal activities of people and institutions whose acknowledged purpose is profit through illegitimate business transactions." To make it simple, white-collar crime is larceny committed by a respectable, legitimate enterprise which is not set up to go out of business like an ordinary fraud or con game. White-collar crime involves embezzlement, forgery, or fraud committed in the course of normal business practice, but is highly unethical and violates accepted accounting principles or the public trust. Like the crime of conspiracy, deception and cover up are the hallmarks of white-collar crime. Sometimes the offender is a government official.

- By the type of offence, eg, property crime, economic crime, and other corporate crimes like environmental and health and safety law violations, some crime is only possible because of the identity of the offender, eg, transnational money-laundering requires the participation of senior officers employed in banks. But the FBI have adopted a narrow approach, defining white-collar crime as "those illegal acts which are characterized by deceit, concealment, or violation of trust and which are not dependent upon the application or threat of physical force or violence". This approach is relatively pervasive in the European countries. The record-keeping does not adequately collect data on the socioeconomic status of offenders which, in turn, makes research and policy evaluation problematic. While the true extent and cost of white-collar crimes are unknown, it is estimated to the cost of dollar annually.
- By the type of offender, eg, by social class or high socio-economic status, the occupation of positions of trust or profession, or academic qualification, researching the motivations for criminal behaviour, eg, greed or fear of loss of face if economic difficulties become obvious. Shover and Wright point to the essential neutrality of a crime as enacted in a statute. It almost inevitably describes conduct in the abstract, not by reference to the character of the persons performing it. Thus, the only way that one crime differs from another is in the background and characteristics of its perpetrators. Most, if not all, white-collar offenders are distinguished by lives of privilege, much of it with origins in class inequality.

- By organizational culture rather than the offender or offence which overlaps with organized crime. Appelbaum and Chambliss offer a twofold definition:
- Occupational crime which occurs when crimes are committed to promote personal interests, say, by altering records and overcharging, or by the cheating of clients by professionals.
- Organizational or corporate crime which occurs when corporate executives commit criminal acts to benefit their company by overcharging or price fixing, false advertising, etc.

Blue-Collar Crime

The types of crime committed are a function of what is available to the potential offender. Thus, those employed in relatively unskilled environments and living in inner-city areas have fewer 'situations' to exploit than those who work in 'situations' where large financial transactions occur and live in areas where there is relative prosperity. Blue-collar crime tends to be more obvious and thus attracts more active police attention such as vandalism or shoplifting. In contrast, white-collar employees can incorporate legitimate and criminal behaviour, thus making themselves less obvious when committing the crime. Therefore, blue-collar crime is more likely to often use physical force, whereas in the corporate world, the identification of a victim is less obvious and the issue of reporting is complicated by a culture of commercial confidentiality to protect shareholder's value. It is estimated that a great deal of white-collar crime is undetected or, if detected, it is not reported.

Corporate Crime

Corporate crime deals with the company as a whole, benefiting the investors or the individuals who are in high positions in the company or corporation. The relationship white-collar crime has with corporate crime is that they are similar as they both are involved within the business world. Their difference is that white-collar crime benefits the individual involved, corporate crime benefits the company or the corporation.

One well-known insider trading case in the United States is the ImClone stock trading case. In December 2001, top-level executives sold their shares in ImClone Systems, a pharmaceutical company that manufactured an anti-cancer drug. The US Securities and Exchange Commission (SEC) investigated numerous top-level executives, as well as Martha Stewart, a friend of ImClone's former chief executive who had also sold her shares at the same time. The SEC reached a settlement in 2005.

A common misconception about corporate crime and white-collar crime is that its effects are mainly financial. However, they can cause harm to the general public, workers and consumers. For example, false claims made by pharmaceutical companies about their products or the dumping of toxic wastes. An example is the Hooker Chemical Company (later acquired by Occidental Petroleum Corporation) dumping toxic waste into the abandoned Love Canal in Niagara Falls and later selling the land after knowing of the problem but choosing not to warn health officials. It was later sold to a private housing developer in the 1950s and in the 1970s the families started experiencing major health problems such as miscarriages and birth defects.

State-Corporate Crime

The negotiation of agreements between a State and a corporation will be at a relatively senior level on both sides, this is almost exclusively a white-collar 'situation' which offers the opportunity for crime. Although law enforcement claims to have prioritized white-collar crime, evidence shows that it continues to be a low priority.

When senior levels of a corporation engage in criminal activity using the company this is sometimes called 'controlled fraud'.

An example of State-Corporate Crime is in Sydney, Nova Scotia, the health of workers and community members at large was jeopardized as a result of being exposed to large.

Organized Transnational Crime

Organized Transnational Crime is organized criminal activity that takes place across national jurisdictions, and with advances in transportation and information technology, law enforcement officials and policy-makers have needed to respond to this form of crime on a global scale. Some examples include human trafficking, money-laundering, drug smuggling, illegal arms dealing, terrorism, and cyber crime. Although it is impossible to precisely gauge transnational crime, the Millennium Project, an international think tank, assembled statistics on several aspects of transnational crime in 2009:

- World illicit trade of almost $780 billion
- Counterfeiting and piracy of $300 billion to $1 trillion
- Global drug trade of $321 billion

Occupational Crime

Individuals may commit crime during employment or unemployment. The two most common forms are theft and fraud. Theft can be of varying degrees, from a pencil to furnishings to a car. Most employees do steal and the expense is high. Insider trading, the trading of stock by someone with access to publicly unavailable information, is a type of fraud.

Occupational Death

A death that occurs while a person is at work or performing work related tasks. Occupational death is the third-leading cause of death in Canada. An example of occupational death is the death of three workers at the Langley Mushroom farm. The three workers died after inhaling fatal doses of toxic fumes in September 2008. Two other workers were left with brain damage. Three operators were fined $350,000 after pleading guilty to charges linked to the death of the three workers.

Intelligence Analysis and Profiling of White-Collar Crime

Unfortunately, there is no uniform white-collar crime reporting system. The investigation agency only tracks crime data on embezzlement and fraud, so the best estimates are that number of arrests for white-collar crimes occur each year. The number of investigations far exceed that number, however. It appears prosecutions for crimes against consumers take priority over crimes against business and government. Offenders typically believe that whatever they've done is not wrong, and is an expected entitlement or fringe benefit of their positions of power. Most research suggests that firms with declining profitability or budget cuts are more likely to break the law. Other research indicates that firms in highly regulated areas and volatile markets (like pharmaceuticals or petroleum) are more likely to break the law.

When approaching the topic of white-collar crime, it is instructive to take a broad view and consider property criminals in general. Property criminals of all kinds tend to be creatures of habit where their classic *modus operandi* consists of the following:

- **Type of Victim**—they usually specialize in a type of prey.
- **Type of Dwelling**—they usually have a turf or place for preying.
- **Means of Entry**—they usually use the same ploy or method.
- **Type of Loot**—they usually are very skilled at getting one thing.

- **Time of Operation**—they are patient no matter how long the crime takes.
- **Presence of Partners**—some work alone; but most work with partners.
- **Trademarks**—some leave calling cards or signatures at the scene.

While the use of *modus operandi* and repeat offender profiles are important, there have been some advances in recent years identifying signature characteristics based on style and the degree of hostility expressed before, during, and/or after the crime. Most of these advances have taken place in a discipline called forensic accounting. For itself, the field of white-collar crime in criminology has long been bogged down in conceptual and definitional debates. However, some things stay the same. It has been frequently remarked that the most common motives for property crime tend to fall into three categories which, in order of being the most frequent, are:

1. to keep the party going (money from the crime is used to purchase drugs)
2. to keep up appearances (money is used to buy expensive clothes, jewellery, or status items)
3. to keep things together (money is used for living expenses, food, shelter, or child support).

The Typical Profile

The typical white-collar criminal is a well-placed, middle class, educated male around 29 years of age with no previous criminal history and no involvement in drug or alcohol abuse. Their offences are characterized by sophisticated planning, and they have carefully considered lessons learned from the extensive histories most corporations have of regulatory violations. Most offenders prefer to work alone, except where the cooperation of others is needed. Almost all criminological theories (strain, learning, control, conflict, and neutralization) have been applied to white-collar crime. The economic costs of white-collar crime are staggering, running well into several billions a year. Perhaps more importantly, economic crime erodes public confidence.

The most common breeding ground, is the 'free-wheeling, self-regulatory' work environment where the lines are blurred between acceptable and unacceptable business practices in pursuit of profit. High levels of both internal and external competition as well as certain kinds of office politics will also create a breeding ground for white-collar crime, as far as the profiles go, by Weisburd et al (2001) who studied 968 offenders over a 3 year period. It may be worth quoting from them, as follows:

> "Most offenders are disproportionately white, middle-aged men who possess high levels of social capital, good income, and higher education (75% of the time). Most are married homeowners who occupy supervisory positions in their organizations. They do not usually have squeaky clean pasts, as about a third of the sample had at least one police arrest in their records, but they tended to stay away from violent crimes, and drifted in and out of property or public order crimes. Compared to ordinary criminals, white-collar criminals begin and end their careers later, and include smaller numbers of recorded criminal events. However, they are similar to ordinary criminals in that they are unlikely to evidence a high degree of specialization and seem to age out of crime."

It is difficult to estimate the amount of planning or foresight that goes on in the minds of white-collar criminals. This is so because most of them see their offending as simply an extension or exaggeration of normal operating procedures. For decades, criminologists have maintained that NEUTRALIZATIONS play an important role in the initial stages of planning a white-collar crime (Hollinger, 1991). Neutralizations are like rationalizations, except they are the kinds of things one says to himself before (not after) the crime is committed. Some offenders, like the ones Horning (1970) describes, engage in a sort of 'cognitive mapping' where certain property and certain procedures in the organization are perceived as 'fair game' for criminal activity. Other, so-called 'rogue' employees sometimes claim they were just following implicit orders. Cressey (1953) used the phrase "vocabularies of adjustment" to describe the many ways in which white-collar criminals comfort or deny their guilty minds, and it has become conventional in criminology to talk about whether such criminals had an unshareable 'problem' or perceived some 'threat'. The 'problem' school of thought holds that something like the 3 Bs (babes, booze, and bets)—a problem with infidelity, alcohol or drugs, or a gambling or debt problem—is at root of the criminality. The 'threat' school of thought holds that something in the competitive environment of the organization or in the potential offender's career path is at the root of the problem. One will find criminologists about equally divided over this issue. The most common neutralizations are as follows:

1. **Denial of Responsibility:** It's not my fault; I didn't have a choice.
2. **Denial of Injury:** It's no big deal; They have too much money.
3. **Denial of Victim:** They had it coming; They had a bad attitude.
4. **Condemnation of the Condemners:** Everybody does it; Why me?
5. **Appeal to Higher Loyalties:** Only cowards back down; protecting.

One of the more prominent theories is that offenders possess an 'unshareable financial problem', the result of living beyond their means, piling up gambling debts, etc (the 3 Bs: Babes, Booze, Bets), and feel they cannot let anyone know about their situation without ruining their reputation. Other theories stress the 'culture at the top' notion, which sets the tone for the ethical climate in the organization. The whole world of business is kept in line by what is called 'economism'—a self-regulating compliance strategy based on the deterrent effects of economic sanctions and civil penalties. This inherently places a lot of trust in the personalities of those who work in business.

Most white-collar crime cases are won on the issue of intent (or motivation). However, offenders are probably as complex as the laws and regulations in this area. The required mental states, for example, range from 'negligently' to 'recklessly' to 'knowingly', depending upon what type of white-collar crime you're talking about. Prosecution, or more specifically, deciding who prosecutes, opens up a cornucopia of agencies, all with joint and/or overlapping responsibilities. In some cases, the level of cooperation is well-known, such as between the FBI (threat of criminal charges) and FTC (civil cease and desist orders), but OSHA inspectors have only recently been equipped with police powers, and the investigative arms of many other agencies are not well-known.

One of the most important things in investigation of white-collar crime is the need for partnership and teamwork. Intelligence work in this area is often disorganized and inefficient, and a team approach can solve this. The Treasury Department, for example, may have the money-laundering analysis expertise, and a local police department may have a proven ability to produce analytical activity charts. The 'strike force' model is one of the most common team approaches in law enforcement. This establishes a network of agencies all working on different aspects of the problem.

Another thing that should not be overlooked is the corporation itself. Businesses spend millions of dollars a year conducting internal audits. Along these lines, one should not neglect the private security force employed by the corporation. Their employees can be valuable sources of information. In addition, sometimes the employees of the organization itself can be induced to 'snitch' or 'whistle blow' on other employees.

The main piece of evidence that will be viewed most strongly in court is any evidence of disguise or cover-up. This will ordinarily be presumed as evidence of intent under most legal standards. Concealment of the violation is therefore the most vital piece of evidence to look for. This necessarily involves unravelling the 'paper trail' and pouring over a large roomful of obscure documents. Many agencies have hired college students or recruited interns to temporarily help them with these chores. Records analysis is something that may take years to complete, but then you have to focus on individual offenders eventually. But with records analysis, you should look for:

- Maintenance of two sets of books or records
- Destruction of any books or records
- Payments to fictitious companies or persons
- False invoices or billings and double payments on billings
- Company loans to employees or other persons
- Large or frequent currency transactions
- Use of photocopies instead of original documents
- Presence of second or third party endorsements on checks

Over the years, a certain number of 'indicators' have tended to be a composite of the white-collar criminal. These indicators include:

- The presence of illegal income
- The presence of large cash transactions
- The presence of multiple bank accounts
- The sudden ownership of one or more businesses
- Multiple businesses at one address

- Corporations with little or no physical assets (paper corporations)
- Out-of-country bank accounts

Beside proof of intent (via habit and character evidence) which satisfies the mens rea element of crime, and proof of destruction or cover-up (via shredded or duplicate documents) which satisfies the actus reus element of crime, AND the testimony of at least one witness (via an informant or snitch co-worker), the intelligence analyst should be prepared for the court to expect the introduction of charts diagramming the scheme or conspiracy. Such charts require an understanding of conspiracy. A conspiracy is difficult to prove, and may only be capable of being demonstrated using forensic science.

Lifestyle Factors and Indicators

CEOs don't travel First Class, they travel 'Their Class' in private jets—no lines, no mingling with the peons, and their favourite toy (business expense) is the Gulfstream's G450 jet, which flies 5,000 miles non-stop, costs $33 million, and is equipped with deerskin seats, mahogany cabinets, Persian carpets, flat-screen video displays with surround-sound systems, walk-in showers, and 24K gold-plated fixtures. Arrogance, rudeness, and imperiousness characterize their relationships with others, and their lifestyles can be described as nothing other than opulent and lavish. Once the adored 'white knights' of the US economy, CEOs and their glamorous lifestyles began to fall from grace with the stock market crash in 2001 and the Enron scandal in 2002. Juries are finding it easier and easier to return findings of guilt or fault because they simply cannot identify with the level of selfish greed involved. What is it, however, that turns a 'pillar of the community' into a corporate criminal? There are several speculations, none of which are really well-supported by criminological research, but interesting nonetheless.

1. **They think they can get away with it**—usually one part of the corporation is doing quite well, and profits are climbing astronomically. The profits from this 'sector' are siphoned off for personal use, but some of it is funnelled back to keep the rest of the corporation from deteriorating. It's usually only when one part of the corporation is experiencing huge losses that attention is attracted.
2. **Pure greed, delusions of grandeur, or megalomania**—usually the executive is mixing in high-class company and wants to impress such folks as having the trappings of power. They want to be seen as brilliant businessmen with the Midas Touch, and will do anything it takes to maintain that impression and fund their lavish lifestyle.
3. **Psychopathic tendencies**—usually they have bullied their way to the top, learned to 'top off' their salary by raiding the corporate coffers, and developed a coterie of followers and yes-people who constantly tell them how great they are. A large portion of these offenders are discovered after a failed office romance or sexual escapade.
4. **Creative opportunities and corruption**—usually the executive is put in charge of an overseas operation and because they want to see those operations succeed, succumb to the bribery and corruption prevalent in many foreign nations, and get caught up in a slippery slope of moral decline where they end up robbing from their own corporation.

There's obviously more speculation that could be made, and one would be hard pressed to explain things like the finding that CEOs usually cheat at golf, but it's clear that an appetite for risk-taking is prevalent among senior business executives. An emerging subject along these lines is the tendency to engage in 'morally reprehensible behaviour' such as cheating on one's spouse. Marital infidelity is so common among the rich and powerful that it merits a close-up view, as follows:

Why do the Rich and Powerful Cheat So Much?

It's easy to say that power corrupts, but that doesn't really explain anything. It's also easy, as feminists do, to point to male dominance or the cultural practice of having mistresses, a custom among the rich and powerful that enjoyed widespread acceptance up to the 1960s. Psychologists, for their part, are divided over whether it's a personality trait or a biological predisposition. Some would say it just involves narcissists who think they can get away with it; and more evolutionary-oriented psychologists would say it's just some kind of testosterone-driven, biological imperative to be promiscuous. Here are some possible criminological explanations:

1. They not only think they can get away with it, but they think they can easily recover and start over if they ever get punished and lose everything for it. This is very similar to the 'double failure' hypothesis in Cloward & Ohlin's (1960) theory where the average criminal becomes a more committed criminal when they come to believe they can easily do prison time 'standing on their head'.
2. It's not the power or privilege, but the build-up of confidence, particularly self-confidence. Cheaters and liars alike tend to keep pushing the limits of how far they can keep pushing their confidence. Their egos are so big that a little self-handicapping is just a way of giving average, less-confident people a fair shot.
3. The opportunities abound, because rich and powerful men tend to have lots of opportunities to meet attractive women who are more than willing to rub elbows (or bump uglies). Unless the man is 'slumming' or engaging in some kind of low-life sexual odyssey, how can they resist such seductive temptations?

4. It's got something to do with the built-in hypocrisy that comes from high moral standards. Power can make a person stricter than they were before, especially when judging others, but along with power and the repeated judgment of others comes a tendency to be morally invincible; that the standards they set for others no longer apply to them, and/or that, in their case, their mistakes are not really moral transgressions nor any indicator of bad judgment, since, after all, they have such a great track record of being good decision-makers getting rich.

One can easily ask why such offenders are treated so lightly. The reason is that between 4,000 and 5,000 top CEOs are part of 'leadership class', and this is a tight, close-knit community, driven by reputation, status-consciousness, and powerful influence. Given the futility of trying to harshly punish such people, many criminologists have said that something like 'reintegrative shaming' or 'woodshedding' might work as a method of deterrence (Braithwaite & Geis 1982). WOODSHEDDING is a unique legal term in corporate law which takes advantage of the so-called 'corporate icon' clause in somewhat rare cases where the corporation as a whole has been found guilty or plead guilty to a crime, but criminologists have been calling for its expanded use. Top executives are frequently so status-conscious that if a judge is willing to consider an alternative sentence like a 'shaming ritual', the theory is that it will have more of an effect than some fine or sanction imposed by an impersonal, remote legal authority. Boards of directors are sometimes involved in these rituals, since "a director's fiduciary duties require them to ensure that an effective information and reporting system is in place" (1991 language of the Organizational Sentencing Guidelines). Prior to 1991, corporate directors followed the Allis-Chalmers rule (from Graham *vs* Allis-Chalmers Mfg 188 A 2d 125, 130 Del 1963) which simply stated: absence of some 'red flag' alerting them to the likelihood that corporate misconduct was going on within the company, a corporation's Board of Directors has no duty to create (or compel the creation of) a programme to detect that misconduct or to insert themselves into the processes of ensuring legal compliance, or in other words, "absent cause for suspicion there is no duty upon the directors to install and operate a corporate system of espionage to ferret out wrongdoing which they have no reason to suspect exists." Shaming rituals usually go like this:

Reintegrative Shaming Rituals

The judge is expected to conduct the proceedings with dignity, and have the CEO (and/or Board of Directors) express remorse and make concrete references to the negative aspects of the corporation's crime. The judge will then urge the participants to internalize a commitment to rules and procedures that prevent future crimes from occurring. The proceedings are conveyed to the public, and the corporation's executives apologize for the social and economic harm their company's misconduct has caused. Woodshedding is generally a compliance credit (for escaping or mitigating punishment) when a corporation admits to the gravity of the crime, accepts responsibility for the crime, hasn't pervasively disregarded the law, and/or self-reported the offence or participated in the investigation of it.

The Psychological Approach

It is often the case that when backed into a corner, the typical white-collar criminal will commit suicide, or in some cases, because they are very old, will die of natural or semi-natural causes. Sometimes, even upon learning they are under investigation, they suffer heart attacks, serious ailments, travel overseas, move or liquidate capital, and hire their own investigators as well as let loose a 'dream team' of lawyers. A certain amount of manoeuvring and resistance is to be expected by people with vast resources, and it is not uncommon for the post-investigation phase to reveal more incriminating information than the pre-investigation phase. It is therefore a common approach that after the suspect dies, an investigation still goes on. The most common criminological technique in this case is known as a psychological autopsy. The elements involved in a psychological autopsy are as follows:

1. Alcohol and drug history, descendent's history of dealing with stress, medical history, family medical history, recent stressors in the victim's life, military history, employment history, educational history, sexual history, dietary history.
2. Interpersonal relationships, writings by the deceased, books and music owned by the deceased, web sites visited, phone calls made, recent conversations with friends, acquaintances, relatives, co-workers, and teachers, interests and hobbies shared with others, old and current enemies.
3. Reactions by any of the above parties to the victim's death, especially as to the degree of lethality, as well as the usual questions about early warning signs and who might have intended harm.
4. Assessment of intention about the role of the descendent in their own demise, including any sub-intentional, covert, or unconscious role, this obtained by analysing the pattern of how the victim went about accomplishing their goals or life plans.
5. Fantasies, dreams, thoughts, premonitions, fears, or phobias of the victim, socio-emotional mood swings, mental status exam, concentration and judgment abilities, IQ.
6. Timeline of events leading up to the day of the deceased's death.

Because investigative resources are almost always limited, investigators also usually follow the standard procedures that criminal justice agencies use in prioritizing cases to investigate. This is sometimes called the triage concept, but it is more commonly referred to as working the solvability factors. Such factors determine which cases are investigated at the expense of others, and include but are not limited to the following: the availability of witnesses and those willing to testify, the amount and kind of loss, the evidence that can be reconstructed, related crimes, and the desires of victimized parties. For white-collar crime, we can add the factor of 'traceability of stolen assets'. The most serious crimes that have the best chances of being solved are usually assigned before the less serious with little or no chance of being solved. Put another way, the method of investigating is similar to triage at an emergency room; someone bleeding will be treated before someone with a sprain, regardless of how long the sprain has been waiting. Police departments only investigate identity theft, for example, when there is cooperation from banks, a collateral crime is involved (eg, forgery), and the victim has filed a complaint in a timely manner. It is important to know these criminal justice procedures if a successful criminal justice prosecution is the goal. Most detective bureaus follow a strict 90-day rule, which can be represented as follows:

If ...	Then ...
The solvability factors are all present	Continue the investigation.
One or more of the factors is missing	Close the investigation.

The science of crime reconstruction also offers some guidance in what to look for, especially in terms of making sense out of all the possible kinds of evidence collected, and how interpretation of this evidence should take place in the investigator's mind. Remember that you are not on a 'fishing expedition' to find out everything bad about a suspect. There is also something called the 'SILVER PLATTER DOCTRINE' which means that you cannot hand over incriminating evidence (possibly collected in violation of the exclusionary rule) to the local or State police if you are a private investigator or a federal one.

Detective science is mostly about induction, which is the process of reasoning where experience, skill, and observation are applied to the particulars of a case and a conclusion or generalization is drawn. Deduction is the process of reasoning that starts with a generalization or premise and then considers the logical consequences of any particulars that follow. Abduction is the process of cycling through both inductive and deductive reasoning by adding known facts until one is able to reject or retain a hypothesis. Typology (aka classification or taxonomy) is the process of arranging known facts into mutually exclusive categories. Synthesis is the process of combining separate parts or elements. Analysis is the process of starting with the whole and breaking it down into its separate parts. A hypothesis is a tentative assertion subject to verification or falsification. A theory is a somewhat verified hypothesis. Serendipity is the factor of chance or luck. Some of these terms, and others, are used in different ways by detectives:

- **Patterns:** Series of similarities that usually indicate the same person or the same *modus operandi* is involved in different crimes.
- **Leads:** Clues or breaks in the case that help move an investigation forward, usually something in a statement that was overlooked, or it could be something that comes up after a records search.
- **Tips:** Leads provided by whistleblowers or informants. Tips by definition involve specifics, like names, dates, places, addresses, phone numbers, or license plates.

- **Theories:** These are beliefs about the case that take you in one direction, at the exclusion of other possible directions.
- **Clues:** These are pieces of evidence that are consistent with the corpus delecti or elements of the crime believed to have been committed or that the suspect will eventually be charged with.
- **Modus Operandi:** Behaviours learned by the offender in order to successfully complete the crime.
- **Signature:** Things about the case that represent the unique psychological or emotional characteristics of the offender.

Crime reconstruction typically starts with inductive reasoning, then proceeds to deductive reasoning, then involves a breaking down or analysis of facts, and then involves a building up of facts or synthesis. The number and kind of facts, together with any ambiguity or doubt associated with them, determine the level of evidentiary value. The process is almost exactly the same as the scientific method:

- **Step 1:** State the problem by looking at what type of crime was committed, the legal elements of the crime, and the characteristics of the jurisdiction where the crime was committed.
- **Step 2:** Form a hypothesis by looking at the physical evidence and interviewing the victim or witnesses to determine motive and possible suspects.
- **Step 3:** Collect data by doing records checks and police checks, re-interviewing the victim, witnesses, and suspects, while trying to obtain additional witnesses and exemplar or comparison samples from suspects.
- **Step 4:** Test hypotheses by evaluating how truthful and reliable the stories are of each party to the crime, and weigh their stories against the physical evidence and any

known physical laws that could possibly reinterpret the physical evidence.

- **Step 5:** Follow up on the most promising hypotheses (theories) with any and all procedures (eg, surveillance, stings) that might prove or disprove that a particular suspect is the offender.
- **Step 6:** Draw conclusions that are supported by court-admissible evidence leading to the arrest, prosecution, and conviction of the offender.

The conclusions of a crime reconstruction should take one of four forms about the sequence of events:

1. it can be shown to have occurred in a given manner;
2. it can be shown to have likely occurred in a given manner;
3. it can be shown to have unlikely occurred in a given manner; or
4. it cannot be shown to have occurred in a given manner.

Dishonesty All the Way Up the Food Chain

At the base of the food chain some home-buyers lied about their income and received loans that were beyond their means to repay. Loan officers required no documentation so that anyone could buy a house, hence the 'liar loans'.

The financial melt-down has been thoroughly described many times before and will not be rehashed here except to point out that the same sort of duplicity worked its way up the feeding chain of the financial system. Banks used fraudulent loan vehicles that were designed to make mortgage holders default, such as the infamous teaser rates. Then they bundled up the junk mortgages into 'investment grade' bonds with the collusion of corrupt rating agencies. Wall Street traders used complex derivatives that levered up the already colossal sums involved in real-estate backed bonds by a factor of about thirty and gambled like drunken sailors.

The ensuing debacle is well-known; the loss of household wealth, the worldwide recession, the loss of tens of millions of jobs. Despite the worldwide chaos and pain, no successful charges have been brought against the banks or Wall Street firms who precipitated in the collapse through their sharp practices and shady dealings despite some trials (eg, Ralph Cioffi and Matthew Tannen).

The real reason may be that it is so difficult to separate the sheep from the wolves. The apparent victims and the apparent confidence tricksters were in cahoots at all levels of a complex worldwide fraud. If you have lied on your loan application, it is hard to complain that the loan officer exploited you.

Past Predicts Future

A good predictor of what someone will do in the future is what he or she has done in the past, a maxim that provides the basis for many of the decisions made by the criminal justice system. Many personality traits and behavioural patterns remain stable throughout life. There is a certain degree of continuity in how we interact with our environment. With respect to criminality, for example, several researchers have shown that the childhood traits of timidity, restlessness, and aggressiveness are remarkably persistent, at least into early adulthood.

Some psychopaths continue to commit offences, especially violent ones, until they die. Although many decrease their criminal activities, they remain egocentric, shallow, manipulative, and callous. Many learn to satisfy their needs in ways that are not as grossly antisocial as before.

Some psychopaths use charm, deceit, and manipulation to gain the confidence of victims. They are the breed of predators whose charming demeanour and anaemic conscience are the basis of white-collar crime, calculated crimes of greed driven by a lust for power. With instincts as savage as the street brute, theirs is the work of incalculable evil. One of their typical characteristics is facile distortion of reality even when they know that others are aware of the facts.

A comprehensive analysis of the white-collar criminal mind reveals a relentless drive to accumulate wealth, the use of people to obtain that end, the abandonment of all emotion and human attachment other than self-love, and the ability to rationalize behaviour toward victims. White-collar criminal psychopaths pretend to wish to be liked by everyone and to fear losing face, but in reality, they consider victims to be stupid in trusting or believing them. Victims deserve the consequences. They betray trust with stunning callousness.

Psychopathic abusers take what's available to satisfy their own needs thinking nothing of the devastating physical and emotional damage upon victims while misusing their positions of power and trust. Because a lot of people are surprisingly gullible, with an unshakable belief in the inherent goodness of others, they are vulnerable to the psychopath. Most people do not want to face the humiliation of being found out to be a sucker.

Intellectual psychopaths construct a facade of normalcy to get what they want with relative impunity as they transcend the bounds of conventional thought, driven by a remorseless need to, supposedly, express themselves.

Without compassion for other human beings, psychopaths are fast talking, charming, self-assured, at ease in social situations, cool under pressure, unfazed by the possibility of being found out, and totally ruthless.

Pathological lying and manipulation are not restricted to psychopaths. What makes psychopaths different from all others is the remarkable ease with which they lie, the persuasiveness of their deception, and the callousness with which they carry it out. They frequently use contradictory and logically inconsistent statement that usually escape detection. They have an uncanny ability to move words and people around easily.

Psychopaths differ from others in the way their brains are organized and in the connections between words and emotion. They seem to have difficulty in monitoring their own speech; they may let loose with a convoluted barrage of poorly connected words and thoughts.

In most people, the two sides of the brain have different, specialized functions. The left cerebral hemisphere is skilled at processing information analytically and sequentially, and it plays a crucial role in the understanding and use of language. The right hemisphere processes information simultaneously, as a whole. It plays an important role in the perception of spatial relations, imagery, emotional experience, and the processing of music.

Bilateral language processes are characteristic of psychopaths. They have an inefficient control over speech. Each hemisphere tries to control speech, which is poorly integrated and monitored. Psychopaths know the dictionary meaning of words, but fail to comprehend or appreciate their emotional value or significance. The heart of psychopathy is that language is two-dimensional, lacking in emotional depth.

It is the emotionally charged thoughts, images, and internal dialogue that give the bite to conscience, account for its powerful control over behaviour, and generate guilt and remorse for transgressions. Beyond the intellectual awareness of the meaning of words, psychopaths lack the related feelings.

If the language of psychopaths is bilateral-controlled by both sides of the brain-it is possible that other brain processes normally controlled by one hemisphere are also under bilateral control in the psychopath. In most people, the right side of the brain plays a central role in emotion. Recent laboratory evidence indicates that in psychopaths, neither side of the brain is proficient in the processes of emotion, implying that their emotions are divided and unfocused, resulting in a shallow and colourless emotional life.

Most language-related hand gestures convey no information or meaning to the listener. Small, rapid hand movements or gestures seem to facilitate speech. High rates of such gestures appear to reflect difficulty in converting thoughts and feelings into speech. Psychopaths use more gestures than do normal people.

Psychopaths' thoughts and ideas are organized into rather small mental packages and are readily moved around. This can be a distinct advantage when it comes to lying. Research indicates that skilled liars are able to break down ideas, concept and language into basic components and then recombine them in a variety of ways, almost as though they were playing Scrabble. The most competent liar often uses a thin truth line to help keep track of what he says and to ensure that his story appears consistent to the listener. The most mischievous liars are those who keep sliding on the verge of truth.

Not Skilled Liar

Psychopaths are not the skilled liars we often make them out to be. Their speech is full of inconsistent or contradictory statements. They fail to integrate the pieces into a coherent whole; their truth line is fragmented and patchy, at best. Most of us are able to combine ideas so that they are consistent with some underlying theme, but psychopaths seem to have difficulty doing so. This helps to explain the wild inconsistencies and contradictions that frequently characterize their speech. They use neologisms (combinations of the basic components of words—syllables—in ways that seem logical to them but inappropriate to others). Their mental packages are not only small, but are also two-dimensional—devoid of emotional meaning. Their words are unencumbered by emotional baggage and can be used in ways that seem odd to the rest of us in that they are logically and effectively incongruous.

Communication Abnormality

The communications of psychopaths sometimes are subtly odd and part of a general tendency to change topics, to go off on irrelevant tangents, and to fail to connect phrases and sentences in a straightforward manner. They are notorious for not answering the question posed to them or for answering in a way that seems unresponsive to the question. They may make it difficult for their listeners to understand parts of their narrative. With them, breakdowns in communication are more frequent, more serious, and possibly indicative of and underlying condition in which the organization of mental activity—but not its content—is defective. It is how they string words and sentences together, not what they actually say, that suggests abnormality.

Psychopaths' responses are often tangential and interpreted as evasive or glib. They often convincingly malinger—fake mental illness—with their ability to manipulate experienced psychiatrists and psychologists. Contradictions, evasiveness, and rationalizations and excuses often mark their statements. Such mental carelessness and lack of continuity indicate a defective self-monitoring of speech. These oddities in speech are often too subtle for the casual observer to detect, and they put on a good show. We are sucked in not by what they say, but by how they say it and by the emotional buttons they push while saying it.

Understand the Rules

Psychopaths meet current legal and psychiatric standards for sanity. They understand the rules of society and the conventional meanings of right and wrong. They are capable of controlling their behaviour, and they are aware of the potential consequences of their acts. Their problem is that this knowledge frequently fails to deter them from antisocial behaviour. They understand the intellectual rules of the game but the emotional rules are lost to them. They know enough about what they are doing to be held accountable for their actions.

Psychopaths see any social exchange as a feeding opportunity, a contest, or a test of wills, in which there can be only one winner. Their motives are to manipulate and take, ruthlessly and without remorse.

It is primarily the show, not eloquent use of language that attracts our attention and cons us. Good looks, a touch of charisma, a flood of words, contrived distractions, or a knack for knowing which buttons to press is the alluring bait that is devastating to the vulnerable victim.

Effective Body Language

Society runs on trust, and we ordinarily pay more attention to what someone says than to the accompanying non-verbal behaviour—hand gestures, facial movements, smiles, and eye contact. However, when the speaker is attractive and gives a really impressive non-verbal performance, the effect can be reversed.

We watch the show and pay little attention to what is said. Psychopaths' effective body language causes us to follow their actions rather than their words as they use intensive eye contact, leaning forward, moving closer, and so forth. Such behaviour tends to distract, impress, control, or intimidate us, drawing our attention away from what is actually being said.

Psychopaths are sure to find and exploit any weak spots in your psychological make-up. They have an uncanny ability to detect vulnerabilities and push the right buttons for personal gain. They callously use the lonely, those needing to find a purpose in their lives, and they prey on the confused, the frail, and the helpless. They recognize and turn to their own advantage the hang-ups and self-doubts that most people have. They use sweet-talk, honey-coated words, flattery, and promises with their uncanny ability to spot and use, for example, nurturing women who have a powerful need to help or mother others.

The psychopathic personality is a person whose development along social and moral lines has not progressed normally and who cannot adjust to social and moral standards. Psychopaths are supremely selfish, caring nothing about anyone else. They live only for what they can get out of life without regard to the consequences.

Most people look to the future as important and strive with hope. To the psychopath, the future is of no concern because he or she is incapable of constructive long-term planning. Psychopaths have no understanding of, and even express contempt for, the future. Normal individuals often make sacrifices for the possibilities of the future, and are willing to defer certain satisfactions in the present for the more important ones in the future. These selfish tendencies are summarized as the secondary symptoms arising from the fundamentals or primary defects are the lack or diminished sense of guilt, absence of sense of gratitude, justification of the means by the end to be attained, complete disregard for the consequences of action, lack of discretion judgment and wisdom, impulsiveness, peculiar ability to ingratiate himself, and inability to profit by experience.

It has become clear during the past years that there is no successful treatment for psychopathy, and the outlook for finding such a treatment is not good. There is no satisfactory treatment for them. Therefore, proficient investigators will consider this group of human beings as a continued challenge. Psychiatrists have, so far, been unable to do any good once the behaviour pattern has been established. Psychopaths do not learn from experience their mode of behaviour is inflexible. Nor can they be corrected by punishment. To them, punishment is always unjust; it has no effect.

Although psychopaths differ from each other in almost all respects, as any cross-section of society does, each has in common an utter lack of empathy and sincerity and an absolute disregard for the consequences of his or her acts. Neither long terms in prison nor restraint in psychiatric hospitals affects their conduct or line of reasoning. When free, they continue in crime.

Use of Pronouns Helps in Detecting Truth

It is often said that though the tongue helps in telling lie yet one's face revolts against him. The research of the British scientist have confirmed this fact and they have succeeded in opening the secret code hidden in the human face. And they can easily identify the face at the time of telling lie. According to research of British Colombia University, they identified the 'five tell-tale muscle groups' which controls the expression of the human face. Through these muscle group they can identify the human face which is not natural at the time of telling lie. In their research they could identify such human face who had murdered their relative but were crying falsely to investigate and find the lost relatives to deviate and mislead the investigators.

In English there are about 500 function words, and about 150 are really common. Content words—nouns, verbs, adjectives, and most adverbs—convey the guts of communication. They're how we express ideas with. Function words help shape and short-cut language. People require social skills to I use and understand function words, and they're processed in the brain differently. They are the key to understanding relationships between speakers, objects and other people. Pronouns tell us where people focus their attention. If someone uses the pronoun 'I', it's a sign of self-focus. Say someone asks "What's the weather outside?" You could answer "It's hot" or "I think it's hot." The "I think" may seem insignificant, but it's quite meaningful. It shows you're more focused on yourself. Depressed people use the word 'I' much more often than emotionally stable people. People who are lower in status use 'I' much more frequently. A person who's lying tends to use 'we' more or use sentences without a first-person pronoun at all. Instead of saying "I didn't take your book," a liar might say "That's not the kind of thing that anyone with integrity would do." People who are honest use exclusive words like 'but' and 'without' and negations such as 'no', 'none', and 'never' much more frequently.

Black Truth

We can also understand truth by the following example—

> You're driving along obeying all the traffic rules when a cop flags you down. He gets in and says he has to be somewhere in a hurry and tells you to step on the gas and go faster than the authorised speed limit. If you listened to him, would you be breaking the law? Or, if you didn't, would you be breaking the law too? The cop could be on the trail of a terrorist who's about to detonate a bomb in a crowded mall full of women and children. He has no way of getting through to his precinct police station and, therefore, it's only up to him (and you) now to stop the bomber from taking innocent lives. Or, he may have got information that his girl friend's going to meet another man in the same mall and he wants to catch her red-handed.

That, in a nutshell, was also Yudhisthira's dilemma when Krishna told him to, well, tell a lie because the battle was basically going nowhere with Dronacharya still alive. However, if he came to know that his son Aswathama had died, he would lose all will to fight on. Luckily, fate had arranged for an elephant of the same name to have been killed recently, so where was the harm, felt Krishna, in Yudhisthira telling Dronacharya that Aswathama is dead"? But Yudhisthira refused and said, instead Aswathama, the elephant, is dead," while Krishna blew his conch loud over the two extra words ... and Kurukshetra went to the Pandavas. Which brings us back to the cop. Would you say something like, "Sorry, my car's just had an engine overhaul and won't go over 50?" After all, you're not God you don't know what's going on in the mall. Better to disobey or tell a black truth.

Human behaviour that lacks integrity leads to value destruction. Some common beliefs, actions and activities in finance that are inconsistent with being a person or a firm of integrity. Each of these beliefs leads to a system that lacks integrity, ie, one that is not whole and complete and, therefore, creates unworkability and destroys value. Focusing on these phenomena from the integrity viewpoint, makes it possible for managers to focus on the value that can be created by putting the system back in integrity and correcting the non-value maximising equilibrium that exists in capital markets. Overall, a purely positive theory of integrity that has no normative elements whatsoever, and demonstrates how it applies to both individuals and organisations.

In effect, integrity is a factor of production just like knowledge, technology, labour and capital, but it is undistinguished—and its affect (by its presence or absence) is huge. Positive theory of integrity that has no normative content, are large gains from putting integrity into finance into both the theory and practice of finance. Integrity as being whole and complete and unbroken. If finance scholars, teachers and practitioners take this approach to applications in finance, there are huge gains to be achieved.

Observe Breathing to Detect Lie

Appearances are very deceptive. They may give you respectability but they cannot give you contentment. The truth has a way of surfacing. It cannot be repressed forever. If it can be repressed forever, then it is not truth. In the very definition of truth, one should include the fact that truth has a way of bubbling up. You cannot go on avoiding it forever. One day or other, knowingly or unknowingly, it surfaces; it reveals itself. A good indicator of whether you are living the truth is the way you breathe, says OSHO. Truth is that which reveals itself. And just the opposite are lies. You cannot make a lie appear as truth forever and ever. One day the truth will surface and the lie will be condemned. You cannot avoid truth. It is better to face it, accept it and live it. Once you start living the life of truth, authenticity, of your original face, all troubles disappear by and by, because the conflict drops and you are no more divided. Your voice has a unity then, your whole being becomes an orchestra. Right now, when you say something, your body says something else; when your tongue says something, your eyes go on saying something else simultaneously. Truth has a way of surfacing one day. Truth can never be repressed forever because it reveals itself.

Watch and Observe

Many times people come. And they say, "We are very, very happy." And it cannot be believed because their faces are so dull—no joy, no delight! Their eyes have no light. And when they say, "We are happy" even the word 'happy' does not sound very happy. It sounds as if they are dragging it. Their tone, their voice, their face, the way they are sitting or standing—everything says something else. Start watching people. When they say they are happy, watch for a clue. Are they really happy?

By and by, watch yourself. When you say that you are happy but you are not, there will be a disturbance in your breathing. Your breathing cannot be natural. It is impossible, because the truth is that you are not happy. If you had said, "I am unhappy"; your breathing would have remained natural. There was no conflict. But you said, "I am happy", immediately you are repressing something—something that was coming up, you have forced down.

In this very effort; your breathing changes its rhythm; it is no longer rhythmical. Your face is no longer graceful, your eyes become cunning.

First, watch others because it will be easier to watch others. You can be more objective about them. And when you have found clues about them use the same clues about yourself. And see when you speak truth, your voice has a musical tone to it; when you speak untruth, there's a jarring note. When you speak truth you are one, together; when you speak untruth you are not together, a conflict has arisen.

Financial Interviewing and Interrogation

In any white-collar crime investigation there may be many sides to every questions and every accusation. Issues are not always simple or easily understood. Each questionable issue may be inescapably intertwined with other ambiguous issues. Nevertheless it remains the duty of investigator to seek out all the facts in question. During an investigation facts will appear from many sources, but the spoken word is potentially the largest source of the various forms of evidence available to the investigator.

Few skills are important to the white-collar crime investigator as having command of the techniques for interview and interrogation. Yet few investigators have mastered the art. Few investigators are fully satisfied with their level of performance in this vital phase of the investigation. There are many reasons for the lack of proficiency in financial investigative techniques. Among these are inadequate training in the field of financial interviewing, inadequate planning, before conducting an interview and a tendency for the investigator to under estimate the mental capabilities of the suspect. The investigator should remember that in financial matters, evidence often develops in small bits and pieces that when viewed separately, may appear to lead nowhere. Frustration is common and tactics and techniques may have to be modified and carefully employed because diligence, patience and persistence are essential to successful results.

Interview vis-a-vis Interrogation

An interview is the systematic questioning of corporative persons who have knowledge of events, persons involved or circumstances surrounding a case under investigation including the obtaining of documentary or physical evidence. And interrogation is the systematic questioning of suspects of uncooperative persons, obtain evidence or proof of significant omissions or to allow the person suspected an opportunity to volunteer facts that might have the exculpatory effect of putting the transactions under investigations in a different light.

In the investigation of embezzlement and fraud, there is little difference in two techniques. Often the line between interview and interrogation is fluid. The investigator may find while questioning a previously cooperative witness that the witness has become hostile, is withholding information or in culpable in the crime. Additionally, even a witness who is at first cooperative may become uncooperative if he becomes aware that investigation has centred on a friend or co-worker. On the other hand while interrogating a suspect the investigator may decide that the suspect in not involved in the crime, but he is willing to discuss all he knows about it. The investigator may also find that the suspect is willing to confess and reveal evidence implicating others in the scheme.

In white-collar crime cases, the major tool of the investigator uses to closed the gap between bits of information and evidence to support prosecution is the interview. It is primarily from the interview that the investigator achieves the following objectives—

1. Information that establishes the essential elements of the crimes.

2. Leads for developing the case and gathering other evidence.
3. The cooperation of the victims and witness in recounting their experiences at the time of trial.
4. Information regarding the personal background and personal and economic motives of suspects, victims and witnesses at trial.

The interview process is dependent on several factors such as personalities of each individual witness, victim and investigator, the complexity of the interview topic and the respective knowledge level of the investigator and the interviewee. Each investigator should nevertheless plan the interview and follow a proven set of guidelines to ensure maximum probabilities of achieving the objectives.

The investigator must concentrate on what the interviewee is saying. Think about one topic at a time and not about the next question. If the interviewee wanders from the question, do not stop him as the response may lead to a new line of questioning. Once the interviewee has completed an answer that strayed from the question, the investigator can bring him back to the topic with specific questions.

Remember that in an interview the investigator necessarily gives information to the interviewee regarding what kind of information the investigator wants to know. If the investigator does not want a piece of information revealed, he must be careful how he is to use it or ask questions about it in the interview.

The determination of whether an interviewee is telling the truth is always a consideration. If untruthfulness is suspected, the investigator must be prepared with facts to refute the untruthfulness. Ending an interview is always better than losing control by a confrontation based on insufficient evidence. Even an untruthful interview may be beneficial later. Witnesses and victims, who are "later confronted with evidence of their untruthfulness, might be more willing to cooperate and testify truthfully."

When an investigator suspects the interviewee is untruthful or may be culpable in the incident, be should consider two options:

1. Stop the interview immediately and make a written record of the reason. This will be especially important if the investigator suspects the interviewee may become the subject of criminal prosecution; or
2. Allow the interviewee to continue to talk on the theory that by confronting the interviewee with his own falsities, he may push the interviewee into giving valuable information.

The investigator should observe carefully the demeanour of the interviewee. They should be at ease from the beginning of the interview and remain at ease throughout.

Quality interrogation is an essential ingredient of any investigation. Unfortunately it also happens to be the most neglected aspect of any investigating process owing to certain extraneous conditions. Firstly the interrogator himself is in teasing hurry to claim the kudos for the speedy results.

Interrogation is essentially an effort to destroy the ego, self confidence and motivation level of the accused. It is a battle of wits between two minds—one trying to conceal and the interrogator inducing him to reveal. The interrogator should always feel that he is in the driver's seat and things will fall in the right place howsoever tough the offender may be. All white-collar criminals have very fat ego but feet of clay which really cannot withstand their body weight. Unjust enrichment in a very short span of time acquired by dubious means is primarily responsible for their such behaviour and with a gentle push they collapse.

Tricks to Catch-Out Liars

Despite decades of trying scientist still have not developed the perfect lie-detector test. Psychological scientists are fascinated by real-life versions of the fictional Gibbs. Detecting lies and liars is essential to effective policing and prosecution of criminals, but it's maddeningly difficult. Most of us can spot barely more than half of all lies and truths through listening and observation—meaning, of course, that we're wrong almost as often as we're right. A half-century of research has done little to polish this unimpressive track record. But scientists are still working to improve on that, and among them is cognitive psychologist Aldert Vrij of the University of Portsmouth, in the UK. Vrij has been using a key insight from his field to improve interrogation methods: The human mind, despite its impressive abilities, has limited capacity for how much thinking it can handle at any one time. So demanding additional, simultaneous thought—adding to cognitive 'load'—compromises normal information processing. What's more, lying is more cognitively demanding than telling the truth, so these compromised abilities should show up in detectable behavioural clues.

Imagine for a few minutes that you're guilty of a murder, and investigator is cross-examining you. To start, you need to invent a story, and you also have to monitor that tale constantly so that it's plausible and consistent with the known facts. That takes a lot of mental effort that innocent truth-tellers don't have to spend. You also need to actively remember the details of the story you've fabricated, so that you don't contradict yourself at any point. Remembering a fiction is much more demanding than remembering something that actually occurred. That's just to start. Because you're naturally worried about your credibility, you're most likely trying to control your demeanour. Surprisingly, 'looking honest' saps mental energy. And what's more, you're not just monitoring yourself; you're also scanning interrogation face for signs that he's seeing through your lie.

Like an actor, you have the mental demands of staying in character. And finally, you have to suppress the truth so that you don't let some damning fact slip out, another drain on your mind's limited supply of fuel. In short, telling the truth is automatic and effortless, and lying is the opposite of that. It's intentional, deliberate and exhausting.

So how can an investigator exploit the differing mental experiences of liars and truth-tellers.

One intriguing strategy is to demand that suspects tell their stories in reverse. Narrating backward increases cognitive load because it runs counter to the natural forward sequencing of events. It also disrupts the normal reconstruction of past events using mental schemes, which give coherence to isolated events. Since liars already have depleted cognitive resources, they should find this unfamiliar mental exercise more taxing than truth-tellers do—which should increase the likelihood that they will somehow betray themselves. And in fact, that's just what happens in the lab in experiment in which half the liars and truth-tellers were instructed to recall their stories in reverse order. When observers later looked at video-tapes of the complete interviews, they detected more clues to deceit in the liars who were burdened by this mental task. Indeed, observers correctly spotted only 42% of the lies in the control condition—way below average, which means they were hard to spot—but a remarkable 60% when the liars were compromised by the reverse storytelling.

Another strategy for increasing liars' cognitive burden is to insist that suspects maintain eye contact. When people have to concentrate on telling their story accurately—which liars must, more than truth-tellers—they typically look away to some motionless point, rather than directly at the conversation partner. That's because keeping eye contact is distracting, and makes narration more difficult. This strategy was tested in the lab, and again observers detected more clues to deceit in those who were required to look the interrogator in the eyes.

Psychological scientists call 'wizards'—those rare people who have extraordinary lie-detection skills. Researchers have been trying, without a lot of success, to unravel these wizards' strategies, but until they do, less sophisticated lie-catchers may be able to exploit the mind's cognitive weaknesses to catch the bad guys in their web of lies.

The world is full of liars. We all tell porkies to some degree in order to get what we want. Of course, some people lie more often than others.

Being able to hide our true intentions is useful in all sorts of areas of life—business, love, career, friendships. That's why children learn how to deceive so early on. In fact, studies have shown that the more intelligent a child is, the more likely they are to tell untruths. All of us have to negotiate this minefield of misinformation. Being tricked by a lie can lead to big disadvantages. It can cost us money, time, opportunity and many other things. Because of this, it's useful to be able to catch liars out.

Some people are excellent deceivers. So good that they make a living out of misleading others. Here are a few good tricks for uncovering them.

Look for What Motivates a Person

If you really want to understand someone, you need to discover what motivates them. Once you have an idea of what someone wants out of life, you have a pretty good shot of figuring out how they're going to behave in a particular situation. When people are focused on a specific outcome, that drive can be so powerful that it's difficult not to give it away. One method of figuring out a person's motivation is to look at the position they're in: a criminal is probably motivated by escaping punishment, an investment banker is probably motivated by a lust for money, a serial womanizer is obviously motivated by sex, and a doting mother is motivated by love for her children.

You can learn a lot about someone just by examining the station in life they've chosen. There's another useful method you can add on top of this for discovering what incentives a person is pursuing—look at their behaviour. How a person acts in certain situations tells you a lot about what drives them. Someone who quibbles over their share of a restaurant bill obviously has a deep aversion to generosity, a man who cheats on his wife doesn't think much of her deep down, a woman who interprets every conversation as being about her is clearly self-obsessed, and a person who throws up bureaucratic barriers to getting something done is probably lazy.

Concentrate on what people are doing, not what they're saying. Most of us have good control over what's coming out of our mouths—and as the old saying goes 'talk is cheap'. But actions are more difficult to manage—not least of which because they're more expensive in effort and other resources. It's easy for someone to say "I'm a generous person", but more difficult to cover the fact that they're not when it's their turn to buy a round of drinks. Once you have a good understanding of what motivates a person, catching them lying is relatively straightforward. If they say something in a situation that doesn't fit with their motivational profile, you can be pretty sure you've caught them out.

There was a technical audit coming up in a bank which meant a lot of very hard and boring work. It was important that we pass this audit, and the CEO gave us a pep-talk about it. He acknowledged we would have to work hard, but assured they would be rewarded if passed. In fact, he said this sentence about five times—"You will be rewarded." Afterwards, someone asked him what specific rewards he had in mind. "Look, you know I can't go into that now, but be assured, it will be something good," he replied.

As soon as he said that, he was lying. If someone refuses to be specific about something, then they're probably not telling the truth. That's because being explicit carries the burden of commitment, which a liar wants to avoid at all costs.

Using general terms such as "it will be good, I promise", or "of course I'll contribute something", or "don't worry, you can trust me on that point" is an almost certain sign that you're being duped. Ask for a specific details and see what reaction you get. Oh yes, and what was our reward for two months hard work on the bank's audit? Chicken sandwiches in the Boardroom on lunchtime.

Most Liars have a Tendency to Overact

There are many people who know how to lie well, but most of them have one fatal flaw—they tend to overdo it. Often, they'll try to act pious and moral while speaking with a forked tongue. If someone's using fine language and assuring everyone how pure and just their motivations are, you're almost certainly being lied to. People simply don't talk that way in everyday conversation. If you say to someone, "You're in love with Jenny, aren't you?", which of the replies below is coming from the liar?

No way am I in love with her! I'm just not interested in being with anyone at the moment. I've got to concentrate on my studies this year and it wouldn't be fair to burden someone with that. I can't believe you'd think such a thing. If you guessed reply 2, then you are, of course right. There's a line in Hamlet, "The lady protests too much, methinks" which sums this up pretty well. Liars usually go too far in trying to convince someone what they're saying is true.

Look for overacting, exaggeration, and claims of moral purity in what someone's saying, and you've almost certainly caught them out in a lie.

Tips that can Let Know if Someone isn't Telling the Whole Truth

A witness to a shooting sat in front of a trained federal agent, skilled in the art of deception detection, tried to tell him that when she heard gunshots she didn't look, she just ran-he knew she was lying. How did federal agent reach this conclusion? The answer is by recognizing telltale signs that a person isn't being honest, like inconsistencies in a story, behaviour that's different from a person's norm, or too much detail in an explanation. While using these signs to catch a liar takes extensive training and practice. Now, the average person can become adept at identifying dishonesty, and it's not as hard as you might think. Experts tell WebMD the top 10 ways to let the truth be known.

1. Inconsistencies

When you want to know if someone is lying, look for inconsistencies in what they are saying. When the woman he was questioning said she ran and hid after hearing gunshots without looking—see the inconsistency. There was something that just didn't fit. She heard gunshots but she didn't look? It is fact that was inconsistent with how a person would respond to a situation like that. So when she wasn't paying attention, he banged on the table. She looked right at him. When a person hears a noise, it's a natural reaction to look toward it, she heard those gunshots, looked in the direction from which they came, saw the shooter, and then ran. Sure enough, he was right. Her story was just illogical And that's what you should look for when you're talking to someone who isn't being truthful. Are there inconsistencies that just don't fit?

2. Ask the Unexpected

About 4% of people are accomplished liars and they can do it well. But because there are no Pinocchio responses to a lie, you have to catch them in it. Sir Walter Scott put it best: "Oh what a tangled web we weave, when first we practice to deceive. But how can you a catch a person in his own web of lies? Watch them carefully. And then when they don't expect it, ask them one question that they are not prepared to answer to trip them up.

3. Gauge Against a Baseline

One of the most important indicators of dishonesty is changes in behaviour," says Maureen O'Sullivan, PhD, a Professor of Psychology at the University of San Francisco. "You want to pay attention to someone who is generally anxious, but now looks calm. Or, someone who is generally calm but now looks anxious. The trick explains O'Sullivan, is to gauge their behaviour against a baseline. Is a person's behaviour falling away from how they would normally act? If it is, that could mean that something is up.

4. Look for insincere Emotions

Most people can't take smile. The timing will be wrong, it will be held too long, or it will be blended with other things. Maybe it will be a combination of an angry face with a smile; you can tell because their lips are smaller and less full than in a sincere smile. These fake emotions are a good indicator that something has gone afoul.

5. Pay Attention to Gut Reactions

People say, "Oh, it was a gut reaction or women's intuition," but what I think they are picking up on, are the deviations of true emotions. While an average person might not know what it is he's seeing when he thinks someone isn't being honest and attributes his suspicion to instinct, a scientist would be able to pinpoint it exactly.

6. Watch for Micro Expressions

A micro expression is a very brief expression, usually about 25th of a second, that is always a concealed emotion, says Ekman, PhD, Professor Emeritus of Psychology at the Universit of California Medical School in San Francisco. So when a perso is acting happy, but in actuality he is really upset abou something, for instance, his true emotion will be revealed in subconscious flash of anger on his face. Whether the concealed emotion is fear, anger, happiness, or jealousy, that feeling will appear on the face in the blink of an eye. The trick is to see it. Almost everyone—99% of those we've tested in about 10,000 people—won't see them. But it can be taught. In fact, in less than an hour, the average person can learn to see micro-expressions.

7. Look for Contradictions

The general rule is anything that a person does with their voice or their gesture that doesn't fit the words they are saying can indicate a lie. For example, this is going to sound amazing, but it is true. Sometimes when people are lying and saying, 'Yes, she's the one that took the money,' they will without knowing it make a slight head shake 'no'. That's a gesture and it completely contradicts what they're saying in words. These contradictions, can be between the voice and the words, the gesture and the voice, the gesture and the words, or the face and the words. It's some aspect of demeanour that is contradicting another aspect.

8. Sense of Unease

When someone isn't making eye contact and that's against how they normally act, it can mean they're not being honest, says Jenn Berman, a Psychologist. They look away, they're sweating, they look uneasy ... anything that isn't normal and indicates anxiety.

9. Too Much Detail

When you say to someone, "Oh, where were you?" and they say, "I went to the store and I needed to get eggs and milk and sugar and I almost hit a dog so I had to go slow," and on and on, they're giving you too much detail. Too detail could mean they've put a lot of thought into how they're going to get out of a situation and they've crafted a complicated lie as a solution.

10. Don't Ignore the Truth

It's more important to recognize when someone is telling the truth than telling a lie because people can look like they're lying but could be telling the truth. While it sounds confusing, finding the truth buried under a lie can sometimes help find the answer to an important question: Why is a person lying?

These 10 truth tips, experts agree, all help detect deception. What they don't do is tell you why a person is lying and what the lie means. Micro expressions don't tell you the reason. They just tell you what the concealed emotion is and that there is an emotion being concealed. When you think someone is lying, you have to either know the person well enough to understand why he or she might lie, or be a people expert. You can see a micro expression, but you have to have more social-emotional intelligence on people to use it accurately. You have to be a good judge of people to understand what it means.

Be Trusting

In general we have a choice about which stance we take in life. If we take a suspicious stance, life is not going to be too pleasant but we won't get misled very often. If we take a trusting stance, life is going to be a lot more pleasant but sometimes we are going to be taken in. As a parent or a friend, you're much better off being trusting rather than looking for lies all the time.

How to Spot a Liar

Not to rely on anyone signal. You'll be more successful if you look for clusters of behaviours (three or four body language cues that reinforce one another). To increase your chances of spotting a falsehood, watch for a cluster of body language clues that include:

1. **Fake Smile:** It's hard for liars to give a real smile while seeking to deceive. (Real smiles crinkle the corners of

the eyes and change the entire face. Faked smiles involve the mouth only.)

2. **Unusual Response Time:** When the lie is planned (and rehearsed), deceivers start their answers more quickly than truth-tellers. If taken by surprise, however, the liar takes longer to respond—as the process of inhibiting the truth and creating a lie takes extra time.
3. **Verbal Cues:** When lying, a person's vocal tone will rise to a higher pitch. Other verbal cues include rambling, selective wording (in which one avoids answering the question exactly as asked), stammering, and the use of qualifiers ("To the best of my knowledge." "I could be wrong..."). It's also been noted that liars use fewer contractions: "I did not have sex with that woman..." rather than "I didn't..."
4. **Under or Over Production of Saliva:** Watch for sudden swallowing in gulps or the increased need to drink water or moisten lips.
5. **Pupil Dilation:** One non-verbal signal that is almost impossible to fake is pupil dilation. The larger pupil size that most people experience when telling a lie can be attributed to an increased amount of tension and concentration.
6. **Change in Blink Rate:** A person's blink rate slows down as she decides to lie and stays low through the lie. Then it increases rapidly (sometimes up to eight times normal rate) after the lie.
7. **Foot Movements:** When lying, people will often display nervousness and anxiety through increased foot movements. Feet will fidget, shuffle and wind around each other or around the furniture. They will stretch and curl to relieve tension, or even kick out in a miniaturized attempt to run away.

8. **Face Touching:** A person's nose may not grow when he tells a lie, but watch closely and you'll notice that when someone is about to lie or make an outrageous statement, he'll often unconsciously rub his nose. (This is most likely because a rush of adrenaline opens the capillaries and makes his nose itch.) Mouth covering is another common gesture of people who are being untruthful, as is covering the eyes.
9. **Incongruence:** When a person believes what she is saying her gestures and expressions are in alignment with her words. When you see a mismatch—where gestures contradict words—such as a side-to-side head shake while saying 'yes' or a person frowning and staring at the ground while telling you she is happy, it's a sign of deceit or at least an inner conflict between what that person is thinking and saying.
10. **Changes in gestures:** Most of the times, in the effort not to let their gestures 'give away' the lie, deceivers will hold their bodies unnaturally still. At other times, especially after being asked a searching question, you may notice liars accelerate pacifying gestures—biting their lips, rubbing their hands together, fidgeting with jewellery, touching their hair.
11. **Micro-Expressions:** Difficult to catch, but if you ever spot a fleeting expression that contradicts a verbal statement, believe what you see and not what you hear.
12. **The Quick-Check Glance:** This may follow a less-than-truthful response: Liars will immediately look down and away, then back at you again in a brief glimpse to see if you bought the falsehood.

One Final Caveat: If a person really believes the lie, there is no way that can detect that falsehood. But, unless you are dealing with a pathological liar or a superb actor, I know you can become better at spotting those who try to deceive you.

Obstacles to Successful Interviewing

The white-collar crime investigator often faces problems and obstacles to interviewing that relate to certain characteristics of victims and witnesses.

Somewhere in the human psyche lies an element that induces many people to hand over their savings rather than risk the possibility that some total stranger might think them stupid. If this element did not exist, neither would the fine art of swindling. This element provides the greatest obstacle to the investigator, first in locating victims, and second in getting victims and witnesses to participate in a situation, such as an interview or court proceeding, in which they must admit being duped. The guile, deception, and trickery common to frauds often silence the victim.

Both privately owned and government enterprises operate based on public trust and confidence. The commission of a white-collar crime involving such institutions may cause not only the initial financial loss, but the attendant publicity may also cause a loss of prestige or public trust. Consequently, the enterprise may elect to suffer the financial loss rather than risk a loss of public confidence.

The victim, whether an individual or corporation, may have already related a false or incorrect account of the incident to family, stockholders or the press and may feel a need to continue with the false account. Most victims do not welcome protracted court proceedings and appearances, especially when they feel they have nothing to gain.

A witness who is not a victim may be uncooperative for a variety of reasons such as fear of reprisal, a dislike for law enforcement, and fear of self-incrimination. Even totally innocent witnesses may feel the problem is not theirs, and it is not worth their time to help in the investigation. Technical experts, such as lawyers or accountants, may be reluctant to participate at the onset fearing the invitation of future civil liability.

Overcoming Obstacles to Interviewing

The investigator can use certain techniques to overcome obstacles to interviewing. The specific situations will determine the proper approach.

When confronting a witness who has made previous denials or given inconsistent statements, the investigator should:

1. persist in following up every question or topic to its logical conclusion;
2. pursue the same topic from a variety of perspectives, any of which might help to generate additional responses; and
3. be ready to use all information obtained earlier, whether from the documents or memory, to refute denials and inconsistencies and to impart varying degrees of damaging information about the scheme and its promoters.

In all cases, especially those involving private and governmental agencies, the investigator should help the victims reduce their embarrassment. When applicable, the investigator should also show that he stands ready to give credit for a victim's or witness's assistance in the investigation. If the investigator is working for a private concern, he should tell victims or witnesses that he will note their cooperation, or lack of it, in whatever report the investigator prepares for his client, usually the victim's or witness's employer.

The investigator may find it desirable to encourage cooperation because cooperation will protect others from similar victimization. He can appeal to the victim's or witness's urge to fight back.

When attempting to gain cooperation, being sympathetic to the victim's or witness's attitudes is always advisable, even if they impede swift resolution to the obstacles. Make the interviewee feel like part of the team.

Most victims are interested in restitution. The investigator may point out that a court may order restitution. He should make sure, however, that the victim realizes restitution is not certain. He can explain to the victim that information uncovered in a criminal investigation is often admissible in a civil action for damages.

Common Mistakes in Financial Interviewing

Often, if the investigator approaches the witness too soon, he will not have developed sufficient incentives for the witness to cooperate. Always take time to analyse what could go wrong in an interview. The investigator should decide in advance what information he needs from the interview, and decide what concessions he can make to obtain it.

Identify the suspect's possible defences, either real or contrived, by analysing his responses to questions concerning the matter under investigation, and by that, find ways to neutralize those defences; or

Confront the suspect with the evidence and allow him an opportunity to provide an explanation or exculpatory evidence.

Whether to Interrogate

The investigator must realize that interrogating the suspect in embezzlement or financial fraud is not always desirable. Obtaining a goal of an interrogation is not assured, and an interrogation is not without risk. Investigators must consider the unique aspects of each case before deciding whether to attempt an interrogation. If the chances of realizing one goal of an interrogation are negligible, the investigator only risks revealing his own information to the suspect. The investigator must consider

1. the type of suspect, his age, education level, status in the community, experience and history; and
2. the scheme itself, the sophistication, the complexity, the scope, and the permanence.

There are many pitfalls inherent in the decision to interrogate a suspect. Such pitfalls are most pronounced when evidence of a suspect's guilt has not yet developed or if an attorney is present. Such pitfalls include:

1. the possibility that they may compromise or stymie the investigation by revealing that an investigation is underway;
2. a chance the suspect may learn something that will enable him to obscure or fabricate evidence or influence witnesses;
3. the possibility that alerting the suspect of an investigation may give him time to flee the jurisdiction before the investigator can file charges; and
4. the possibility that the investigator may waste time following fictitious leads or information the suspect gives.

The likelihood of an experienced white-collar criminal exposing information or making incriminating statements is not good. Many white-collar criminals have above average intelligence and, as a normal prerequisite for the trade, are accomplished liars. Investigators are not always immune to those skills.

The interrogation of a suspect may be totally unnecessary when the investigation reveals overwhelming evidence. It may be demoralizing for the suspect to believe that the case against him is so strong that investigators never felt it necessary to speak with him about the accusations.

When considering whether to interrogate a suspect the investigator should also know legal consequences may imperil the case. A court may suppress evidence crucial to the investigation gathered from such an interrogation, thereby destroying the possibility of prosecution.

The investigator should also consider foregoing an interrogation when the suspect's lawyer is present. While denying a suspect his Constitutional right to counsel is never proper, the risks to the case go up, and the prospective benefits go down when the attorney accompanies the suspect.

There are, of course, many arguments in favour of interrogating suspects. Confronting a suspect with overwhelming evidence already gathered during a thorough and comprehensive investigation may have such a psychological impact as to provoke admissions of guilt. Additionally, such an impact may cause the suspect to be more conducive to a later plea bargain agreement.

A meeting with a suspect, before gathering substantial evidence, rarely results in an admission of wrongdoing. Such a meeting, however, can be beneficial. The suspect is much more likely to discuss his business dealings openly when the investigator explains that someone has made a complaint, and that the investigator is merely trying to decide whether there should be a formal investigation. Such a discussion may reveal many investigative leads.

Suspects experienced in embezzlement or financial fraud often have contingency plans and explanations should the scheme be investigated. An inexperienced suspect, however, may not have developed such plans or explanations, and is therefore, more likely to reveal information. The shock of being discovered may even result in the suspect making incriminating admissions. It is also unlikely that such inexperienced suspects can gather any useful information from the investigator during the interrogation.

Depending on the circumstances, speaking with the suspect to avoid the perception of a rush to judgment may be desirable.

Juries do not look favourably on an investigation that does not allow a suspect the opportunity to explain himself, especially if he can present a viable explanation at trial. The jury is left wondering why the investigator never bothered for hearing the suspect's side of the story before rushing to file a criminal complaint.

Interrogation Planning

Once the investigator has decided that an interrogation is in order, preparations are vital. The investigator cannot be too prepared. The success of an investigation and prosecution may depend upon the investigator obtaining a confession.

In preparing for the interrogation, the investigator should use the basic steps employed in preparing for an interview:

1. collect and review all the pertinent evidence and statements already collected;
2. organize the evidence logically; and
3. determine the objectives or goals or the interrogation.

Additionally the investigator must review the legal elements of the case and compare them with the evidence to decide whether he must cure any deficiencies in the case.

Generally, questioning of a suspect begins only after the investigator has interviewed another known witnesses and gathered all available information and documents. Sometimes, however, interrogating the suspect early in the investigation may be advisable, especially if he already knows an inquiry is underway. This may prove helpful in developing financial information about a suspect. There should never be an attempt to question the suspect, however, before the investigator has had an opportunity to find out a few facts about the nature of the scheme. The investigator will seldom obtain an admission if he does not know as to what the suspect is to admit.

In most white-collar cases such as embezzlement and fraud, the suspect is generally aware of the investigation long before the investigator is ready to approach him. He has probably heard from witnesses already interviewed. As a general rule, it is best not to let the suspect know the interrogation has been scheduled; it will simply permit him to develop exculpatory answers to the questions and make obtaining a confession more difficult.

Questioning the suspect without first making an appointment may not be possible, however. Many white-collar criminals, at the first hint of an investigation, will obtain legal counsel. The attorney will advise the suspect never to talk to anyone regarding the allegations or investigation unless the attorney is present. Unlike common crime defence work, which typically begins only after an arrest has been made, the white-collar crime attorney is intimately involved in the case from the first stages of official investigation, when there may be only the whisper of a suspicion of wrongdoing and rarely a smoking gun. Instead of being on the receiving end of a set of largely pre-established facts the attorney is in a position to influence and shape the very pool of facts that becomes the focus of legal argument. It is clear, that therefore, there is little hope of developing substantial information from a suspect who has already obtained counsel.

Setting for the Interrogation

In most situations, the investigator cannot control the location of the interrogation. It is nearly impossible to arrange for a suspect to meet the investigator at some pre-arranged location without allowing the suspect substantial time that he might use to prepare for questioning. The investigator must usually surprise the suspect at his home or place of business to catch him unprepared for questioning. In such cases, it is imperative that the investigator attempts to reduce distractions.

The room or location established for the interrogation should be as quiet and private as possible. There must be a minimum of distractions, thus enabling the investigator to conduct the interrogation with the suspect's full attention. Unless the suspect is under arrest, the investigator should not lock the door to an interview room. The suspect should feel that he is free to leave whenever he wants. The room should be free of large objects, such as opaque drapes, that may cause the suspect to feel that someone else may be secreted in the room. The room should be adequately well-lighted so that the investigator can see the suspect's facial features and expressions. The investigator should remove noise distractions such as televisions, radios, and telephones since they impair both parties' abilities to concentrate.

The suspect should not sit behind a desk or any other physical barrier to allow the investigator full view of the suspect's body posture and language. The suspect and investigator should sit about five to six feet apart, far enough to allow the investigator to maintain a safe distance, but close enough to converse in a normal tone of voice.

Once all the interested parties to the interrogation arrive in the room the investigator, suspects, attorneys etc, the investigator should introduce himself to the suspect, stating his name and position. If the investigator intends to record the proceedings (and he should), he must inform the suspect of that fact. The investigator should then immediately start the recorder and make a short introductory statement. This statement should identify everyone in the room and give a brief description of the nature and purpose of the investigation. It should also include the date, time of day, and location of the interview.

The investigator should then explain to the suspect why he has been asked to appear and answer questions. The investigator should not divulge specifics, but he should give the suspect a general description of the allegations under investigation. This helps define the limits for the interrogation, by assuring the suspect that the interrogation will not become an inquisition.

The next step is to inform the suspect of his Constitutional rights. It is generally desirable to inform the suspect from a written form to ensure that no pertinent language is overlooked or confused. It is strongly recommended that the language used to inform the target of his constitutional rights and the manner in which it is administered be cleared either with the local prosecutor, the State Attorney General, or appropriate agency legal counsel in order to ensure that it conforms with local State or Federal policy custom and/or procedure. The investigator must make sure that the suspect positively asserts that he understands his rights.

Anatomy of an Interview

Conducting a third-party or corroborative interview is a key step. In most fraud Investigations and should be conducted by experienced professionals. There may be only one chance to interview an individual in an investigation, so investigators must make the most of it. It is important that a trained investigator conduct that interview. Interview are 'the stock-in-trade' of investigators.

There are legal implications that should be considered. Tape recording interviews, issuing Miranda rights and using interrogation techniques are areas that should be left to experts.

Interviewing techniques vary. Trained experts can help you understand the process. The basics follow.

Being Prepared

The most efficient and productive interviews are accomplished by advanced preparation. Questions should be prepared ahead of time along with evidential material that will be introduced during the interview, co-relating the query with the available evidence.

Having documents at your fingertips will move things along more quickly and offer the impression that your case is organized and solid.

Employees have a duty to cooperate during an internal investigation as long as what is being requested is reasonable. The fraud investigator must be careful to voluntarily seek the assistance of the subject and not restrict his or her ability to leave the interview.

During the introductory phase of the meeting, the objective should be to reduce the subject's anxiety, establish a rapport and set the format of the discussion, in a normal atmosphere.

Notes can be taken as the interviewer works through the initial stages of the interview. Always note the date, time and place when the subject is being interviewed. Changes in body language and tone to specific areas of questioning should also be noted.

Once background data is gathered, the interviewer should introduce the purpose of the task without giving away too much information. For example, you might explain that you are seeking the individual's cooperation in learning about possible inventory shrinkage at the warehouse, not necessarily that the subject is the suspected target of the investigation.

While questioning an individual, the interviewer should consider certain protocol.

Use open-ended questions that offer little information but force the subject to speak about the topic. For example, "Explain to us how the cash deposit is prepared each evening." Don't interrupt. Allow the subject to speak freely and offer ample time before directing additional questions. Don't offer information and don't do most of the talking. The investigator's role is to gather information. Clarify ambiguities without challenging. Inconsistencies may reveal lies that have been told. Be sure to follow up on these points, but don't alienate the subject. Your job is to use the information gathered as one piece of the investigation.

The interview should be wrapped up once you have exhausted your questions and determined that no more relevant information can be gleaned. Be sure to inquire whether the subject has anything more to add or whether something else should be discussed.

Provide subjects with your contact information in case they think of something later. Likewise, request their permission to contact them for additional information or clarification as your investigation proceeds. Finalize by thanking them for their cooperation.

Once the interview is completed, promptly type up your notes. It's best to summarize while thoughts and observations are fresh in your mind. If another individual was in the interview with you, compare notes and discuss relevant points revealed during the discussion. Depending on the success of your interview, your fraud case can be set in motion. Experienced investigators use this opportunity to build their case. It could be the most rewarding aspect of an investigation.

Methods of Interrogation

These are the approved methods of interrogation taught by SERE (Survival, Evasion, Resistance, Escape)—US military training programme. The use of these techniques is highly controversial and many people say that they are essentially methods of torture and illegal under the Geneva Convention.

1. Isolation

Isolation is the idea that a person should be left entirely without stimulation by another person. When left for the right amount of time in this state, it leads to a deep feeling of anxiety. The KUBARK document (1) states:

> "Little is known about the duration of confinement calculated to make a subject shift from anxiety, coupled with a desire for sensory stimuli and human companionship, to a passive, apathetic acceptance of isolation."

The document recommends that the interrogator should determine whether the person being interrogated has been imprisoned in the past, to better judge the amount of solitary time that will have the greatest effect.

2. Sleep Deprivation

The most common method of sleep deprivation is to keep the prisoner awake for several days. When they are finally allowed to fall asleep, they are awakened and interrogated. Ex-Israeli Prime Minister Menachem Begin describes his experience of this technique when he was a prisoner of the KGB: "In the head of the interrogated prisoner, a haze begins to form. His spirit is wearied to death, his legs are unsteady, and he has one sole desire: to sleep.... Anyone who has experienced this desire knows that not even hunger and thirst are comparable with it."

Besides leading to hallucinations, sleep deprivation for periods longer than 24 hours can lead to a state of temporary insanity.

3. Sensory Deprivation

In a study on sensory deprivation, 17 paid subjects were placed in a tank-type respirator that blocked all sensory stimulus. The subjects could breath for themselves through open vents. The time limit for staying in the tank was 36 hours. Only six of the subjects completed the full time. Four of the eleven who left the study early complained of anxiety and panic.

> "The chief effect of (...) solitary confinement, is to deprive the subject of many or most of the sights, sounds, tastes, smells, and tactile sensations to which he has grown accustomed."

It is believed that a few hours in this environment is equal to weeks or months of imprisonment in an ordinary cell.

4. Stress Positions

This is posing a detainee in an erect standing position for a period of several hours. No restraints or external devices are used. Variations of this technique include the extension of one's arms outward to the side.

According to one Army intelligence officer with personal knowledge of these practices, soldiers in the field developed harsher variations of the stress technique. In one position reportedly improvised by soldiers in the field, known as a 'short shackle', detainees are bound at the wrist and ankle with metal or plastic handcuffs and then doubled over with their wrists bound to their ankles, either while lying on the ground or sitting.

Stress positions are commonly used by the US Military. Recruits are often put in stress positions during basic training, the most common being the 'front leaning rest' which is the military term for the push-up positions.

5. Sensory Bombardment

This includes being bombarded with loud noises or music and flashing or bright lights. These methods are designed to overload the senses, interfering with sleep, cognition, and concentration. An Iraqi dissident reported his experience of this form of interrogation technique:

> He was made to stand or kneel facing a wall for seven-and-a-half days, hooded, and handcuffed tightly with plastic strips. At the same time a bright light was placed next to his hood whilst distorted music was played.

6. Forced Nudity

Forced nudity is the most common technique used by US forces in Iraq when interrogating prisoners. It involves stripping prisoners in front of other prisoners and forcing them to remain naked for long periods of time. The technique has also been used on people caught looting or stealing. The effect of this act is to cause great shame.

7. Sexual Humiliation

Sexual humiliation comes in a variety of forms and it takes in to account the beliefs and views of the prisoner. For example, a person whose religious beliefs are strongly opposed to homosexuality or transvestitism may be forced to participate in acts of this nature with other prisoners. This may be extreme, or mild (in the case or prisoners being made to wear female underwear). This can also include being subjected to forced displays of sexuality (such as lapdances) in the case of those with extreme views towards women.

8. Cultural Humiliation

Cultural humiliation can include any acts which are contrary to the religious or cultural views of a person. For example, a Muslim may be forced to eat foods forbidden by his religion, or made to witness or commit acts considered blasphemous.

This can also include verbal abuse which is meant to lead to feelings of shame and disgust, further breaking the will of the prisoner.

9. Extreme Cold

This is a particular favourite of the Chinese government towards political or religious prisoners. In many cases they are routinely doused with cold water and left outside or in unheated cells to freeze. Some have been forced to stand in or run through snow wearing only a thin layer of clothing. Thousands are left to sleep on the concrete floors of unheated prison cells in the dead of winter. To make the cold even more unbearable, prison staff have been reported to leave the windows open in practitioners' cells during the night. Many practitioners are kept in such cells even when badly injured or on the verge of death.

On occasions, extreme heat is also used. In this case the prisoner is locked in a 'hot box'—a small hot room which due to lack of ventilation, essentially functions as an oven. When the prisoner cooperates, he or she is finally released.

10. Phobias

Phobias are able to incite extreme amounts of panic in people. For this reason, a prisoner who has a fear of spiders may be forced to remain in a room filled with spiders. Once he achieves the useful state of anxiety or panic, he is interrogated.

The threat to inflict pain, can trigger fears more damaging than the immediate sensation of pain. The same principle holds for other fears: sustained long enough, a strong fear of anything vague or unknown induces regression.

11. Water Boarding

Water boarding consists of immobilizing an individual and pouring water over his or her face to simulate drowning. Water boarding has been used to obtain information, coerce confessions, and also to punish, and/or intimidate. It elicits the gag reflex, making the subject believe his or her death is imminent while ideally not causing permanent physical damage.

Journalist Julia Leyton, describes the method:

> "Water boarding as it is currently described involves strapping a person to an inclined board, with his feet raised and his head lowered. The interrogators bind the person's arms and legs so he can't move at all, and they cover his face. In some descriptions, the person is gagged, and some sort of cloth covers his nose and mouth; in others, his face is wrapped in cellophane. The interrogator then repeatedly pours water onto the person's face. Depending on the exact

> setup, the water may or may not actually get into the person's mouth and nose; but the physical experience of being underneath a wave of water seems to be secondary to the psychological experience. The person's mind believes he is drowning, and his gag reflex kicks in as if he were choking on all that water falling on his face."

On average, CIA officers who allow themselves to be tested upon, last for an average of fourteen seconds.

White-collar criminals are the human blasts. The reason why white-collar criminals rarely go to prison is that white-collar crime is very hard to detect.

Humans everywhere have an evolved finely-honed sense of justice. This protects the community against selfish individuals who harm others for their own benefits. Yet, white-collar criminals recently brought the world economy to its knees, and our complex criminal justice system is almost powerless to deal with them. They escape justice mainly because it is so difficult to establish that a crime has taken place, or even to distinguish between criminals and victims. They vaporize the assets of innocent people. Once unmasked, it is clear that they have committed crimes and that their numerous victims have suffered terrible harm and losses. When prosecuted, they are relatively easy to convict and pay stiff penalties.

In the recent worldwide financial chaos, it has been difficult to separate the sheep from the wolves, however. At least two issues are salient. First, dishonesty prevailed all the way up the food chain. Second, bad actors at each level of the financial system were ignored by financial regulators.

4. Black Money and Political Leaders

AugustaWestland

The Italian court's judgment exposes the role of Sonia Gandhi, Manmohan Singh in AgustaWestland Chopper Deal. The judgment also reveals that Sonia's Political Secretary accepted the commission of €15-16 million from the middlemen. The judgment of the appeal court in Milan convicting AgustaWestland chopper company chief Giuseppe Orsi described how the firm paid bribes to top Congress leaders in India and lobbied with them to bag the ₹3,600 crore deal. Reproducing the handwritten notes seized from middlemen, the judgment says that the political leaders accepted the commission of 15-16 million Euros (around ₹120-125 crores) in the controversial purchase of 12 VVIP chopper deal. It also names the role of Sonia Gandhi's trusted aide and AICC General Secretary Oscar Fernandes and the then National Security Advisor MK Narayanan.

Sonia Gandhi's name (signora GANDHI) is mentioned four times in the judgment, convicting Orsi and other officials of Finmeccanica, the firm which manufactures AgustaWestland VVIP Choppers. Orsi and other officials were convicted for four and a half years.

A letter seized by investigators shows the main middleman Christian Michel, who is still a fugitive, writing to Peter Hulet, then India region sales and liaison head of the helicopter company. The letter states that Sonia is the main driving force behind this deal and she will no longer fly in the existing MI-8 choppers. The letter is quoted verbatim in the judgment. Details of lobbying and corruption of Congress leadership, writing to the then British High Commissioner in India that he should target top Congress leadership for clinching the deal are clearly explained.

The judgment also says Haschke had identified all the Congress leaders including Sonia Gandhi and Ahmed Patel in the court when their photos were shown to him during the trial by the Italian prosecution.

The Italian court judgment names Manmohan Singh and details that Orsi used Italian leadership and diplomats to contact the then Prime Minister to scuttle the probe by non-cooperation from Indian government side.

Sanjay Bhandari

Sanjay Bhandari, the defence consultant whose premises were searched by the Income Tax Department, has admitted that the email trail recovered from his computer was indeed that of messages exchanged between him, Robert Vadra and Vadra's assistant Manoj Arora. Officials in the Department have confirmed just before the search operation was over, Bhandari was confronted with the batch of emails, including one dated April 4, 2010—the only one sent from Vadra's own email ID and signed off by him—and he acknowledged the exchanges on the subject of finalising interiors for an apartment in London. An attachment to one of the mails shows that while the cost of refurbishing was earlier estimated by Sumit Chadda, a relative of Bhandari, to be £28,000 pounds, additional items were added to the worklist and the estimate went up to £35,000.

IT's investigation wing had assessed the significance of the mail trail and sent as many as seven requests to countries for details of this and other property deals involving Bhandari. The requests have since been sent to the British Virgin Islands, United Kingdom and Dubai and replies are awaited.

(*Courtesy: The Indian Express*)

When income tax officials descended on his residence in Greater Kailash, Sanjay Bhandari, the man at the centre of the controversy for allegedly holding Benami properties for Robert Vadra, damaged his SIM card to keep his 'contacts' under wraps. Indeed it was his 'contacts' that the government agencies were after.

In 2014, after the BJP came to power, a top secret report of the Intelligence Bureau (IB) listed Bhandari as a close aide of Vadra, son-in-law of Congress President Sonia Gandhi, and mentioned that he was friends with the son of a former senior BJP leader.

In fact, Bhadari's contact list was so impressive that after the IT raids, he could send word to Prime Minister Narendra Modi through two influential people to explore possibility of immunity in exchange of information. However, his request received a cold response and he went into a shell, deserted by his powerful friends, including cabinet ministers, senior intelligence officials, industrialists, senior judicial functionaries and power brokers.

Before entering the defence industry, Bhandari looked after his father's homeopathic clinic in Connaught Place. Things, however, changed in 2008. Bhandari was introduced to Delhi's elite power circle by a property dealer in Defence Colony, and he made his debut in defence. In January 2010, he booked a stall at the defence expo in Pragati Maidan, but failed to attract interest. Though he had little to offer, Swiss firm Pilatus decided to engage Bhandari's Offset India Solutions (OIS) and in 2012 Pilatus won a ₹4,000 crore basic trainer for an aircraft contract.

Bhandari received one million Swiss francs from Pilatus, even before the trials for Basic Trainer Aircrafts (BTA) in September-October 2010. It was also revealed that OIS was not listed as an offshore provider of the firm in documents filed with the Indian Air Force. The report revealed unexplained payments to the tune of ₹69 crore his companies received. ₹69 crore came from a known Hawala operator, Deepak Aggarwal, who being scrutinised in a separate case involving funding to the Aam Aadmi Party.

By virtue of being a security service provider, Bhandari knew the nuances of keeping secrets—he routinely erased his hard drives, snooped on his staff and installed high-level security applications. Despite such extraordinary precautions, an email trail connecting him to Vadra was revealed.

(*Courtesy: Hindustan Times*)

Sanjay Bhandari, a defence dealer being investigated for allegedly buying a benami or proxy-owned house for Robert Vadra in London, and Aviation Minister Ashok Gajapathi Raju's top aide Appa Rao, exchanged 355 phone calls over the last one year, according to documents collected in raids on Sanjay Bhandari. Appa Rao, who is officer on special duty or OSD to the minister, denied that Bhandari had made hundreds of calls to him; they were so few that he could not recall an exact number, Rao said.

Eighteen properties owned or linked to Sanjay Bhandari were raided by investigators who allege he has committed a variety of financial crimes. As reported, emails they claim to have accessed from his computers and phone allegedly show that Robert Vadra and his executive assistant, Manoj Arora, sent messages which promised to arrange payments and discussed the interiors of a house in central London.

(*Courtesy: NDTV*)

Vijay Mallya

Once called the 'King of Good Times' and 'Playboy of the East' due to his extravagant lifestyle, Mallya and his companies have been embroiled in financial controversies and difficulties in recent years, and especially since 2012. Mallya left India on

2 March 2016 after saying he wanted to move to Britain to be closer to his children. A group of Indian banks is trying to collect approximately ₹7,000 crore in loans, they have made to Mallya and his businesses, and the Attorney General said that Mallya's assets abroad are "far in excess to loans taken by him". Seventeen banks petitioned the Supreme Court of India to try to prevent Mallya from leaving the country, but the Indian government indicated that he had already left. The Enforcement Directorate of India also filed a money laundering case against him for allegedly sending abroad ₹900 crore that had been loaned to his airline. High Court of Hyderabad issued a non-bailable warrant against Mallya for his failure to appear in the court regarding an allegation of cheating the GMR Hyderabad International Airport Ltd by issuing them a dishonoured cheque for ₹50 lakh.

Kingfisher owes banks about ₹9,000 crore, which comprises of principal of about ₹6,000 crore along with accrued interest. At the hearing Mallya's counsel offered to pay ₹4,000 crore along with additional ₹2,000 crore, subject to settlement of a claim Kingfisher has filed against GE. Lenders told the court that they were open to a meaningful negotiation, they expect at least the principal amount of ₹6,000 crore to be paid, along with some portion of the interest. They further added that for any settlement to take place, Mallya must show bonafides to court, disclose all his assets and preferably be present in court.

The Supreme Court wants loans defaulter Vijay Mallya to declare all his assets by April 21, 2016 and by that same date inform the court when he can appear before its bench. On 7th April 2016, Supreme Court told Mallya—who owes more than ₹9,000 crores to as many as 17 banks—to deposit a 'substantial amount' with it to 'prove his bonafide'.

SBI has the highest exposure of ₹1,600 crore to Kingfisher Airlines. Other banks with exposure to the airline include PNB and IDBI Bank (₹800 crore each), Bank of India (₹650 crore),

Bank of Baroda (₹550 crore), Central Bank of India (₹410 crore). UCO Bank has to recover ₹320 crore, Corporation Bank (₹310 crore), State Bank of Mysore (₹150 crore), IOB (₹140 crore), Federal Bank (₹90 crore), Punjab & Sind Bank (₹60 crore) and Axis Bank (₹50 crore).

Industrialist Vijay Mallya figures in the offshore leaks by International Consortium of Investigative Journalists (ICIJ), whose Panama Papers have rocked the world. Details accessed from the ICIJ website showed a British Virgin Islands firm—Venture New Holding Limited—which has been operational from February 15, 2006, is linked directly to Vijay Mallya, and not to any of his companies. Tax haven entities of Mallya, a non-resident Indian, have been in focus after the Karnataka High Court observations in January 2014 that "Mallya had not come to the court with clean hands" in reference to a possible diversion of ₹4,000 crore to a subsidiary in British Virgin Islands.

State Bank of India (SBI) has seized the Kingfisher Villa of debt-strapped liquor baron Vijay Mallya in Panaji, Goa. The District Magistrate gave an order in favour of banks to take physical possession of ₹90 crore villa.

Government of India has revoked the diplomatic passport of Vijay Mallya, in an effort to bring the business tycoon back to India. Prevention of Money Laundering Act (PMLA) court declared Vijay Mallya a 'proclaimed offender' on the request of the Enforcement Directorate (ED) in connection with its money laundering probe against him in an alleged ₹900 crore loan default case. Enforcement Directorate provisionally attached nine movable and immovable properties worth ₹1,411 crore of Vijay Mallya and United Breweries (Holding) Limited, as part of a money laundering probe against him. Vijay Mallya sold off two properties worth several crores before the Enforcement Directorate (ED) could seize them. ED is trying to find out whether Mallya received money from the sales and if that money has been remitted to him or to his firms abroad. ED had information about Mallya disposing of assets so that the provisional attachment action could be 'frustrated'.

Subrata Roy

Subrata Roy, founder-Chairman of Sahara India, a conglomerate with diversified businesses and ownership interests that include London's Grosvenor House, New York's Plaza Hotel, Aamby Valley City and Force India. Roy founded the company in 1978. In 2012, he was named among the 10 most powerful people of India by *India Today*. In 2004, the group was termed by the *Time* magazine as 'the second largest employer in India' after the Indian Railways. Since March 2014 he is under judicial custody with a bail amount of ₹100 billion. Supreme Court ordered the arrest of Subrata Roy for failing to appear before it in connection with the ₹24,000 crore deposits his company has not refunded to investors. He was eventually arrested by UP police on Supreme Court's warrant, in a dispute with Market Regulator—SEBI. Subrata Roy has been in custody in the Tihar Jail, his bail plea has been rejected by the Supreme Court. Sahara was allowed to sell a part of its assets in India to raise part of the money in question. He was granted interim bail by Supreme Court for the same on condition of depositing ₹10,000 crore with SEBI. His deposit of ₹10,000 crore has not been made and Subrata Roy is still in jail.

Supreme Court asked SEBI to initiate the process of selling 87 'unencumbered' properties of Sahara group, whose title deeds are with the market regulator, to generate the bail money for release of its chief Subrata Roy who has been in jail for two years now. A three-judge bench headed by Chief Justice TS Thakur also the regulator not to sell any of the properties of the beleaguered group below 90 per cent of the circle rates. The bench, also comprising Justices AR Dave and AK Sikri, said the regulator will have to take its prior nod before going ahead with the sale of any property if it (SEBI) receives bids even below 90 per cent of the circle rate. "You (SEBI) evolve mechanism and start selling the properties and we are passing the order to this effect," the bench said when the counsel for SEBI alleged that nothing concrete was happening on the ground.

Sahara chief Subrata Roy, in Tihar Jail since March 2014, has been allowed to leave prison for four weeks for the funeral of his mother Chhabi Roy. In a breather to Sahara chief Subrata Roy, Supreme Court extended his parole till July 11 to enable him to deposit ₹200 crore with SEBI.

Panama Papers

The Panama Papers are a leaked set of 11.5 million confidential documents that provide detailed information about more than 2,14,000 offshore companies listed by the Panamanian corporate service provider Mossack Fonseca, including the identities of shareholders and directors of the companies. The documents show how wealthy public officials hide their money and identify current government leaders from five countries—Argentina, Iceland, Saudi Arabia, Ukraine, and the United Arab Emirates—as well as government officials, close relatives, and close associates of various heads of government of more than 40 other countries, including Brazil, People's Republic of China, Peru, France, India, Malaysia, Mexico, Pakistan, Romania, Russia, South Africa, Spain, Syria, and the United Kingdom.

The Indian Express, which is among 107 media organisations in 78 countries that has access to the documents, has revealed that as many as 500 Indian names figure on Fonseca's list of offshore clients, including those of politicians, businessmen and movie stars.

According to the front page report in *The Indian Express*, an eight-months-long investigation has revealed that corporates, including DLF owner KP Singh and nine members of his family and Gautam Adani's elder brother Vinod Adani, are also part of the list. Shishir Bajoria and Anurag Kejriwal are the politicians whose names allegedly come up in the list.

Allegations of money laundering and tax evasions are levelled against prominent politicians, celebrities and public figures in India. Media reports have suggested that Bollywood superstar's brother Ajitabh Bachchan might have been handling the former's businesses and finances during the time that the companies in question were incorporated. The report says that at least one major political family's money was also allegedly routed through this account.

The Indian Express claimed it checked the authenticity of over 300 addresses of Indians on the list. Other names include that of Mumbai ganglord Iqbal Mirchi, businessmen with addresses in non-descript neighbourhoods in Panchkula, Dehradun, Vadodara and Mandsaur.

These include cricket franchise deals and, in several cases, linkages to those who have previously been under CBI or Income Tax scrutiny.

Prime Minister Narendra Modi has ordered an investigation into the 500 Indians who are among those named in the 'Panama Papers'—a list of some of the richest and most powerful people whose offshore accounts have been divulged in what's being described as the 'world's biggest leak'. Ministry of Finance said,

> "The Government is committed to detecting and preventing generation of black money. In this context, the expose of Panama Papers will further help the Government in meeting this objective.... The Government will take all necessary actions as required to get maximum information from all sources including from foreign governments to help in the investigation process."

Last year, it was Swiss Leaks, a global list with over 1,100 Indians with secret bank accounts in HSBC Geneva, which shaped the debate over black money parked overseas.

First Conviction in Coal Scam

In the first judgment in the coal block allocation scam case, a special court has awarded four-year jail term to RC Rungta and RS Rungta, Chairman and Director, respectively, in Jharkhand Ispat Private Ltd (JIPL).

The court also imposed ₹5 lakh fine on each of the convicts held guilty for deceiving and defrauding the government to bag a coal block in Jharkhand. Besides, a fine of ₹25 lakh was imposed on JIPL, also convicted in the case.

This is the first coal block allocation scam case in which the special court, set up to exclusively deal with coal scams, has delivered its judgment. After a Comptroller and Auditor General (CAG) report in 2012 alleged ₹1.86 lakh crore windfall gain to companies, the CBI had started probe against allotment of coal.

JIPL and the Rungtas were earlier put on trial by the court, which had framed charges against them for securing allotment of North Dhadu coal block in Jharkhand allegedly on the basis of false and forged documents.

In its chargesheet, CBI said JIPL 'grossly misrepresented' a number of aspects before the steel and coal ministries to inflate their claim, thereby inducing coal ministry officials and the screening committee to allocate the coal block to them.

In its judgement, the court held that the "intention to defraud on the part of accused persons is writ large on the face of record."

RS Rungta had last year moved an application before a special court seeking to summon former Prime Minister Manmohan Singh and former Minister of State for Coal Dasari Narayana Rao as witnesses in his defence in the case. Singh was also the Cabinet Minister for Coal at the time of allocation of mine. The court, however, rejected the plea.

The court acquitted both RS Rungta and RC Rungta for the alleged offences under IPC Sections 467 (forgery of valuable security), 468 (forgery for the purpose of cheating) and 471 (using a forged document as genuine) saying they were not proved against them.

Rungta Brothers?

RC Rungta is the Chairman of the RC Rungta Group. JIPL is one of the six fully owned companies under the Rungta Group. The websites of these two companies mention RC Rungta as the promoter "who hails from the reputed business family having business network across the country and having interest in mining, highway and civil project, steel industry, cement industry, manufacturing of irrigation system, leasing and finance, transportation and education etc." The website also mentions him as an eminent industrialist of Jharkhand, with business experience of more than 20 years. There is no mention of his brother RS Rungta on any of the websites even though the court submissions mention him as one of directors in JIPL.

Second Conviction in Coal Scam

In the second conviction in the coal scam, Special CBI Judge Bharat Parashar sentenced RSPL's CEO Udit Rathi and MD Pradeep Rathi to three years imprisonment while AGM Kushal Aggarwal was awarded two years in jail. The court also imposed a fine of Rs 50 lakh each on RSPL and its CEO, Rs 25 lakh on the MD and Rs 5 lakh on the AGM.

Raninder Singh, Son of Captain Amarinder Singh

The Enforcement Directorate has summoned Raninder Singh, son of former Punjab Chief Minister and State Congress chief Captain Amarinder Singh, under the Foreign Exchange Management Act for questioning. According to the Directorate, the summons was served to probe suspected foreign exchange violations. Raninder Singh is believed to have received funds from United Kingdom-based Jacaranda Trust. Movement of funds to Switzerland and some legal entities in British Virgin Islands are also under scrutiny.

The Income Tax Department had probed four companies having assets worth about ₹460 crore. According to the agency, documents of these companies and their bank accounts established that they were associated with Raninder Singh. In March, the agency filed a challan against Raninder Singh in a Ludhiana court, which issued summons asking him to appear. Through the challan, the agency had also alleged that his father was a discretionary beneficiary of the UK-based Trust. The four companies were identified by the IT Department as Chillingham Holdings Limited, Mulwala Holdings Limited, Allworth Venture Holdings Limited and Limerlock International Limited. The agency, in its challan, accused Raninder Singh of lying on oath and furnishing fake accounts and bogus documents pertaining to the Trust and the companies. It also alleged that when he was shown his signatures on the Trust deed, he changed and disguised his signatures. His statements were recorded twice in 2015.

The Enforcement Directorate summoned Raninder Singh on June 16, 2016 but after he did not appear before the ED on that date citing health reasons, he was issued fresh summons on July 4 to appear on July 14. Raninder Singh was summoned for allegedly violation of Foreign Exchange Management Act (FEMA). He sought exemption from appearing in ED office on the pretext that since he was president of National Rifles Association of India and due to his engagement in the Rio 2016 Olympics he was unable to come, said sources. ED sources said that the next date of summoning him is yet to be decided.

He has already been summoned by a Ludhiana court on July 26, 2016 on charges that he had provided false information to Income Tax Department pertaining to transactions through offshore companies and a trust based in the British Virgin Islands.

5. Conclusion

There is always a freedom for an individual to choose between capitalism and democracy. Capitalists are crooks it is said. They milk you for all they can get. They cheat you in a thousand ways. *Banias* are notorious for using 'fixed' weighing scales and adulterating goods. They black-market goods subject to price controls, ranging from urea to kerosene. They filch subsidised grain and sugar from the public distribution system and sell it in the open market. Big industrialists are worse. They make fancy claims about their products in advertisements, but deliver substandard stuff. They demand—and typically get, in return for bribes—sundry subsidies and tax breaks. They wallow in tax evasion and black money. They manipulate import and export invoices to illegally accumulate dollars abroad in tax havens. They pay lip-service to competition, but actually succeed by using money, muscle and influence to buy or bully their way through the system. Where's the morality in this lot?

Capitalism empowers people through the freedom to choose what to buy or produce. Freedom to choose is a high moral principle. Democracy is based on the same principle. Paradoxically, democracy has a high moral cachet while capitalism is looked down upon. Yet, democracy can match capitalism flaw for flaw. Businessmen make fancy claims and don't deliver. But don't politicians also promise the moon, and not deliver? Are promises in election manifestos less bogus than those in commercial advertisements? Businessmen claim they want to serve the public interest by creating jobs in backward areas, while their actual aim is to get rich. But don't politicians also claim to be promoting the public interest while lining their pockets? Businessmen may adulterate their products. But don't politicians constantly adulterate their supposed policies and principles? Capitalists may wallow in black money. But are politicians any different? They spend thousands of crores on elections—where does the cash come from? Politics is supposed to be public service. In fact, it has become the shadiest of businesses, in which you invest black money (in elections) in order to make even more black money (through bribes and extortion). Crony capitalism, a sadly widespread phenomenon, is a perversion of capitalism. It is a perversion of democracy too. Businessmen use money to promote their interests. So do politicians. US politician Jesse Unruh said, "Money is the mother's milk of politics."

Once politicians used to hire musclemen for dirty work. The musclemen have now entered politics themselves in thousands. In the recent Uttar Pradesh election, 47% of those elected had pending criminal charges. Businessmen use influence to get what they want. Politicians are surely ahead of them in this game. Just ask Congressmen: if you have access to 10, Janpath, all doors open to you. In sum, politicians in a democracy are opportunistic scoundrels. Yet, democracy is viewed as a highly moral system. Because it empowers citizens through free choice. That makes it superior to any other form of government.

The Communist criticized democracy on exactly the same ground that many criticize capitalism. He said elected politicians were opportunistic scoundrels representing their own class interest and not the public interest. So, he proposed replacing them with a politburo of noble intellectuals genuinely working for the masses. Alas, this endeavour ended in mass murder, misery and ultimate collapse. Democracy has a thousand flaws. But as Churchill once said, "It is the worst system except for all the others." Benevolent dictators often felt they were more principled and moral than crooked politicians in democracies.

Yet, the autocracies ultimately failed because of a fatal flaw: they did not give citizens the freedom to choose their leaders. For the same reason, centrally planned economies also failed. These too aimed to create noble economic systems free of the greed and grab of capitalism. Yet, they failed for the same reason as autocracies: they did not empower citizens to choose.

People repeatedly fled from communist to capitalist countries: from East Germany to West Germany, from Red China to Hong Kong, from North Korea to South Korea. Now, the communist States had full employment and assured security for the aged and handicapped. Yet, people fled to capitalist countries where neither jobs nor welfare were assured. What was assured was freedom to choose, and that mattered above all. They wanted freedom to choose their political leaders, freedom to choose their job or business, and freedom to buy goods they liked. Capitalism, like democracy, is "the worst system except for all the others." It too has scoundrels parading as leaders. But it too turns out to be the best. This is not just a matter of efficiency. It is, above all, a matter of high morality. Freedom is a fundamental human right. Adam Smith, father of capitalism, disliked capitalists. He said businessmen rarely met without concocting some scheme to milk consumers. But, he said, once capitalists had to compete in a market system, they had to woo consumers with ever better goods and services, thus producing a social good that was never part of their original aim. Smith said capitalists were scoundrels, but capitalism was a good system. He could have said the same of politics: democratic politicians are scoundrels, but democracy is a good system. Both systems are saved from rascality because they rest on the same moral principle—freedom to choose.

Ghost of Harshad Scam

To build a robust corporate bond market, unless regulators forget the past and move on, the price of an liquid bond market will be much more than any scam. It is time to bury the ghosts of Harshad Scam. The story that broke 20 years ago still haunts many in the market. The '92 scam was a story where the government market bond was used to pay stocks. Many blame the scam for slower reforms in the bond market. It created a distrust between the regulators and brokers. Bankers and regulators have to bury the past and develop the corporate bond market. Fears of another Harshad lurking has held back the opening of the market.

"Were you around when the Scam happened?" The question was tossed to an official of a private bank, a man in his late '30s who shook his head and smiled. He had unintentionally provoked one of the Reserve Bank of India officials sitting around the table with his suggestion to bring back a money market transaction that was banned almost two decades ago. They had gathered a few months ago to discuss ways to revive the bond market, which was yet to heal from the scar left by the '92 securities scam. For the bankers and traders of his generation, who have read about the scam and heard from senior colleagues stories of buccaneer brokers and their sharp practices, it's an almost forgotten fiasco caused by clever operators and some bankers who took advantage of opaque financial markets with low regulations. The men who caused it are either dead or living in obscurity; some are still fighting court cases that followed the scam; those who stepped back before the music stopped escaped unscathed while a few laundered their way to respectability. It's a story that broke 20 years ago at this time and is cherished. It's natural for today's bankers and stock traders to shrug it off as an old event captured in sepia-toned images that don't matter anymore. They are partly right. But the point they miss is the collective paranoia it triggered among financial market regulators—a glimpse of which one catches in occasional conversations to reform the money and bond market that was the playfield of Harshad Mehta, the brash and flawed icon behind the ₹6,000 crore stock market scam. The damage by the scam to the market ten years back is better described by senior stock exchange officials.

While the scam brought about dramatic changes in market infrastructure, transparency in dealings, clearing mechanism, demat shares, exchange reforms and risk control mechanisms in equities as well as bonds, the fear of another scam and another Harshad lurking around the corner has held back the opening up of the market. To avert another scam, the government securities market (that constitutes 90% of the bond market) works like an exclusive club: not all can trade on the exchange, the Central Bank acts as the depository, and while a retail window exits for individuals and provident funds to buy gilts, it's yet to take off. Such baby steps partly owe their origin to the scam that rattled the regulators. No broker can be member of the government bond exchange the way it can be a member of a stock exchange to buy or sell equities on behalf of clients. The distrust towards brokers, the fear of intermediaries shorting the market and a continued ban on transactions that can add liquidity in bonds partly owe their origin to deals cut by Harshad.

How to Stop a Thief by Thinking Like a Thief

The success of detection of fraud depends upon the ability of the investigator to think like a thief. Just as a chess master understands the numerable but finite opening sequences to a chess game, an anti-fraud professional should know the numerable but finite fraud schemes. Frauds include many types of inventory fraud, manifold check-kiting schemes and techniques with colourful names like cash lapping. The beauty of a taxonomy is that it's universal. Naturalists can classify newly discovered flora and fauna in the existing Linnaean system. Likewise, newly discovered fraud schemes are just fresh takes on established schemes in taxonomy.

While members of team understand frauds generally, there's a lot of crimes to master. So it commissions specific team members to become subject matter experts. The goal is to have one person thinking like a specific kind of thief rather than everyone thinking about fraudsters in general. This expert will gain a deep understanding of a specific kind of fraud, the type of person who commits it and his motivation, and tools and techniques to combat it. There should be one person focus on inventory fraud, and they'll know to periodically check eBay, for example, to see if goods are being sold there illegally. Another who knows benefits fraud inside and out, and so forth.

To think like a thief, you have to know how a thief's mind works. The best place to start is with Dr Donald Cressey's landmark work on the psychology of fraud and his 'fraud triangle'. According to Cressey, the three elements of all fraud are opportunity, motivation and rationalization.

Sometimes we associate thinking like a thief with thinking like a bad guy, but they are not one and the same. In order to successfully understand fraud, you need to throw out some prejudices about the type of person who commits fraud. To start, it's rarely a bad guy, a malicious person with purely malicious intent. Not only bad people committed fraud. In fact it's usually good people who make a bad decision and a bad rationalization, who think the pain they're causing is less than the gain they get. They could be a company's Board member. These are usually fairly intelligent people. Typically male, higher up in the organization and typically, for internal fraud, they have long tenures with the company." In other words, fraudsters are criminals but not archetypical criminals. Rather, they're the same people you work with, have lunch with and socialize with every day.

Countermeasures Against White-Collar Crime

An ancient Chinese proverb, Akera's Dragon tells of a man, Akera, and his search for a dragon. Akera came from a place where any man who slayed a dragon would be considered the mightiest of the warriors. He spent his whole life searching far and wide for the dragon he sought. After 100 years of searching, he collapsed. On his deathbed, he thought back on his life, and realized his mistake. He had wasted his life searching for a fictional beast, for the dragon he sought was the dragon within.

Akera looked for his dragon the same way we look for crime. We look for the disgruntled employees, murderous lunatics, and gun-toting bandits. When we plan our security, we focus on locks and barriers. The typical business of medium or large size will hire a small team of security personnel to guard against vandalism, theft, and workplace violence, but, at the same time, gives one person full access to accounting information without direct supervision. That one person could embezzle thousands, millions, or even billions. And he can cause the business to file for chapter 11, the last thing this company will do. This is the result when trust is given away.

Most people shrug off the white-collar crime (WCC) as a rare event, fooling themselves into believing that the damage is small. In actuality, the cost is very big per year for fraud based on white-collar crime worldwide. To be even more specific, “the total cost of all American bank robberies in the last 100 years is less than the cost of … a single corrupt. However, money isn’t the only cost. The ripple effects of human suffering are quite substantial. While it’s less likely today, some families affected by WCC in the past have lost so much money that they starve or commit suicide.

In addition to being surprised by the cost of WCC, people are often surprised by the variety of WCC. Sutherland, the man credited with coining the phrase ‘White-Collar Crime’, defines WCC as “crimes committed by a person of respectability and high social status in the course of his occupation.” Put simply, WCC is a crime committed by someone trusted who makes crime a part of his career. This includes tax fraud, ID theft, and even environmental crimes. Some even say that wars are sometimes considered a type of WCC. Once knowledge of these crimes is obtained, the next step is protecting against them.

The Psychology of Fraudsters

We often wonder why people commit fraud, why they steal things that do not belong to them and what goes through their minds when they do such awful things. The answers can be explained by Donald R Cressey's famous concept, which was developed in the 1950s to explain why people commit fraud. Cressey, a criminologist came up with a theory which he called the 'fraud triangle' to understand the basics of fraud. According to Cressey, there are three elements present in every fraud: Motivation, Opportunity and Rationalization.

Motivation

In this element, Cressey says that a person always feels pressure or feels a need to commit fraud. It might be a financial need such as high medical bills or debts or it can be a desire for material goods that makes a person want to commit fraud. Sometimes, there may even be a need for good results at work or gambling and even drugs. So, it does not necessarily have to be a financial need or pressure that makes one commit fraud.

Motivation can be understood as a potential force. Different employees can experience the same motivation and yet behave differently. What might motivate a 'good' employee to commit fraud? Consider these five common motivators:

Fear: If I don't do this something bad will happen to me

Entitlement: I deserve this because…

Anger: I am angry, and since I cannot express it directly I will…

Perceived need: This is the only way I can get what I need

Temptation: I don't need this but I want it, and I can get it if…

Motive looks for opportunity. Opportunity can present itself in any number of ways. Perhaps the most common motivation can be a lack of proscription. If there are no barriers then there is no impedance to me doing what makes me feel better. For example, there may be no rule prohibiting what I want to do and/or it can be ɔne without significant difficulty. Add to that a lack of perceived ɔnsequences and the psychological barrier to improper conduct even lower. If I believe that even if I'm caught doing what I'm ɔnsidering nothing bad will happen to me, that further rengthens the attractiveness of the opportunity. Another ement often associated with opportunity is overconfidence. If I elieve that I can get away with this, even if, perhaps, a 'lesser' erson could not, then why not seek what I want?

Opportunity

Vhen there is a need, the fraudster usually looks for opportunities) commit fraud. And the workplace is always a good target. mployees may have certain access to records, valuable ocuments or other information that would allow them to ɔmmit fraud. They may also have heard stories from other nployees, who may have cheated the employer before, and may ave gotten away with it. Therefore, internal access as well as nowledge about what goes on in the company may make it asier for them to commit fraud.

Opportunities for fraud abound in nearly every organizational ɔntext. In almost every organization employees have the pportunity to perform critical tasks without direct supervision. Vhether it is completing paperwork, dealing with a customer, ıpplier, competitor or fellow worker, the details of that ıteraction are often unobserved by those in charge. For many mployees there can be dozens of opportunities to commit petty 'auds every day of the week. And, the opportunity for gnificant fraud may be just as readily available.

Rationalization

raudsters always rationalize their behaviour by convincing ıemselves that committing fraud is okay. For instance, "I eserve it. I only want my share", "After this, I'm done", "They'll low their money anyway" etc. Fraudsters will also rationalize their behaviour by convincing themselves that they are jus 'borrowing' money and will pay it back one day. Some fraudster may say that the company has enough money and it won't affec them in a big way.

Therefore, employers must take action to avoid fraud from happening at their companies. Learn about the fraud triangle and take control especially when there is an opportunity to commit fraud. Limit access to valuable information and documents and allow employees only to handle internal information when it is necessary for the job.

Rationalization as "the lies we tell ourselves to give us permission to do what we know is wrong". Some of the classic rationalizations include:

- No one will get hurt (no harm—no foul).
- If I don't someone else will.
- Everybody else does it.
- I'm entitled because of how I was treated (classic Feeding the Hog).
- I have no choice.
- It's worth the risk—nothing bad will happen to me.

We can revisit the spark testing example where employees were intentionally under-producing or the case of the supervisor who was intentionally under-reporting, 'sandbagging' work and saving it for a rainy day. I suggest that for each we can find motivation, opportunity and rationalization.

What the fraud triangle suggests is that we need to ask ourselves what can we, individually, do to identify, address and eliminate feeding the hog and silent sabotage as part of our organization's reality?

Why Good People Do Bad Things

According to data from the Ethics Resource Centre derived from their National Business Ethics Survey, National Government

Ethics Survey, and National Non-Profit Ethics Survey, it can be concluded that fraud remains a problem.

Just a sampling of findings from the 2009 National Business Ethics Survey makes the point.

- 49% of the survey respondents report observing misconduct on the job.
- Examples of the fraudulent behaviour reported include: lying to employees, lying to external, stakeholders, benefits violations, falsifying time and/or expenses, document alteration, misrepresenting financial records, bribing public officials and insider trading.
- Exacerbating the problem was the observation that 36% of those who observe misconduct opted not to report what they had observed to their management.
- And, of the 64% who did report what they observed 15% of those experienced retaliation.

In the broadest sense a 'fraud' is a deception made for personal gain. The legal definitions of what constitutes a fraud vary by legal jurisdiction, as do the punishments. Fraud is both a criminal and civil law violation, typically defined as the deliberate deception of another in order to damage them, usually to obtain property or services unjustly.

To examine the psychology of fraud we rely on Freud. In Freud's structural model of the psyche he posits that the inner desire is responsible for our basic drives. It is amoral (not governed by external values), egocentric and ruled by the pleasure-pain principle. The ID is illogical and will not take 'no' for an answer. "If it feels good, do it."

Freud goes on to describe the Ego, which balances our primitive drives and reality. The Ego provides defense mechanisms that are often used when a behaviour conflicts with either society's morals, norms and taboos or the individual's expectations as a result of the internalization of those morals, norms and taboos. One defense the Ego employs when faced with such ethical conflicts is to find justification or rationale for doing what we want to do, even when we know it to be wrong.

The third Freudian concept is the Superego, which acts as our conscience, maintaining our sense of morality and proscription from taboos.

If we juxtapose Freud and fraud we get: fraud is often the fulfilling of an inner/personal desire through the use of self-deception, thus giving us permission to act in a manner that violates societal morals, norms or taboos.

Fraud is different from other forms of misconduct in that it relies on trickery or deception, often including self-deception by the Ego.

Retaliatory Behaviour

Consider an example from a Pacific Northwest lumber mill, first noted several years ago. A consultant was brought into the lumber mill because management had noticed that profits were in decline while other measurements, such as productivity and quality, were constant. The consultant's task was to find out where the money was going. As is typically the case, the consultant went to the source, interviewing employees.

His conclusion was that the employees were angry and felt powerless. From their perspective, management kept demanding more and more, and even when employees delivered, management was harsh, arbitrary, and disrespectful. The employees felt powerless to protect themselves against the powerful. We know that people who feel powerless often find ways to punish those in power for how they are being treated. In this particular lumber mill the employees chose to punish management.

The lumber mills comes from childhood cartoons where Dudley Do-Right routinely rescued Darling Nell from the hands of the evil Snidely Whiplash. If Whiplash wasn't tying Nell to the railroad tracks, he was tying her to a big log in a sawmill. As the log progressed down the conveyor, closer and closer to the saw blade Dudley invariably came to her rescue—and good triumphed over evil once again.

Today's sawmills are much more sophisticated. The incoming log is trimmed of branches and bark. Lasers measure its cross-section to determine the maximum usable lumber that can be extracted and the computer plots the path of the saws so that the log is transformed into the maximum amount of finished, high profit, product.

Even with today's technology there is waste. The bits and pieces of scrap wood that are too small to become 'lumber' drop to a conveyor belt where they are transported to a wood crusher which grinds them into the particles that go into making particle board, the lowest-profit product to come out of the lumber mill.

Disgruntled employees at this mill reported that when management made them angry they would simply 'Feed The Hog'. 'The Hog' was the nickname for the wood crusher. Like its animal namesake, the Hog would eat anything. Any time management yelled at, ridiculed or embarrassed an employee, they 'empowered' that employ to strike back—to get even. What the now disgruntled employee would do is take high profit product (finished lumber) and feed it to the wood crusher (the Hog) turning it into low profit product. Once the product is wood chips management has no way of knowing whether it was derived from the high profit core of the log or from the bits pieces and scraps that normally fell to the conveyor below.

Thus, 'Feeding The Hog' has come to mean any behaviour that disgruntled employees use to strike back. It is retaliatory and it is wrong. But, in the moment it feels good and evens the playing field for those who feel powerless.

Defensive Behaviour

Not all counter-productive behaviour is retaliatory. Some is a self-defensive in nature. When employees feel threatened they find ways to protect themselves from what they consider a hostile environment. If, in the process of protecting themselves, they might inflict a little pain on the powerful, that is a bonus.

The acronym 'SABOTEURS' to describe this retaliatory behaviour. Looking at each of the letters in the word saboteurs we get the following:

- **S** = **Scapegoating:** If you fear being blamed for something one of the easiest ways to avoid blame is to deflect it to another. Find someone or something to blame. Just so long as it isn't you.
- **A** = **Abdicating:** If you fear being blamed you can avoid the blame by avoiding the task. Find a way to not take on the responsibility and the risk of failure, and thus blame, is deflected.
- **B** = **Budget Games:** These are the games we play to ensure that we have the money needed to do the work at hand despite what appears to be the best efforts of the organization to deprive us of what we need to succeed.
- **O** = **Overpromising:** The easiest way to get an overbearing manager to go away is to promise to deliver whatever it is they might be asking for. That is a short-term solution but a solution nonetheless.
- **T** = **Turf Guarding:** Turf can be understood as a form of power. It comes from a variety of sources: position, information, relationships, resources, ideas.... If I characterize those sources as 'mine' then I will guard them jealously because to share them means to give others access to the same power that I currently enjoy.
- **E** = **Emperoritis:** This harkens back to the story of the Emperors' new clothes. Like the townspeople

cheering the naked Emperor as he walked down the street, we lie to our leaders, praising their ideas and actions, knowing full well they are doomed to fail.

U = **Underdelivering:** This is the flipside of overpromising. Once we have promised more than we can do we now delivered the barest minimum that will allow us to satisfy the demand and avoid punishment.

R = **Risk Avoiding:** While for the adventuresome risk yields reward, for the downtrodden risk yields anxiety and pain. The unempowered employee fears risk and thus will avoid it at any cost, even if the potential reward is extraordinary.

S = **Sharp Penciling:** This is the technique that nearly every fearful or threatened employee masters in order to make mediocre or substandard performance appear, at least on paper, to have been satisfactory, perhaps even exemplary.

Interestingly, two relatively recent and related shifts in management philosophy have helped to encourage both Feeding The Hog and Silent Sabotage. The first is MBO (Management By Objectives). In 1983, in a landmark article in the *Harvard Business Review*, sociologist Robert Jackal noted that the shift to Management By Objectives refocused employees on attaining personal goals rather than team, unit or organizational goals. He underscored the point that what you measure is what you get and if you focus on individual performance you should not be surprised when your employees do likewise.

MBO led to the second change by encouraging managers to rank team members so as to facilitate individual performance-based compensation. From the employee's point of view visible competition discourages collaboration at any level. Why would I support/assist a colleague if their success puts me in a relatively weaker position regarding performance-based rewards?

Preventation of Fraud

Leadership can in fact do several things to prevent or at least reduce fraud. If the fraud triangle calls for motive, opportunity and rationalization then perhaps leaders can start there. Leaders traditionally have done some of the things necessary to reduce the opportunity for fraud. They create rules, policies and procedures. They enforce those rules, policies and procedures. They measure nearly everything that can be measured, and some things that, at least reliably, cannot. They apply significant, consistent and visible consequences for the failures to abide by those rules, policies and procedures. Leaders can also limit or reduce the motivation for fraud. One way is to balance workplace fear of failure with preparation for success. If we help our employees develop the skills, obtain the knowledge, and gain the confidence necessary for success we may reduce the attractiveness fraud represents. We can also make the consequences for failure to abide by rules, policies and procedures visible, consistent and significant.

Leaders can also address the motivation for fraud. We can try to find a better balance between the consequences for failure to meet interim goals and our investment in preparing employee for success. Leaders can do a better job of understanding and addressing some of the fears, tensions, uncertainties and anger that exist in our workforce. Leaders can openly discuss the challenges that may lead some of the workforce to resort to feeding the heart and/or silent sabotage. Leaders can look for and understand the sources of the anger and frustration in their workforce and mitigate those forces. But leadership alone cannot prevent a person intent on committing fraud from doing so. So, in addition to the psychology of leadership we have to look at other factors including environment, motivation and rationalization.

A key word when looking at organizational work environments for the past 15 or 20 years has been 'culture'. The idea of organizational culture gets talked about a good deal. We should start by reaching agreement on what the word 'culture' means. Culture is a shared understanding of how things really work around. Culture is the net result of the admixture of policies and procedures, the formal aspects of culture, and leadership, the informal aspect of culture. Policy and procedures defined the way things should be done. Leadership defines how things actually are done. And culture reflects the shared understanding within the organization of both the priorities and the consequences inherent in both sets of rules, the congruencies and conflicts. It is the answer to the question,

> "If I were a new employee here and you wanted to help me succeed, what one thing would you tell me that I really need to know/understand, but won't find written down anywhere?"

Embedded in culture are the measures and rewards the organization uses to motivate the behaviour it is trying to encourage. Both measures and rewards can be tangible or intangible. Culture also includes the operational values of the organization—principles that drive its people and its systems. For some motivation is driven by formal systems: what gets measured and what gets rewarded in terms of salary, authority, position, and status. For others motivation can also be driven by the values inherent in the organization's culture: things like fairness, respect, honesty and compassion. The third component of culture can revolve around the organizations' 'self talk'. How does the organization, be it the entire corporation, a specific department, or a single workgroup, view itself and its place in the greater scheme of things?

There is near universal agreement among those who study such things as organizational culture that it is both a product of and the shaper of leadership behaviour, where leadership is defined with the lower case 'l'—not exclusively the province of those with formal titles, positions or authority. Some argue that informal leadership, the leadership exerted by those lacking formal authority, is in fact an even more powerful than formal authority. The goal, then, is to create and sustain an ethical culture. At a minimum ethical culture presumes a clearly articulated and defined set of core values or principles that the organization promotes, measures and rewards. Typically that Statement of principles or values would include things such as honesty, integrity, fairness, respect, compassion, courage, and accountability.

Value statements have become very popular in the past couple of decades. But being popular is not always the same as being effective. Anecdotal evidence of the power of ethical cultures can be instructive but it doesn't necessarily teach us how to shape and sustain an ethical culture. There is in fact a well-tested conceptual model that does inform the shaping and sustaining of an ethical culture. There are seven conditions that shape and sustain the culture and organization. They can be characterized as:

- Stated position
- Formal systems
- Informal systems
- Measures and rewards
- Communication and education
- Reaction to critical events
- Leaderships perceived motives

While all seven factors are a necessary precondition, they are increasingly significant as you go down the list. As we review this list we will find that the first five are somewhat intuitive. Given the opportunity to consider how organizational culture is formed and sustained we might very likely have come up with a similar list. The last two, however, are not as intuitive and it is those that truly cement the culture into the organization.

Stated Position

This is where the organization articulates its fundamental values, principles and beliefs. This can run the gamut from

Nordstrom's focus on customer service to Walmart's focus on price, J&J's focus on customer well-being or LLBean's focus on customer satisfaction. Stated position, however, merely creates a target that points the organization in a direction. It is not sufficient to ensure movement in that direction.

Formal Systems

It is the formal systems of the organization that create the first movement in the direction stated above. The formal systems say that if we believe in customer service, for example, then we have to have systems to train our employees to monitor customer satisfaction and to determine whether or not the service we are aiming for is being delivered. It then extends into the internal management of the organization. What do our policies and procedures provide? What do our measures suggest we truly value and what does the reward system prove we truly value?

Informal Systems

As noted above, informal systems can trump formal systems. The informal systems are leader-specific as opposed to organization-specific. These are the priorities, standards, criteria and methods that my immediate superior holds me to and I in turn am expected to hold up for my subordinates.

Measures and Rewards

The combination of position, formal systems and informal systems all feed into what gets measured and what gets rewarded. And ultimately, as we have all heard repeatedly, what gets measured gets managed. If we don't care enough to measure it and if we don't care enough to reward it then we don't really care.

Communication and Education

Little if any of the above, gets 'off the page' and into the workplace unless it is effectively communicated and unless the key persons are effectively educated as to what the standards are, what behaviours they demand, and how they will be measured and rewarded. Had you been asked to identify the things that influence ethical culture my educated guess is that you would have come up with a list very similar to the first five listed above. So far, nothing new. The 'new' really begins and ends with the last two elements that contribute to shaping and sustaining an ethical culture.

Leaderships Perceived Motives

The final, and the single most important, component of shaping organizational culture is the perceptions of people within the organization and outside of what leaders actual motives are. Are we waiving the ethics flag because it is the popular thing to do and will create a positive image of our company, or are we raising the banner of our values and standards because we are committed to meeting those standards and honouring those values in everything we do?

It is these last two elements, reaction to critical events, and perceptions of leadership's actual motives, that are most powerful in both shaping and sustaining organizational culture.

Ethical Maturity

There is one additional conceptual framework that can inform the dialogue about fraud, its sources and its prevention, from President of the Ethics Resource Centre. In it we found as to how individuals mature and posited that there might be an organizational analog. In simplified language it can summarize the understanding of individual maturation in the following way. Small children, infants through toddler, rely exclusively on authority to define what is right and wrong. If Mommy or Daddy says something is good, it's good. If they say it's bad, it's bad. Very young children generally accept the legitimacy of parental authority in defining boundaries. As children's approach school age a second source of authority regarding what is right and wrong emerges. It can be captured in the near universal experience of a child saying to a parent, "I want to do X (you can fill in the blank"). Mommy or Daddy says, "No, you cannot do that." And the child replies, "Johnny (or Sally) gets to do it. His/her mommy says it's okay." Our near universal response to that has, for generations, been, "Well, I'm not Johnny's (or Sally's) mommy (or daddy)." At this point the youngster has two influences on the definition of what is right, good fair and appropriate—the authority of his/her parents and that of other adults and/or his peers.

As we get older our horizons broaden and our definitions of what is good, right, fair and just broadens with it. Either through direct contact or indirect experience such as movies and television we learn that not everyone operates from the same assumptions or has the same experiences as we do. Society is much broader and more diverse than our limited social circle. And we discover that the definition of what is right, good, fair and just can be much more complex and diverse than we had earlier believed. And finally, there is the concept of self-actualization, where the individual decision-maker has a fully developed ethos and is able to judge what is right, fair good and just based on an inner compass, informed by authority, peers and society but not limited by them. With that very quick overview of how individuals attain ethical maturity we can draw a parallel to the concept of organizational maturity.

The lowest level of ethical maturity for the individual is authority. In the organizational context 'authority' can be seen as compliance with laws regulations rules, policies and procedures. As individuals mature they broaden their ethical reference base to include peers. In the business world we see that acted out as a focus on compliance and 'best practices'—a reference to selected peers whose ethical standards one admires.

The individual's focus on the stand as a society as a broader basis for decision-making has an analog in the business world as well. Starting in the 1990s the majority of leading corporations formally adopted processes and procedures to allow them to fulfil a broader social contract than the simple return on shareholder investment. Environmentalism, consumerism, and the special interests of a plethora of narrowly defined social standards became standard fare in organizations. It's a fairly simple process. It begins with the leadership focus on developing and sustaining an ethical culture. That process typically includes the development of a formal statement of values, the standards to guide us in policy and procedure are inadequate to the task. It includes a code of ethics, which 'behaviouralizes' those values describing what they look like when they're put into action. The code is further supplemented with ethics training where employees are not only exposed to what the code requires but are given the opportunity and the safety of classroom environment to develop confidence in their ability to apply and abide by those standards to the day-to-day decisions in the workplace. Finally the organization puts in place the supporting systems necessary for an ethical culture to flourish.

The measurement and rewards systems are expanded beyond financial and temporal goals and objectives to examine whether or not the resulting measures were achieved in ways consistent with the values and ethical standards of the organization. An ethics infrastructure is created so that the ethics message can be effectively communicated, employees can be trained, policies and procedures can be reviewed to ensure their congruence with the adopted standards and questions and concerns can be managed. Employers are not merely encouraged to raise ethics issues, ask questions, or report observed or suspected misconduct. Mechanisms are created to facilitate the safe reporting or questioning. And those mechanisms go beyond merely noting concerns to investigating and addressing concerns that are raised and ensuring that appropriate action is taken to both address any misconduct and to understand how better to prevent such misconduct in the future. And the means by which it is addressing ethical concerns to ensure that it consistently rises to higher and higher standards. And, as a commitment to the entire employee body and the broader society, results are published as to the types of issues the organization is facing and the means by which it is addressing ethical concerns to ensure that it consistently rises to even higher standards. This process is true in large corporations, midsize companies and small entrepreneurial operations. The basic steps are unchanged. What varies are the details in terms of complexity and sophistication of the infrastructure. What does not very is a commitment to high standards and the use of all appropriate means to attain the standards.

The final observation regarding the psychology of fraud and its counterpoint, a commitment to organizational ethics, that ultimately you manage what you value. If it's all about the numbers you'll manage to the numbers. If the goal is financial success achieved in a manner consistent with a set of ethical values you will manage for success according to an in-line with those values. There's an interesting parallel in building an ethical culture as a result of ethical leadership and building a customer service culture as a result of service-oriented leadership.

If as a leader you consistently model the values you espouse, hold your employees to a high standard, and then hold yourself to an even higher standard you will create the ethical culture. Risk of making that statement is that it may sound simple, perhaps too simple. In truth creating an ethical culture is fairly simple. However, it is extraordinarily difficult to create and sustain a culture in a complex organization that reflects fundamental ethical values day in day out, without exception, and ever-higher standards.

The psychology of fraud means that one must be ever vigilant. Fraud is, if not natural, at least easy. It can even seem logical or reasonable. To be effective we have to consider the motivation to commit fraud, the opportunity for fraud the rationalizations and justifications that might be employed and the likelihood that it could go undetected and or unaddressed in your organization. It is just as important that we spend moment on the psychology of fraud prevention. If we believe something to be wrong we have to choose whether or not to address that wrong, to make a good-faith effort to turn it in the direction toward becoming a right.

One of concrete things we can resort to is trying to understand the risks we and our organization might face. Looking inward, we might consider a few simple questions:

- What are we going to do in the next 30 days to reduce the likelihood of financial fraud, in our organization, among your employees, among our suppliers, competitors, colleagues, and customers?
- How might we do a better job of detecting fraud in our organization, finding it earlier and preventing it more effectively?
- How might we help our organization, employees, clients et al to address the common fraud motivators that may be present—thereby preventing future fraud?

Fraud is a real problem. We know that. All we have to do is look around us. The last several years have been filled with the names of once respected organizations and TV images of individuals who've been brought down by their inability or unwillingness to resist or combat fraud in their organizations. This is not an abstract or hypothetical issue. Fraud is at the root of the worst economic crisis we have faced since the Great Depression. We cannot undo the past. But we can shape the future.

Ethical people armed with effective processes and information can create organizations that operate to the highest ethical standards, effectively resist incidental and intentional efforts to perpetrate fraud within the organization and from within the organization to the outside world.

Fighting Financial Crimes

More than 150 delegates from over 54 countries participated in the first international Tax and Crime Conference organised on 21.0.2011 by the OECD and hosted by the Norwegian government in Oslo, Norway. The conference brought together representatives from a range of OECD and non-OECD governmental agencies, including tax administrations, finance and justice ministries, Financial Intelligence Units, central banks, FATF, international organisations, as well as business and NGOs. Participants from OECD and G20 countries as well as developing countries from Africa, Asia and Latin America shared ideas to find better and more effective ways to counter financial crimes, including tax evasion and other illicit flows through better inter-agency and international cooperation. The aim was to deliver better results, in shorter time frames, with lower costs and less duplication, building on the strength and expertise of different agencies.

Issues of financial crime and illicit flows are of concern to all countries, but particularly to developing countries. Illicit financial flows resulting from financial crimes strip resources from developing countries that could finance their long-term development and undermine the foundation of democratic governance.

Mr Richard Boucher, Deputy Secretary-General of the OECD emphasised how inter-agency cooperation can enhance financial integrity and good governance by improving the effectiveness of countries' abilities to fight financial crimes.

> "Unfortunately, criminals operate across borders and sectors quite easily. They make harmful use of telecommunications innovations and liberalisation of trade to carry out illicit activities with greater speed and on a wider stage. They can also more readily hide their traces by using multiple jurisdictions and by recycling the proceeds of their

crimes at dizzying speeds. So, we need to operate across borders and between agencies as well. The question we are addressing is how to do so effectively."

Accounting Scandals

Accounting scandals, or corporate accounting scandals, are political and business scandals which arise with the disclosure of misdeeds by trusted executives of large public corporations. Such misdeeds typically involve complex methods for misusing or misdirecting funds, overstating revenues, understating expenses, overstating the value of corporate assets or under-reporting the existence of liabilities, sometimes with the cooperation of officials in other corporations or affiliates.

In public companies, this type of 'creative accounting' can amount to fraud and investigations that are typically launched by government oversight agencies. Scandals are often only the 'tip of the iceberg'. They represent the visible catastrophic failures. Note that much abuse can be completely legal or quasi-legal.

For example, in the domain of privatization and takeovers, it is fairly easy for a top executive to reduce the price of his/her company's stock—due to information asymmetry. The executive can accelerate accounting of expected expenses, delay accounting of expected revenue, engage in off-balance sheet transactions to make the company's profitability appear temporarily poorer, or simply promote and report severely conservative (e g pessimistic) estimates of future earnings. Such seemingly adverse earnings news will be likely to (at least temporarily) reduce share price. (This is again due to information asymmetries since it is more common for top executives to do everything they can to window dress their company's earnings forecasts). There are typically very few legal risks to being 'too conservative' in one's accounting and earnings estimates. A reduced share price makes a company an easier takeover target. When the company gets bought out (or taken private)—at a dramatically lower price—the takeover artist gains a windfall from the former top executive's actions to surreptitiously reduce share price. This can represent tens of billions of dollars (questionably) transferred from previous shareholders to the takeover artist. The former top executive is then rewarded with a golden handshake for presiding over the first sale that can sometimes be in the hundreds of millions of dollars for one or two years of work. (This is nevertheless an excellent bargain for the takeover artist, who will tend to benefit from developing a reputation of being very generous to parting top executives).

Similar issues occur when a publicly held asset or non-profit organization undergoes privatization. Top executives often reap tremendous monetary benefits when a government owned or non-profit entity is sold to private hands. Just as in the example above, they can facilitate this process by making the entity appear to be in financial crisis—this reduces the sale price (to the profit of the purchaser), and makes non-profit organisations and governments more likely to sell. It can also contribute to a public perception that private entities are more efficiently run reinforcing the political will to sell-off public assets. Again, due to asymmetric information, policy makers and the general public see a government owned firm that was a financial 'disaster'—miraculously turned around by the private sector (and typically resold) within a few years.

All accounting scandals are not caused by top executives. Oftentimes managers and employees are pressured or willingly alter financial statements for the personal benefit of the individuals over the company. Managerial opportunism plays a large role in these scandals. For example managers who would be compensated more for short term results would report inaccurate information since short term benefits outweigh the long-term ones such as pension.

Notable Accounting Scandals

The Enron scandal turned in the indictment and criminal conviction of one of the Big Five auditor Arthur Andersen on June 15, 2002. Although the conviction was overturned on May 31, 2005 by the Supreme Court of the United States, the firm ceased performing audits and is currently unwinding its business operations. The Enron scandal was defined as being one of the biggest audit failures. The scandal included utilizing loopholes that were found within the GAAP (Generally Accepted Accounting Principles). For auditing a big sized company such as Enron, the auditors were criticized for having a brief meeting few times a year that covered lots of material. By January 17, 2002 Enron decided to discontinue its business with Arthur Andersen claiming they had failed in accounting advice and related documents. Arthur Andersen was judged guilty of obstruction of justice for getting rid of many emails and documents that were related to auditing Enron. From this incident little less than 1,00,000 employees lost their jobs. Although later the ruling was overturned by the US Supreme Court, the image of the auditing firm has been damaged beyond repair, and was never able to come back to its full operation capacity.

On July 9, 2002 George W Bush gave a speech about recent accounting scandals that had been uncovered. In spite of its stern tone, the speech did not focus on establishing new policy, but instead focused on actually enforcing current laws, which included holding CEOs and directors personally responsible for accountancy fraud.

In July, 2002, WorldCom filed for bankruptcy protection, in what was considered the largest corporate insolvency ever at that time.

These scandals re-ignited the debate over the relative merits of US GAAP, which takes a 'rules-based' approach to accounting, versus International Accounting Standards and UK GAAP, which takes a 'principles-based' approach. The Financial

Accounting Standards Board announced that it intends to introduce more principles-based standards. More radical means of accounting reform have been proposed, but so far have very little support. The debate itself, however, overlooks the difficulties of classifying any system of knowledge, including accounting, as rules-based or principles-based. This also led to the establishment of Sarbanes-Oxley.

On a lighter note, the 2002 Nobel Prize in Economics went to the CEOs of those companies involved in the corporate accounting scandals of that year for "adapting the mathematical concept of imaginary numbers for use in the business world."

In 2003, Nortel made a big contribution to this list of scandals by incorrectly reporting a one cent per share earnings directly after their massive layoff period. They used this money to pay the top 43 managers of the company. The SEC and the Ontario securities commission eventually settled civil action with Nortel. However, a separate civil action will be taken up against top Nortel executives including former CEO Frank A Dunn, Douglas C Beatty, Michael J Gollogly and MaryAnne E Pahapill and Hamilton. These proceedings have been postponed pending criminal proceedings in Canada, which opened in Toronto on January 12, 2012. Crown lawyers at this fraud trial of three former Nortel Networks executives say the men defrauded the shareholders of Nortel of more than $5 million. According to the prosecutors this was accomplished by engineering a financial loss in 2002, and a profit in 2003 thereby triggering Return to Profit bonuses of $70 million for top executives.

In 2005, after a scandal on insurance and mutual funds the year before, AIG was investigated for accounting fraud. The company already lost over 45 billion US dollars worth of market capitalisation because of the scandal. Investigations also discovered over a billion US dollars worth of errors in accounting transactions. The New York Attorney General's investigation led to a $1.6 billion fine for AIG and criminal charges for some of its executives. CEO Maurice R 'Hank' Greenberg was forced to step down and is still fighting civil charges being pursued by New York State.

Guarding Against the Shadow Crime

Crime Prevention Through Environmental Design (CPTED), is a well-known crime prevention strategy. Even though its focus is traditional street crime, its principles can be applied to WCC. Crime Prevention Through Awareness and Procedural Design (CPTAPD), is a more appropriate system for preventing WCC. By creating a heightened level of awareness and procedures designed to combat these losses, a business can be better prepared for WCC.

White-collar crime occurs when the four components are present—Money, Trust, Greed, and Opportunity. By removing access to any of these, the chance of becoming a victim significantly decreases. Money, Opportunity, and Trust can be dealt with differently for each type of WCC. However, Greed, being a part of human nature, cannot be removed from a person, but it can be overcome. Edwin Sutherland once said that white-collar crime can happen "if, and only if, the weight of favourable definition (to crime) exceeds the weight of the unfavourable definitions."

A person will only commit a crime if he or she believes that the benefits outweigh the risks. So, by showing what happens to criminals (increasing awareness), knowing that committing a crime is not worth the risks will become a part of the corporate subculture. We will take a closer look at a few of the different types of WCC and address countermeasures against each one.

Consumer Fraud

Most businessmen believe that consumer fraud only affects individuals, not a business. That is simply untrue. Any business that buys something is at risk. Here are some examples to illustrate that point:

- A supply manager buys 100,000 pens at an unbelievable $0.04 each. After receiving the pens, the supply manager realizes that the pens are only 1/8 full of ink. He could have bought the pens from a reliable, well-known, supplier for $0.09 each, but instead took the lowest bid without looking at who the bidder is.
- A manager buys a delivery truck. The seller said it was rarely used and the odometer read 30,000. A week later, the truck breaks down. After having it fixed, the manager does some research. It turns out that it had 90,000 miles. Meanwhile, the seller has moved on to another town and another business.
- A security director buys 35 uniforms from a catalogue he received in the mail. They are $20 each, and only require a $10 deposit each. The uniforms never arrive and the business's phone number has been disconnected.

In each of these examples, it was an individual who was the victim, but he was spending the company's money. These companies gave one person a responsibility to buy. A procedure for buying must be created for all businesses and should include the following:

- Board approval before contracting with a vendor/supplier.
- An investigation period before buying from new suppliers or individuals.
- Most importantly—fraud awareness programmes for all employees.

A business is more prone to being an offender of securities fraud than a victim. However, with the recent cases of Enron and WorldCom, it has become obvious that companies will face the consequences for their actions. The best way to combat this is to prevent corruption of both management and low level workers. Increasing employee awareness of Enron and other scandals is one way to do this. In many recent cases of corruption, the corruption starts at the top and works its way down. If someone in management fears that a whistleblower will come forward, he or she is less likely to commit the fraud, knowing what will happen. Remember, it is every employee's responsibility to prevent securities fraud; if a business fails, all its employees are out of work.

Embezzlement is one WCC that is well-known among management and, to a lesser extent, security. This may be because the damage is more obvious. Embezzlement is someone taking money, normally by playing with the books. Over time, one person can take millions from a business. This can happen when one person has access to the accounts, but is not supervised, and his or her work is not double-checked. One method for minimizing damage is to hire a forensic accountant, who finds errors and inconsistencies in accounting.

Forensics also can be used in a more positive way to help prevent fraud. A number of accounting firms and law firms offer forensic accounting services in which they run background checks on key employees or red flag odd cash or material flows. However, a forensic accounting generally is not part of a healthy company's routine book-keeping, but it is an extra tool that can be used to fight white-collar crime. If properly applied, these special techniques can stop irregularities before they grow into crises. (Martin, 1998a, 15)

Running background checks before hiring someone for an important position is another preventative measure. Stephen Nelson, an author for Inc, shows the importance of hiring the right people by pointing out a simple fact: "In my experience, someone who has embezzled once is likely to be a repeat offender."

While ID theft affects individuals more than businesses, it should still be an area of concern to asset protection professionals. Typically, someone will claim to be a representative of a reputable business to create trust and then use that trust to commit fraud. After the victim realizes he has been taken, he will blame the business. While, in most cases, he has no evidence to seriously pursue criminal or civil charges, he may harm a small or medium sized business by defaming its image. Often, the perpetrator is a former employee of the business they claim to represent. Businesses must be very careful when placing employees in a position of trust where they have access to personal data. Many consider information the most important asset of the new millennium.

Computer crimes are believed to be the fastest growing type of crime. Unlike the other types of WCC, computer crimes are not normally the crime itself, but rather a means of committing, a tool used to reach the criminal's goal. Hacking into a bank's system and illegally transferring money is one example. A small or medium sized business should focus more on protecting information stored within its computers. While espionage by competitors may be an issue for some, protecting customer data (credit cards, bank accounts, etc) is a more realistic concern. Not only are computer crimes rarely discovered, they are often committed by employees themselves. Friedrichs observes both of these facts in *Trusted Criminals:*

> Most cases of computer crime are discovered by accident because people who use computers to commit crimes are more likely than not to be bright enough and skilful enough to cover their tracks. In one study, a third of those committing computer crimes were managers.

Like security fraud, businesses are normally the offender of Environmental Crimes. The solution in this case would be the same: making examples of what has happened to other offenders. However, sometimes, even a big company can become the victim:

- Pleezer Inc buys property for a measly $5,000 per acre. After starting construction, it finds 30 yellow barrels buried underground, all filled with a hazardous substance. The required clean-up cost is one million dollars.

- XYZ Corp pays ABC Waste Removers $678,000 to remove 15 barrels of substance GC-161. ABC dumps the barrels in a nearby lake and leaves the country. XYZ may be criminally prosecuted, even though they were only careless, not the actual business that dumped the barrels.

In both of these examples, carelessness left a business responsible for someone else's criminal behaviour. Environmental Crimes may be subject to strict liability, the ability to be prosecuted even if no intent to commit the crime is shown. Though, it is noteworthy that strict liability is only imposed in some States, including Pennsylvania. Once again, the key to preventing this is to research a business before striking a deal. Best of all, a business could create a policy requiring just that.

'Crime Prevention Through Awareness and Procedural Design' is an idea all businesses should incorporate. They should include articles about white-collar crime in a newsletter or make flyers. Next, businesses should create checklists of things to do, such as researching a seller, and distribute them to anyone who has buying power. Having good awareness and well-thought-out procedures are the best ways to combat white-collar crime. By creating such, a business will be ready for the next con man who comes to town, and well-aware of what will happen if it become the next Enron. Unlike Akera, this business won't only be prepared for the physical beast, but the one who builds trust and uses it as a weapon as well.

Risks Faced by Business

A risk is a threat or potential disruption to any business and its profitability. Risks may come from poor recruitment, unreliable suppliers, health and safety incidents, fraud etc. If a 'risk' eventuates, there is a problem of loss of revenue, a disruption to operations, a decline in profit and may have to go to court either as a witness or a defendant. Those who commit fraud often do so because they think no-one knows what is happening.

The 2010 Report to the Nation on Occupational Fraud and Abuse by the Association of Certified Fraud Examiners (ACFE) found typical organisations lose 5% of its annual revenue to fraud. Applied to the estimated 2009 Gross World Product, this figure translates to a potential total fraud loss of more than $2.9 trillion. The median loss caused by the occupational fraud cases in the ACFE study was $160,000. Nearly one-quarter of the frauds involved losses of at least $1 million.

Frauds Lasted a Median of 18 Months Before Being Detected

Whistleblowing (Tips) from employees, customers, vendors, and other sources remained the most common detection method (40.2%), catching nearly three times as many frauds as any other form of detection. This is consistent with the findings of ACFE reports since 2002. Tips remain by far and away the most common means of detection. Management review and internal audit were the second and third most common forms of detection, uncovering 14% and 15% of frauds. The report highlighted that only 25% of Australian (Oceania) organisations had whistleblowing hotlines compared with more than one-half of USA entities even though disclosures (tips) were the major source for highlighting fraud. The ACFE recommended:

> "Organisations should implement hotlines to receive tips from both internal and external sources. Such reporting mechanisms should allow anonymity and confidentiality, and employees be encouraged to report suspicious activity without fear of reprisal."

Whistleblowing Reduces Fraud and Theft

Whistleblowing has helped reduce up to 50% of corporate fraud and theft in the United States. Australia is lagging behind in implementing independent, anonymous whistle blowing services. Employers have a duty of care to provide a safe working environment for their employees. The definition of safety extends to emotional and psychological safety. Companies that use whistleblowing services find they learn of bullying and harassment behaviours earlier and can act to stamp them out faster before the behaviours become out of control. Naturally this is of great benefit to the victims but also provides business owners with comfort as it limits their exposure to legal and reputational risks including potentially hefty OHS fines and now even significant prison sentences.

The purpose of this legislative change should be to address the issue of serious bullying and deter people from engaging in the use of abusive or offensive words to or in the presence of the victim, and acting in a way that could reasonably be expected to cause physical or mental harm to the victim, including self-harm or arouse apprehension or fear in the victim for his or her own safety or that of another. Employers must take responsibility to ensure that employees can work in a safe environment that is free from these types of risks.

Most employees have access to the internet and making a secure online report has many advantages compared to simply the telephone, email or post. The employee making the report can remain anonymous if they choose. A private online feedback forum can be used to help clarify the information being provided. An encrypted, secure independent reporting system available 24/7 means your staff can provide the knowledge you need to manage risks as soon as they become aware of any threat or risk to your business. It is about options and designing a whistleblower programme which best suits your organisation's culture and people whether that be by our Web based Solution alone or with our PLUS option of telephone.

20 Ways to Detect Fraud

If you suspect any of the following items are occurring in a company, fraud may be suspected and detected as well.

1. Unusual Behaviour

The perpetrator will often display unusual behaviour, that when taken as a whole is a strong indicator of fraud. The fraudster may not ever take a vacation or call in sick in fear of being caught. He or she may not assign out work even when overloaded. Other symptoms may be changes in behaviour such as increased drinking, smoking, defensiveness, and unusual irritability and suspiciousness.

2. Complaints

Frequently tips or complaints will be received which indicate that a fraudulent action is going on. Complaints have been known to be some of the best sources of fraud and should be taken seriously. Although all too often, the motives of the complainant may be suspect, the allegations usually have merit that warrant further investigation.

3. Stale Items in Reconciliations

In bank reconciliations, deposits or checks not included in the reconciliation could be indicative of theft. Missing deposits could mean the perpetrator absconded with the funds; missing checks could indicate one made out to a bogus payee.

4. Excessive Voids

Voided sales slips could mean that the sale was rung up, the payment diverted to the use of the perpetrator, and the sales slip subsequently voided to cover the theft.

5. Missing Documents

Documents which are unable to be located can be a red flag for fraud. Although it is expected that some documents will be misplaced, the auditor should look for explanations as to why the documents are missing, and what steps were taken to locate the requested items. All too often, the auditors will select an alternate item or allow the auditee to select an alternate without determining whether or not a problem exists.

6. Excessive Credit Memos

Similar to excessive voids, this technique can be used to cover the theft of cash. A credit memo to a phony customer is written out, and the cash is taken to make total cash balance.

7. Common Names and Addresses for Refunds

Sales employees frequently make bogus refunds to customers for merchandise. The address shown for the refund is then made to the employee's address, or to the address of a friend or co-worker.

8. Increasing Reconciling Items

Stolen deposits, or bogus checks written, are frequently not removed, or covered, from the reconciliation. Hence, over a period of time, the reconciling items tend to increase.

9. General Ledger Out-of-Balance

When funds, merchandise, or assets are stolen and not covered by a fictitious entry, the general ledger will be out of balance. An inventory of the merchandise or cash is needed to confirm the existence of the missing assets.

10. Adjustments to Receivables or Payables

In cases where customer payments are misappropriated, adjustments to receivables can be made to cover the shortage. Where payables are adjusted, the perpetrator can use a phony billing scheme to convert cash to his or her own use.

11. Excess Purchases

Excess purchases can be used to cover fraud in two ways:

- Fictitious payees are used to convert funds.

- Excessive purchases may indicate a possible payoff of purchasing agent.

12. Duplicate Payments

Duplicate payments are sometimes converted to the use of an employee. The employee may notice the duplicate payment, then he or she may prepare a phony endorsement of the check.

13. Ghost Employees

Ghost employee schemes are frequently uncovered when an auditor, fraud examiner, or other individual distributes paychecks to employees. Missing or otherwise unaccounted for employees could indicate the existence of a ghost employee scheme.

14. Employee Expense Accounts

Employees frequently conceal fraud in their individual expense account reimbursements. These reimbursements should be scrutinized for reasonableness and trends, especially in the area of cash transactions on the expense account.

15. Inventory Shortages

Normal shrinkage over a period of time can be computed through historical analysis. Excessive shrinkage could explain a host of fraudulent activity, from embezzlement to theft of inventory.

16. Increased Scrap

In the manufacturing process, an increased amount of scrap could indicate a scheme to steal and resell this material. Scrap is a favourite target of embezzlers because it is usually subject to less scrutiny than regular inventory.

17. Large Payments to Individuals

Excessively large payments to individuals may indicate instances of fraudulent disbursements.

18. Employee Overtime

Employees being paid for overtime hours not worked by altering time sheets before or after management approval.

19. Write-off of Accounts Receivable

Comparing the write-off of receivables by customers may lead to information indicating that the employee has absconded with customer payments.

20. Post Office Boxes as Shipping Addresses

In instances where merchandise is shipped to a post office box, this may indicate that an employee is shipping to a bogus purchaser.

India should adopt OECD's residence-based tax system to attract investments. This will entice pension funds and TEIs to bypass tax havens and invest directly here. Drug smugglers and third world dictators laundering-ill-gotten wealth through secretive banking systems in tax havens is an anachronistic image from crime novels. Leveraging US's remarkable success in compelling tax havens to block terrorist financing, the G20/ OECD have successfully persuaded tax havens to improve tax transparency and participate in an international regime of information exchange. All tax havens have committed to OECD standards for tax transparency and are executing Tax Information Exchange Agreements (TIEA) wherever needed. Stringent know-your-customer (KYC) regulations and TIEAs are making it difficult, albeit slowly, for round tripping black money through tax havens. However, tax havens continue to suffer an image problem due to a Swiss tradition that has gone with the wind, ie not accepting tax evasion as grounds to lift the veil of banking secrecy.

Today, capital is globally mobile seeking to optimise risk adjusted returns from international investments. Investors are willing to take higher risk by investing in emerging markets and seeking to reduce 'capital gains taxes' (CGT) to optimise risk-adjusted returns. Three large investor categories, controlling significant part of global capital, use tax havens to optimise risk-adjusted returns from emerging markets. The largest demand comes from tax-exempt investors (TEIs) such as pensions funds and university endowments domiciled in OECD countries. Initially, TEIs chose international investments only in other OECD countries, where the OECD model of 'residency-based taxation' exempts non-residents from taxation. In recent years, TEIs have sought tax havens to access emerging markets that follow the UN model of 'source-based taxation', which requires non-residents to pay taxes at source. For example, being a tax-exempt US resident, a pension fund, will not be subject to source country taxes on its OECD investments or home country taxes in the US. But source-country taxes would make risk-adjusted returns low for the same fund unless it channelises its emerging market investments through funds domiciled in tax havens (FTH).

Demand also comes from residents in countries that don't tax capital gains and/or that don't tax global income. For example, financial investors from Hong Kong (no CGT) and US (15% CGT)—would find India (22% CGT on unlisted investments), a competitive destination only through FTH. Another source of demand arises from residents in jurisdictions that limit overseas tax credits to what is paid directly and not through an intermediate vehicle. For example, Indian investors will seek to invest in an international fund only if it has a tax pass through status and/or through FTH.

Our country has periodically gone through convulsions about 'black money' and 'phoren investors' coming through tax havens. Unfortunately, public debate on this subject has been driven solely by the tax havens' image problem instead of the need to be competitive to access capital from one or more of the 'investor categories listed above. Also no distinction has been made between strategic investors, who may invest directly and financial investors who will only come through FTH.

Public debate must focus on the OECD model versus the UN model taxation. Government following our induction as the 34th member of the OECD Financial Action Task Force, India intends to adopt the OECD model. Implementing this model will be a dramatic step in making India a competitive investment destination. The OECD model will also transform Mumbai into a financial powerhouse and will enable the growth of a globally-competitive Indian fund management industry. But Budget 2012 is taking India in the opposite direction with amendments that stretch the limits of 'source-based taxation'. It also proposes to rush through the implementation of GAAR, without adequate safeguards, which could significantly impact India's attractiveness as an investment destination. With the rupee near its all time low, foreign reserves at a 15-year low and investors struggling to make positive returns, this is not the time to be messing with capital flows. Decline in trading volumes since April 1, 2012 are a stark reminder that foreign financial investors may stay away.

Tax evaders could be in for trouble as the government is mulling placing tax crimes on a par with money-laundering offences that have severe criminal and financial implications. India could bring income tax offences under its anti-money-laundering law, making way for easier prosecution, rigorous imprisonment, fines and shifting onus on the accused to prove he is not guilty. An inter-departmental group has been set up to examine the changes required. The group's recommendations could then be placed before Parliament and changes made to the Prevention of Money Laundering (Amendment) Bill, 2011. The offences will include concealment of income, failure to deposit tax deducted at source and false evidence. These changes are consistent with a global plan drawn up by the Financial Action Task Force, an inter-governmental body to combat money-laundering and terror financing, of which India is a member.

Many countries have already incorporated these offences in their money-laundering laws even though the FATF adopted them as part of new standards in February this year.

If these offences become scheduled of fences under the anti-money-laundering law, they will attract rigorous imprisonment of three to seven years and a fine of up to ₹5 lakh. A proposed amendment to PMLA has suggested open-ended penalty, to be decided by courts, as opposed to a maximum of ₹5 lakh fine now. The trial in these cases will be faster as offences under PMLA are tried in special courts and the onus to prove innocence lies on the accused. The apex direct taxes body, the Central Board of Direct Taxes, had earlier written to the revenue department, the nodal department for PMLA, to bring some tax evasion offences under its ambit. However, the suggestion made two years back was put on the back burner since there was no compulsion on India to bring them under the PMLA.

India, which became a member of the FATF in 2010, is obliged to make changes in its own anti-money-laundering law now. Under the current rules, the Income Tax department has to take law ministry's permission to initiate prosecution against tax evaders. The cumbersome procedure has meant that so far no evader has been put behind the bars although there is a provision for six months imprisonment and penalty on tax evasion. The tax authorities prefer not to invoke these provisions as prosecution could take many years.

Significant changes have already been made through the Finance Bill, 2012, passed by the Lok Sabha on May 8 that will allow for easier prosecution. India has submitted a detailed action plan that lists various short-term, medium term and long-term measures required to conform to FATF standards and some of the amendments proposed in the PMLA Bill are in line with these commitments.

In Moral Origins, anthropologist Christopher Boehm charts the history of how humans developed a sense of right and wrong. In particular, he focuses on why being nice to people lacking any blood ties is a matter of everyday practice. Boehm's theory is that moral virtues evolved according to the principle of natural selection as a by-product of social selection that rewarded impulse control and punished aggressive behaviour. So far so good; it's the standard evolutionary explanation these days that goes down well with mainstream science since it deconstructs things like altruism and empathy to genes and reproductive advantages. But then, Boehm runs headlong into a will when he tries to grapple the issue of internal ethics that govern values and principles that separate moral human beings from amoral apes. His solution is to say that our ancestors were 'pre-adapted' for morality that then worked as the first step towards developing a conscience something Boehm describes as a 'Machiavellian risk calculator'. There are two problems with this view. The smaller one is that if we think of every conscience-driven act of goodness or decency as a 'calculated risk', then forget theology, even biology has no credible future left. The bigger problem of so-called pre-adaptiveness for morality springs from. Surely, not from the ancestors of our ancestors because that would mean they were pre-adapted too, along with their own ancestors—till we get back to the original ancestor of all living things a little one-celled amoeba, pre-adapted for morality.

Vodafone Case

Vodafone is in talks with the government to pare its tax dues aggregating to ₹20,000 crore. A settlement is the right thing to do. The government should accept the company's demand to waive interest and penalty for failure to withhold tax and collect only the capital gains tax of around ₹7,900 crore on Vodafone's purchase of Hutchison's interest in its mobile telephony venture with Essar held through a holding company registered in Cayman Islands. Charging capital gains tax will validate the basic principle that what counts for the government is whether value accrues to the company changing ownership because of its economic activity in India. The Budget has already proposed a change in the language of law to make it clear that indirect transfer of capital assets in India would attract capital gains tax on par with direct transfer. A retroactive clarification on the intent of the tax law is perfectly in order, so as to remove any uncertainty or ambiguity. An amicable settlement with Vodafone makes sense as long as the government does not give up its underlying right to tax capital gains created out of India's economic activity. India cannot be a tax haven. There is a precedent in an out of court settlement—the government did one with ITC in an alleged excise evasion case in 2005 after the company secured a favourable verdict from the Supreme Court. However, a settlement with Vodafone will trigger similar demands from other companies involved in such deals and on whom tax demands have already been raised. The government must waive penalty and interest in all these cases too. Pragmatism is in order to avoid legal wrangles. The government should withdraw other retrospective moves that seek not so much to clarify extant law as to create a fresh tax burden. These include a key proposal in the Budget to retroactively change the meaning of royalty, and that too from 1976, on computer software. Such retroactive changes bring in business uncertainty and must be eschewed. This would show foreign investors complaining about retrospective taxation that India means business and respects their sentiments, too.

An Improvement Agenda for Investigatory Agency

The investigating agencies requires overhauling, the law requires amendments and the approach requires re-fashioning to reverse the prevalent perception as well as experience. A general perception of selectivity, politically pushed agenda, below par investigation which results in large scale dismissal of cases and the pyrrhic effectiveness where result is manifested in prosecution and arrest rather than truly bringing the culprits to the book is the hub of the matter. With enormous expectation from investigation agencies must be strengthened, made independent of politics, but systemic flaws ingrained in them should be corrected too.

Arrest, imprisonment and prosecution could be like 'vigilante justice' ahead of final findings. But they are not likely to have sustainable impact on the systems and the society when prosecution fails, decoupled from initial flash work associated with seemingly, quick retribution. But the litmus test is whether the investigation and prosecution stand the judicial scrutiny though for the *vox populi*, Taliban-like *be-dalila, be-wakila au be-apela* (no arguments, no advocate and no appeal) legal system looks perfectly acceptable with cheerleaders and media actuating our thinking.

Investigation Agencies develop institutional culture and institutional strategies of their own. Draconian provisions help the agents in capturing the process. They develop their own style, approach and method though not being in consonance with the objective arid being violative of legal principles. It is finally the principle of fairness, fair functioning and fair super-ordinate goal which ensures legitimacy of institution as well as disciplined response from the agents.

For issues like white-collar crimes including corruption with vanishing trail, a multi-disciplinary of team consisting of people trained in law, taxation, chartered accountancy and police are required. Now limited to policemen, often the investigation is considered far below the desired quality required, but prosecution is launched nevertheless. Among several ways of achieving the same goal, people gravitate to the least demanding course of action, that is chargesheeting in the instant case. Just accepting that there is no case, requires effort and explanation which is difficult to come by in a public institution. When a case goes to the special court, the judge is more likely to give conviction order with minimum acceptable level of evidence, even though he knows about gaping holes in evidence as the price involved in acquittal can be high in terms of his reputation. Cases go on appeal and very often fail there. Meanwhile, a dumb charade of action has taken place relentlessly without anyone being accountable. Arrest, imprisonment and high percentage of conviction by the original court has been achieved.

While investigation agency independence of the government is a necessity, the process control of investigation and prosecution must be done by some independent authority as in the US and the UK. Clamour for autonomy from process control may be self-serving but will not be in the interest of achieving the objective mandated and will do long term damage to the institution. When the rules of the game are poorly written, the loopholes will be evident sooner than expected. This is exactly what has happened. In the backdrop of rampant corruption, only a few cases are taken up with, not so edifying result except for 'vigilante justice' of arrest and chargesheeting. When execrable perception about impartiality of several enquiries is widespread, likening enquiry (to quote Clausewitz in the context of war) to extension of politics by other means, is natural. Public systems like need, to be strengthened but along with it weaknesses in the law, process and institutions should be corrected.

Index